UNEXPECTED
RECOVERIES

UNEXPECTED RECOVERIES

Seven Steps to Healing

Body, Mind, and Soul

When Serious Illness Strikes

TOM MONTE

ST. MARTIN'S GRIFFIN

New York

For Toby

A NOTE TO READERS

This book is for informational purposes only. It is not intended to take the place of individualized medical advice from a trained medical professional. Readers are advised to consult a physician or other qualified health professional regarding treatment of all of their health problems or before acting on any of the information or advice in this book. The fact that an individual, organization, Web site, magazine, or book is mentioned in this book as a potential source of information does not indicate an endorsement of this book or its contents by those sources and does not mean that the author or publisher of this book endorses any of the information those sources may provide or recommendations they may make.

The names and identifying characteristics of some individuals described in this book have been changed.

Calorie densities of foods from *The Pritikin Principle,* available on-line at www.pritikin.com. Reprinted with permission from the Pritikin Organization, LLC, and the Pritikin Longevity Center, Aventura, California.

www.stmartins.com

Design by Patrice Sheridan

LIBRARY OF CONGRESS CATALOGING-IN-PUBLICATION DATA

Monte, Tom.
    Unexpected recoveries : seven steps to healing body, mind, and soul when serious illness strikes / Tom Monte.—1st ed.
        p. cm.
    ISBN 0-312-26262-0
    EAN 978-0-312-26262-4
    1. Catastrophic illness. 2. Sick—Psychological aspects. 3. Terminally ill. 4. Chronically ill. 5. Healing. I. Title.

R726.8.M665 2005
616'.029—dc22   2005041985

First Edition: July 2005

10 9 8 7 6 5 4 3 2 1

Contents

Acknowledgments

This book is the culmination of twenty-six years of writing about health and healing. Though it would be impossible to thank all the people who have contributed to my limited understanding of these endless mysteries, I would like to mention a handful of special people.

First, I want to express my infinite gratitude to my great mentors, Michio and Aveline Kushi and Nathan and Ilene Pritikin, who gave me a foundation for understanding health and healing from both the Eastern and Western perspectives.

I want to thank some of my teachers and friends, especially Robert Pritikin, John A. McDougall, M.D., Richard Fleming, M.D., Michael Rossoff, Denny Waxman, Leonard Jacobs, Luc De Cuyper, Wim Mestdagh, Bill Tims, Michael Jacobson, Ph.D., director of the Center for Science in the Public Interest, and Anthony Sattilaro, M.D., now gone, but whose inspiration still lives in many people.

My gratitude goes out to the many hundreds of people who have shared their stories of recovery with me during the past twenty-five years, and the healers with whom I have worked. Not all of you appear in this book, but all of you have contributed to it.

My sincerest thanks to my wonderful publisher and editors at St. Martin's Press, George Witte, Elizabeth Bewley, and Heather Jackson.

I must thank Ken and Sherry Courage, Peter and Maryla Wallace, and Phiya Kushi, who also supported me in this work.

I want to thank my mother, Kathryn Monte, who gave me so many things, including a love of books, and the memory of my father, who had such a good heart.

Finally, I want to thank my wife, Toby, who wrote the menus and the recipes for this book, but more important, gave me a life that would make such a book possible.

Introduction

People overcome the most devastating diseases. Choose any illness that is now considered incurable and with a little effort you will find dozens of people who have performed the unexpected feat of defeating that disease.

Over the past twenty-five years, I have written about many hundreds of people who have conquered illnesses that were labeled "life-threatening" and even "terminal" by medical doctors. Those who restore their health have much in common. Indeed, I have found that they follow a similar healing path, one that has at least seven steps. These seven steps might be understood as seven healing behaviors, each of which transforms a specific part of the person's life and, for many, leads eventually to the restoration of health. These seven steps are:

1. The person is shocked and humbled by the diagnosis of his or her disease. In that state of humility, the person develops a new relationship with himself or herself, one based on compassion, self-acceptance, and love.

2. The person takes responsibility for his or her recovery.
3. The person adopts a healing diet that is composed largely of plant foods.
4. The person has a strong support system that includes loving, intimate relationships, social support groups, and a network of healers.
5. The person makes a commitment to life. That commitment is expressed in practical ways, especially by adhering to a healing diet and getting regular physical exercise.
6. The person develops faith, which is strengthened through regular prayer and meditation.
7. The person discovers a larger purpose for living that transcends his or her own survival.

Each of these seven steps moves a person further along his or her healing journey. While all of the people in this book have these seven steps in common, some emphasized one or two steps more than the other five or six. There are no hard-and-fast rules to the healing journey, only guidelines that point the way.

In the chapters that follow, I have included practical ways to incorporate the information described in each step into your life. In Chapter 9, I have provided a healing diet and a twenty-one-day menu plan. Recipes and a resource guide for people who want to explore alternative therapies in greater depth are provided in the back of the book, as well.

The potency of these seven steps is based to a great extent on the spirit of the person using them. A sincere commitment to getting well is fundamental to the healing process (Step 5). Yet no one step has as much power to heal as when all seven are used together. As with so many other examples, this is another case of the whole being greater than the sum of its parts.

The vast majority of people described in this book suffered from illnesses that were life-threatening. Many were told by their doctors that they needed a high-risk form of treatment in order to have any chance of surviving. Others were informed that their diseases were incurable and would very likely end their lives. Rather than accept such pronouncements of doom, these people took matters into their own hands and found methods of healing that eventually led to recovery.

That being said, I have stressed throughout the book that people who use the methods described here should remain under the supervision of their doctors. As you incorporate the changes described in this book, your doctor can monitor you, inform you of any changes in your condition, and advise you of your medical choices. While it is important to remain in contact with your physician, it is essential that you explore other sources of information and take responsibility for your own recovery. Only by becoming fully engaged in your own healing journey can you marshal all of your body's healing powers.

Healing Versus Curing

Many people, including many doctors, believe that there is a fundamental conflict between orthodox and complementary medicine. We can overcome this conflict if we distinguish between two forms of health care—one that focuses on curing and another on healing.

In the conventional medical model, illness reveals itself as signs and symptoms. Curing is the act of eliminating the signs and symptoms of a particular disorder. The underlying causes of that disorder, and the conditions that support it, remain unchanged, however. A cure comes from a source outside of ourselves. One submits to a doctor's treatment and is cured. A cure requires little or nothing from the patient. Once cured, the person essentially resumes his life as before. He is largely the same person he was prior to becoming ill.

To heal means to alter the internal conditions that created the illness in the first place and now sustain its existence. Every serious illness, no matter whether it's heart disease, cancer, diabetes, high blood pressure, digestive disorders, or AIDS, arises because the conditions within the body supported the birth of the illness and nurtured its life. To heal means to reduce or eliminate those conditions and replace them with conditions that support health.

When a doctor tells a patient that there is no cure, it means that there is no treatment that the doctor can administer to eliminate the illness. It does not mean that the person cannot be healed. There is no cure for heart disease, for example, but we all know that a person with heart disease can be fully healed and the illness eliminated from the body. To be healed, the patient must change his behavior.

Healing is more often the domain of competent complementary healers, while curing is the domain of medical doctors. Depending on the situation, both approaches may be necessary. In many instances, each approach is enhanced by embracing the other.

This book is about healing. Healing requires that we strengthen the conditions within the body that support health. Some degree of health already exists within your body. It has not been extinguished entirely, no matter how sick you may be.

The healer and shiatsu specialist Waturo Ohashi, with whom I wrote the book *Reading the Body,* used to tell a story about a husband and wife who one day came to see him for help. The wife gave a long list of disorders her husband suffered from. When she was finished, she said, "Isn't my husband very ill, Mr. Ohashi?"

Ohashi stood back in awe of the man and said, "You are so healthy. If I had half of your problems, I'd be dead. But because you have so much health, you can hold all those problems and still survive." Ohashi maintained that health and illness are always present within us at the same time. As long as we are alive, health sustains our bodies.

"Health carries sickness," Ohashi said. "Even when we suffer from the most severe symptoms, we still have health. The only time that health does not exist in us is when we are dead. That's when sickness has triumphed over health. Wherever there is life, there is health. Health keeps us alive."

Like many traditional healers, Ohashi maintained that healing was the act of strengthening the forces within us that sustain life and restore health. Unlike curing, healing requires effort on the part of the person who is sick, because only through changes in behavior, thinking, and emotions can those healing forces be enhanced. Healing, therefore, is a much deeper experience than curing, and requires a great deal more from us in the process.

Healing: A Broader Definition

Healing is the act of bringing together that which has been separated. Illness arises when parts of the body are separated from, or deprived of, what they need to sustain health. When cells and tissues do not receive adequate blood supply, oxygen, nutrition, and lymph flow, or when they are overwhelmed by toxic substances, they naturally decay and fall into illness. Any number of degenerative diseases are possible, including heart disease and cancer. As long as some part of the body is prevented from getting what it needs to maintain health, it is cut off from the whole. Healing is restoring these separated parts of the body to optimal circulation and thus to the forces that support health. Healing is not unlike bringing water to the thirsty parts of the body. We become aware of the thirsty parts of us by acknowledging our symptoms, then changing the behaviors that create such symptoms. To use the example of heart disease again, healing requires that we change our diet, exercise, and lifestyle patterns in order to restore circulation to the heart. As we will see, similar changes can alter the course of other serious illnesses, such as type 2 (adult-onset) diabetes, high blood pressure, and even the common cancers, such as those of the breast, prostate, and colon.

Healing is the bringing together of the separated elements of our lives—whether they be blood and tissue, the rejected parts of our own psyche, or the love between people who have been separated by conflict. It begins by listening, either to the body and its symptoms, or to the inner voice that cries out for attention, or to the person from whom we are estranged. It is made possible by changing the behaviors that created and sustain the injury. In the end, the act of bringing together that which has been separated is an act of love, whether it is within the context of the body, mind, or a relationship.

One of the beautiful and inspiring aspects of the healing journey is that each step offers us the opportunity to heal some vital part of our lives and to restore that part to reconciliation and love. This is the core of healing: to bring us back to a compassionate, nurturing, and loving relationship with ourselves and with the world around us.

Unlike curing, healing is not confined to the physical body. People who heal themselves do so by changing their behaviors, thinking, and emotional lives. In the process, they are transformed. For some, these changes bring about a physical recovery. For others, they restore harmony to their lives and their relationships, which allows them to pass into the next world in a state of greater wholeness and peace. Since all of us die, all of us consciously or unconsciously seek such healing before we pass on. Thus, the healing path beckons us all, even before we are confronted with a life-threatening illness.

How Complementary Systems Heal

All too often, those who want to utilize complementary treatments have little understanding of the healing modalities they are choosing, or any overall plan for healing. The consequence is that they end up stringing together a disparate array of therapies that seem to have some value individually but have no organic relationship to one another. Desperate to get well, they swallow pills and potions that may, in the end, do more harm than good. If we are to have any chance at success, we must understand what we are doing, and why we are doing it, so that we can create a unified and effective healing program. For that, we need a deeper understanding of illness, healing, and health. We also need a set of principles to guide us in our choices.

Traditional medicine, that is to say, Chinese, Ayurvedic, Greek, and other ancient systems, was founded on such a set of principles.

- The first is that health is a consequence of wholeness, which can be understood as unity of body, mind, and spirit.
- Second, the body is animated by a life force, or what we refer to today as electromagnetic energy. Health is established by the unfettered and abundant flow of the life force through the body, which restores optimal function of organs and the unity of body, mind, and spirit.
- Third, health is the natural consequence of balance in one's life. In many traditional systems, balance had a very specific meaning. It is established by effectively manipulating dynamic forces within the body—and in all of life—that are both complementary and antagonistic. Among the many ways to regulate such forces are food, herbs, physical therapies, prayer, meditation, and lifestyle choices.

- Fourth, the body knows how to heal itself. The body is imbued with an intelligence that is rooted in our cells and, at the same time, maintains a holistic perspective on the overall function of the body. This intelligence is continually striving to overcome the sources of illness and sustain health and life.

Using these four principles as our guide, we can define illness as the disruption of the body's underlying intelligence. In essence, illness causes cells, organs, and systems to behave chaotically and in ways that counteract the body's attempts to maintain orderly function and overall integrity. Consequently, the body fragments into competing parts that function independently and threaten the health and life of the whole organism.

Healing is the act of creating the conditions that allow the body's natural intelligence to dominate the system. Once that intelligence regains the upper hand, balance, integrity, and wholeness are restored, and health is experienced.

The question, therefore, is, How do we restore order within the body so that healing can occur? It would be best if we understood this process from both the scientific and traditional perspectives.

The Twin Causes of Degenerative Diseases

Two degenerative forces drive most of the illnesses that people suffer and die from today. They are inflammation and oxidation. Inflammation is an immune reaction that causes swelling, heat, redness, and physical changes in cells and tissues. Your immune system causes inflammation when it releases substances that destroy bacteria and viruses, or when it attacks substances such as fat and cholesterol that cause disease. Oxidation is the breakdown or decay of molecules, cells, tissues, and organs. The same process that causes an apple to brown occurs in your body.

Today, most of us create the conditions for high degrees of inflammation and oxidation by eating a diet rich in fats and processed foods, by drinking excess amounts of alcohol, by smoking cigarettes, and by living sedentary lives. Such behaviors lead to overweight, elevated blood cholesterol, and high levels of an amino acid called homocysteine that rises to toxic levels when we eat too much animal protein and not enough vegetables and fruits. These substances, and the inflammation they cause, increase our chances of suffering from heart disease, the common cancers, high blood pressure, and adult-onset diabetes.

Ironically, inflammation, by itself, is not a bad thing. It's part of our defense system and therefore is largely responsible for keeping us alive. The real issue is balance. The more exposed you are to illness-causing substances, the more inflammation you experience, and the greater your risk of major illness. You don't want your body to be chronically inflamed. Yet, that is exactly what happens to most of us who eat the standard American diet and live a sedentary lifestyle.

One of the by-products of inflammation is oxidation, or the creation of oxidants, also known as free radicals. Oxidants break up molecules and deform cells and tissues. Those altered tissues become cholesterol plaques in the arteries and scar tissue in the brain, liver, and intestines, just to name a few important sites. Free radicals also cause cells to mutate, turning some healthy cells into cancer. Free radicals are now recognized as the cause of aging and more than sixty illnesses, including cardiovascular diseases, cancer, asthma, cataracts, Parkinson's and Alzheimer's diseases.

As with inflammation, moderate production of oxidants is a natural consequence of living. We increase the body's oxidant burden by eating certain kinds of foods, living sedentary lives, and being exposed to a wide variety of environmental pollutants. The more oxidants, the more decay of cells and tissues—and the more disease.

Among the things that jump out at us when we examine the effects of inflammation and oxidation on our tissues is that they create biochemical chaos. Inflammation and oxidation turn healthy cells and tissues into bulbous masses and cancerous renegades.

In health, the body functions with unimaginable precision and orderliness. It knows when to eat, sleep, and expel waste. The heart beats, the lungs breathe, and wounds heal, and it all takes place without our ever having to think twice about such activities. On a microscopic level, cells know when to stop replicating so that they do not create a threat to the overall system. The orchestration and balance that exists between the tiniest and largest functions within the body are awe-inspiring.

Orderly behavior points to intelligence and even wisdom. When we consider that the body is composed of an estimated three trillion cells, we are talking about an order and an intelligence on a scale that cannot be imagined.

Unfortunately, the more the body is subjected to inflammation and oxidation, the more this underlying intelligence is thwarted. Cells can no longer function properly. Instead, they become deformed and behave in ways that are antagonistic to the body's overall goals of healthy function and even survival. The disruption of the intelligence can be seen as symptoms, disease, and premature death. Unless the two primary disrupters of the body's intelligence are dramatically diminished or removed, it is extremely difficult, if not impossible, to heal. In study after study, researchers have shown that if we remove the causes of excessive inflammation and oxidation, health can be reestablished.

In order to do that, we must significantly reduce, and in some cases eliminate, the causes of excess inflammation and oxidation. We can do that by eating a diet composed largely of plant foods, engaging in regular exercise, ceasing the use of tobacco products, and avoiding chemical and environmental toxins, including excess exposure to the sun's ultraviolet rays. We must also address the causes of stress in our lives, including our beliefs, and the degree to which we are able to give and receive love. As we make positive change, the levels of inflammation and oxidation are reduced, and the body's natural intelligence and order begin to be restored. At that point, the body very often is capable of restoring health.

The most effective healing programs are those that radically reduce and eliminate the most severe causes of inflammation and oxidation. This explains, in part, why diet is such an important factor in virtually all remarkable recovery cases, including those cited in this book. A healing diet, composed mostly of plant foods and small amounts of low-fat animal products, specifically fish, dramatically reduces inflammation and oxidation throughout the body. It also explains why the macrobiotic, Pritikin, McDougall diets—and others like them—are associated with such dramatic recovery stories. These approaches, which rely on plant foods as the primary source of nutrition, go directly to the very cause of disease. They rapidly reduce inflammation, lower oxidation, and boost the immune system—virtually a formula for recovery. At the same time, they encourage an increase in exercise, lower weight (overweight is highly inflammatory, as we will see), and dramatically reduce toxic substances that otherwise support the life of the illness. By reducing inflammation and oxidation, these approaches restore order to the body and allow its native intelligence to do its job.

The healing diet described in Chapters 3 and 9 is an essential part of an effective healing program. Diet is not the single, magic bullet, but it is the foundation for recovery. The other steps described in this book are also important. Indeed, these other six steps strengthen the body's healing powers, relieve the body from so much fear and tension, and often make it easier for people to follow a healing diet.

One of the first things that the body does when returned to a state of low inflammation and oxidation is to restore optimal blood flow to cells and tissues throughout the system. In essence, improved blood flow restores unity and integrity throughout the body. Also, a plant-based diet is rich in nutrients, antioxidants, and plant-based chemicals that boost immune function, fight cancer, and dramatically lower inflammation and oxidation. In such an environment, the body is optimally nourished. Meanwhile, disruptive toxins are reduced, and the body's intelligence once again is allowed to reassert its influence over the entire system.

Physical therapy is important, as well. Moderate exercise is anti-inflammatory. Healing touch, such as acupressure, therapeutic massage, chiropractic, shiatsu, and Jin Shin Jyutsu, can dramatically reduce tension in the tissues and improve circulation, thus reducing inflammation and oxidation.

Many people want to use a complementary herbal formula or supplement program as part of their healing program, as well. In the right circumstances, these can be helpful, and sometimes even essential, but only if the foundation is taken care of. Herbs, supplements, and other approaches cannot overcome the widespread, disease-causing effects of inflammation and oxidation. Therefore, unless the more fundamental approaches are incorporated into one's life, especially a healing diet, the other complementary modalities will have little, if any, effect.

An Electrical Basis for Healing

Oxidation and inflammation are scientific concepts and part of our Western understanding, but other factors are involved in the healing process that do not fit into the current scientific model—at least not yet. For thousands of years, Chinese medical doctors treated illness by enhancing what they perceived as an underlying energy, or life force, that animates the physical body. The Chinese refer to this energy as *chi,* or *Qi.* They developed a highly sophisticated medical system designed to manipulate this energy in order to promote healing. One of the system's most important tools is acupuncture. The Chinese maintained that the life force, or *Qi,* flows through the body in twelve distinct channels, or meridians. Along these pathways of energy are acupuncture points, which are said to act as generators of energy when stimulated, either by the shallow insertion of a needle at the point's precise location on the skin, or by applying finger pressure or heat. By stimulating the acupuncture point, the healer increases the flow of energy to the organ associated with that meridian. This increase in energy provides the basis for the restoration of health.

Acupuncture has been the subject of significant scientific research. The World Health Organization maintains that acupuncture is effective in the treatment of more than sixty disorders. Although science has shown that acupuncture works for a wide array of disorders, most scientists have dismissed the Chinese theory that describes how it works.

In fact, the human body is a highly complex electrical system. The heart, for example, is an electrical pump, or rather two pumps working in a highly coordinated manner. Electrical impulses originate from two nodes within the heart—the sinoatrial node (SA) and the atrioventrical node (AV)—which fire electrical current along electrical conductive fibers within the heart muscle, causing it to expand and contract. The nervous system is a complex electrical wiring that runs throughout the body, connecting every part of the body to the brain. Electricity is present in the blood.

An increasing number of researchers are now discovering that the body's electrical impulses run along the very meridian lines described by acupuncturists. One of the pioneers in this area is Robert Becker, M.D., an orthopedic surgeon and professor at the State University of New York, who has demonstrated in the laboratory that the Chinese theory accurately describes what takes place in the human body.

In his book *Cross Currents: The Perils of Electropollution, The Promise of Electromedicine,* Dr. Becker states that:

> We found that about 25 percent of the acupuncture points on the human forearm did exist, in that they had specific, reproducible, and significant electrical parameters and could be found in all subjects tested. Next, we looked at the meridians that seemed to connect these points. We found that these meridians had the electrical characteristics of transmission lines, while nonmeridian skin did not. We concluded that the acupuncture system is really there, and that it most likely operates electrically.

Becker also showed that health is dependent upon electromagnetic energy. Illness, he found, occurs when there is a diminution of electricity in the system. Any reduction in the overall flow of electromagnetic energy in the system makes it vulnerable to disease. The body responds to illness by attempting to increase electrical energy throughout the system, thus stimulating the immune system, and blood-cleansing organs.

Becker found that numerous tools can be used to boost electrical charge throughout the system, and thus promote healing. Among them are acupuncture, diet, herbs, homeopathy, massage, visualization, and placebo. These methods restore health in many ways, to be sure, but they appear to have a distinct impact on the body's electrical system, which may, in the end, be one of the keys to good health, if not the basis for it.

I have described healing as bringing together that which has been separated. In essence, this is the act of creating greater wholeness or integration. The key to integrating the body is to enhance circulation of blood, lymph, and electromagnetic energy. All three mediums—blood, lymph, and *Qi*—must flow optimally in order for the physical body to experience unity, integration, and wholeness. The program described in this book does just that. A healing diet, exercise, and various body-therapies, such as massage and acupuncture, enhance the circulation of blood, lymph, and electromagnetic energy throughout the system. These same approaches help to create oxygen- and nutrient-rich blood. They lower the quantities of toxins and waste products in the blood and lymph. And they boost electromagnetic energy.

The ancient understanding of health and illness is still the only integrated approach to health and illness. And indeed, from that understanding springs an array of healing tools that medical science is proving to be remarkably effective. Thus, for people searching for solutions to intractable health issues, the wisdom of our ancestors becomes ever more relevant to health and survival.

STEP 1

✳

Your Move from Shock to a Humble, Compassionate, and Loving Relationship with Yourself

The healing journey begins while you are still in a state of shock. A medical doctor discovers the presence of a life-threatening illness for which there is no medical solution. The inescapable message is that you are about to die. Though your loved ones gather around you and offer support, there is no one who really understands your situation or how alone you feel.

Remarkable as it may seem, untold numbers of people who find themselves in precisely this situation also find a way back to health. Through a series of experiences, some of which they initiate, others that appear unexpectedly, they discover healing tools, transform their lives, and overcome their disease. Marlene McKenna was one of those people.

On March 20, 1986, Marlene was informed by her surgeon at the Massachusetts General Hospital in Boston that she had malignant melanoma that had spread throughout her small intestine. The best she could hope for was six months to a year of life. She was forty years old. Marlene and her husband, Keven, both longtime residents of Providence, Rhode Island, had four children, two of their own, and two more from Keven's previous marriage.

Shocking as the diagnosis was, it did not come as a complete surprise to Marlene, nor to her doctors. During the previous eight years, Marlene had been manifesting a series of cysts and moles that appeared sporadically throughout her body. Her medical record reads like a precancerous tour of the human body, with each new cyst being documented with its own name and location: a chalazion on her right eye; a lipoma on her back; a subcutaneous nodule on her back; a kerototic lesion on her chest; a pigmented lesion on her right palm; another on her abdomen; and yet another on her neck. The list goes on.

Marlene would discover these and other strange eruptions at odd moments of the day. "My mind would be elsewhere—on my job or with my children," she told me, "and then my hand or eye would stumble upon an unusual bump. It was almost as if some part of my brain knew it was there and was directing my attention to it. When I would find one of these growths, which wouldn't be any bigger than a pea, I would be terrified. 'What's happening to me?!' I'd be screaming inside my head. Then I'd run to my doctor."

Finally, in August 1983, a mole found on Marlene's back was diagnosed as malignant. This new growth was surgically removed and analyzed. The pathology report was unequivocal: "Clark's level III melanoma," which meant that the cancer was malignant and perhaps had spread.

Despite the removal of the cancerous mole, the disease kept coming. For the next three years, more cysts appeared, each one a terrifying sign that the cancer was advancing. In March 1985, Marlene's doctor recorded the presence of a "flesh-colored papule with some dark reticulated pigmentation in it." That one was followed by two more papules, one on each eyebrow.

In August 1985, Marlene suffered acute abdominal pain after horseback riding. A gastrointestinal specialist diagnosed the problem as "spastic colon." A barium scan of the small and large intestine done at Miriam Hospital in Providence proved inconclusive. But the pain persisted, and by February 1986, it was accompanied by vomiting and dizziness. By that time, Marlene's weight had fallen to 105 pounds and there seemed little doubt that cancer had spread to her intestinal tract.

On March 20, 1986, renowned Mass General surgeon Dr. A. Benedict Cosimi performed exploratory surgery on Marlene and discovered that the small intestine had been "infiltrated extensively" by cancer. Dr. Cosimi removed twenty-two inches of Marlene's small intestine, excising as much cancer as possible. He recorded his findings in Marlene's medical record: "Not unexpectedly, rather extensive metastatic disease to the small bowel was encountered. There were two segments of small bowel containing a total of five separate lesions that required resection . . . there was considerable lymphadenopathy throughout the mesentery of the small bowel." His report left no doubt about Marlene's condition: "Undoubtedly, she has other positive nodes [cancerous tumors in her lymph system] in the mesentery and perhaps other occult lesions in the bowel as well." All of which meant that the cancer had spread beyond the length of intestine Dr. Cosimi had removed.

Little else could be done. Metastatic melanoma is among the most lethal of all cancers. It is considered incurable. Marlene's only hope lay with one or another experimental treatment offered at several large cancer centers. As Dr. Cosimi noted: "It would be appropriate, therefore, to proceed with some form of adjuvant therapy at this time. We recommend combined chemo/immunotherapy . . . Certainly reasonable for her to look into the interferon program at Yale."

Marlene did just that. She met with doctors and researchers at the Yale Medical Center in New Haven, Connecticut, and at the New England Medical Center and the Dana Farber Medical Center, in Boston. None of these specialists offered any tangible reason for hope. Marlene and Keven concluded that they were better off avoiding the experimental treatments. Not only were they ineffective, but they increased the suffering of the patient during his or her remaining months of life.

Soon Marlene's terror turned into deep depression. She was alive, but barely. Marlene had been an associate vice president at a major stock brokerage firm, serving as both a broker and financial planner. But work was now out of the question. As far as she was concerned, her career was meaningless, or worse: it robbed her of precious time with her children.

Her oldest son, Sean, was twenty; Christopher was seventeen; Damian, twelve; and Mary Kathryn, nine. Though they understood that their mother was ill, none of the four knew how desperate Marlene's situation really was. Damian and Mary Kathryn, both still young and dependent on their mother, concerned Marlene most. Their vulnerability and impending loss brought back memories of Marlene's own childhood trauma.

Marlene's father had died when she was eleven years old. Their relationship had been close and affectionate, and losing him devastated her. Not only did Marlene miss him terribly, but she grew up feeling unprotected and anxious. Now she feared that her own children, especially the two youngest, would suffer a similar fate.

"Part of me wanted to hold them and hug them and tell them everything—that we had only some weeks or months left together," Marlene said. " 'Let's make them special,' I wanted to say. But another part of me wanted to hold back, to protect them. They're going to have enough pain later on, I told myself. Spare them for now."

Meanwhile, Marlene's condition continued to deteriorate. Her weight fell to the low nineties. Her cheeks were dark hollows, her skin sallow gray. Her eyes drooped with exhaustion. She was essentially skin and bones. She could not walk up a flight of stairs without feeling exhausted. It seemed to those who knew her that it was only a matter of months, perhaps weeks, before the inevitable end. But then something unexpected happened.

Marlene's brother, Albert Marcello, who was studying biochemistry and civil engineering at Tufts University in Boston, happened to be listening to a late-night radio talk show that featured a guest who claimed to be psychic. At one point in the show the host opened the telephone lines and encouraged people to call in and ask the guest personal questions. Albert got through and asked about his sister.

"My sister is very depressed," Albert told the woman. "Is there anything I can do for her?"

"Your sister is ill, isn't she?" asked the woman.

"Yes, she's very ill. She has cancer," Albert said.

"She's given up all hope," the woman replied. "But she shouldn't. Tell her about macrobiotics. Many people are benefiting from using that diet. I believe your sister can be helped if she adopts a macrobiotic diet."

The words landed on Albert like lightning. Macrobiotics? What's macrobiotics? he said to himself. He got a pencil and paper, wrote down the word, and went to the bookstore the next day to find out more about this strange-sounding diet.

That same afternoon, Albert appeared at Marlene's front door with two large bags of groceries in his arms. When they entered Marlene's kitchen, Albert removed from the bags bunches of vegetables, brown rice, and an array of foods that Marlene had never seen before, foods with strange names like "miso" and "tamari."

"Albert, what is this stuff?" Marlene asked.

"These are macrobiotic foods," Albert said, unable to restrain his enthusiasm. "Here," he said, and handed her a book. "This book explains what this is all about." The book was entitled *The Cancer Prevention Diet*, by Michio Kushi, with Alex Jack (St. Martin's Press, 1983). Marlene took the book and looked at her brother incredulously.

"Albert, I'm way beyond cancer prevention," Marlene said. "I'm into cancer treatment."

"No, no," Albert replied, overlooking Marlene's condescension. "This book can help you now. It can show you how to get well. Read it, please. It's all about the cause of cancer, even the cause of melanoma. It also shows how you can use food to recover."

Marlene didn't believe Albert's words, but she was moved by his love. What he was saying made no sense to her at all, but she couldn't bring herself to reject him.

"Okay," Marlene said, "I'll read the book tonight," and then embraced her brother. "I love you. Thank you."

The *Cancer Prevention Diet* made little impression on Marlene, and she was ready to drop the idea of macrobiotics entirely, but the next day Albert called and asked her what she thought about the book. "I don't know, Albert," she replied. "I don't really believe diet can cure my cancer." Albert would not be put off. He had found a woman in Providence by the name of Eileen Shae who taught macrobiotic cooking. He gave Marlene the telephone number and insisted that she call. Reluctantly, Marlene did. Eileen Shae was warm, intelligent, and supportive. After listening to Marlene, Eileen told her to call Dr. Marc Van Cauwenbergh, M.D., who counseled people in the macrobiotic approach to diet and health. Marlene decided to call Dr. Van Cauwenbergh, in large measure because he had the credibility of being a physician.

A week later, she met Dr. Van Cauwenbergh, who gave her a dietary program which she followed religiously. He became her medical guide through the healing process, adjusting her diet and lifestyle to meet every new challenge she faced.

Meanwhile, Eileen Shae introduced Marlene to a substantial and active macrobiotic community within the Providence area. Eileen gave cooking classes and held weekly potlucks, where people gathered and occasionally listened to guest speakers who provided in-depth information about macrobiotics.

Those who attended these dinners were a varied lot. Some were healthy and followed macrobiotics because they believed in the diet and lifestyle. There were a handful of people in the same boat as Marlene, who were using the program in an effort to save their lives. There were even a few people who had successfully navigated the crossing that Marlene and so many others were attempting: These people had already overcome serious illnesses, including cancer. Hence, the dinners were a great source of support and information.

In the weeks and months that followed, Marlene made what could be described as a miraculous transformation. By mid-June, just six weeks after she began the macrobiotic diet, she felt an unmistakable increase in energy. Her skin appeared to be getting pinker and brighter. She slept deeper and more restfully, and woke up with more vitality. During the day, her mind was clearer and her memory better. But one symptom seemed particularly persuasive to her. Marlene had noticed during the months preceding her diagnosis that her menses were dark and thick. It had occurred to her one day that her blood seemed almost dirty. But in July of 1986, Marlene noticed that her menstrual blood was becoming bright red. Was it possible, she wondered, that her blood contained more oxygen and less toxicity? That might explain the healthy, bright red color, she speculated. It might also explain some of the other improvements in her health. If her blood was carrying more oxygen, she would likely experience greater energy and mental clarity. More oxygen in her blood might also explain her improved skin color. Could other benefits be possible? Marlene wondered. Could blood that is richer in oxygen and less burdened by fat, carbon dioxide, and other poisons be a better medium for her immune system?

While her physical health appeared to be improving, Marlene made other important changes in her life. She took short walks every day. She attended a gym twice a week and, with the help of an exercise physiologist, worked out with a five-pound bar, which was all she could lift. She did some gentle exercises on the resistance equipment, as well, and, once a week, she also received a light massage from a shiatsu therapist. Meanwhile, she managed to get lots of help in her daily life. A retired emergency room nurse helped her with her housekeeping and shopping; friends ran errands for her; others picked up her children when she was tired or had to visit her doctor.

The differences between her current and former lives were striking. In the past, her entire day was caught up in a stressful whirlwind of meetings, deadlines, and the ever-changing fortunes of the stock market. She was always running late, it seemed. She had little time for her children and husband, and even less for herself. She took her meals on the run—which meant fast foods—and hurried her children through their lives so that she could attend to the ceaseless demands of her own. Her illness changed all of that. The first thing it did, of course, was force her to leave her job, which freed up lots of time. But she also responded to her illness by caring for herself—indeed, loving herself—in a multitude of new ways. For the first time in her adult life, she had to listen to and care for her body. She had to accept help from others. And she had to get as much out of the present moment as she could, which meant that her focus shifted from the people who paid her salary to those she loved and who loved her.

During the summer of 1986, Marlene's health continued to improve. Since being discharged from Mass General, Marlene underwent monthly blood tests to monitor her condition. Her doctors expected those tests to reveal that her cancer was advancing. But by the end of the summer, her blood tests had all returned to normal, including her SGOT and alkaline phosphatase (both liver function tests and important markers for cancer), bilirubin, hematocrit, and hemoglobin. Her body had stopped producing cysts and tumors, and every sign and symptom suggested that her cancer was being defeated.

At one of her checkups, Marlene asked her doctor which test she could undergo to establish more firmly if she was free of cancer. A magnetic resonance imaging (MRI) might give them more information, she was told. An MRI uses electromagnetic fields and radio signals to detect both subtle and profound changes in the body. MRIs can "see" through bone, but can also detect the presence of cancerous tumors. Marlene scheduled an MRI for October 1986.

Before she underwent the test, her doctor informed her that he expected the disease to be in essentially the same state as when she left Mass General seven months before. At that time, there was still considerable evidence of inflammation and cancer throughout her small intestine. She was instructed not to get her hopes up.

Contrary to what the doctors expected, Marlene's MRI showed no sign of cancer anywhere in her body. The results from the test were normal. Her doctors were at a loss to explain her recovery.

Marlene McKenna's story does not end at this happy moment. In January 1988, she discovered that she was pregnant. Her doctors insisted that she abort the pregnancy for fear that it would trigger the return of her cancer. After weeks of soul-searching, and very much against her doctors' advice, Marlene decided to go ahead with the pregnancy. As with so many of her other decisions on the healing path, this one proved to be the right one, as well. On September 24, 1988, Joseph Matthew McKenna was born in Providence, Rhode Island. Contrary to all expectations, both baby and mother were healthy.

Marlene continues to be active and in good health at the time of this writing in the fall of 2003.

Shock Must Lead to Compassion

To be shocked is to be overwhelmed with fear. Since all of us, at one time or another, have been shocked, we all know the experience of feeling instantly isolated and stripped of all that, just moments before, appeared to protect us from harm. For those who have just been told that they suffer from a serious illness, the shock comes while standing in the face of their greatest fear.

For many people, the diagnosis of a life-threatening illness is followed by a period of grim detachment. The person is numb and thrown into despair. All the old demands that used to preoccupy him or her now have little or no importance. Former duties that were previously viewed as essential now seem grotesquely irrelevant.

As the old lifestyle gives way, the old identity erodes. People ask themselves: Who am I if not my work, my daily routine, my responsibilities, my body as I knew it? These things were my life? I don't even recognize myself anymore, they say. Making the situation even worse is the fact that many old friends and, in some cases, even some family members start to identify the person with his or her illness, as if that is all that was left.

Marlene McKenna put the problem this way: "Dying is lonely. People don't want to associate with you because you remind them of their own mortality. After the people in my community found out that I had cancer and wasn't expected to live for very long, every encounter with old friends was awkward and tense. Very often, people would look away when they saw me and pretend that they hadn't seen me. Others who stopped to talk to me didn't know what to say to me. What could they say? It was very hard for everyone."

No one can deal rationally with a diagnosis of a terminal disease. Shock is a kind of protective reaction to the overwhelming nature of the events and all the feelings exploding inside. Shock dims the conscious mind while allowing the unconscious processes to do their job, which is to rearrange one's life on the basis of this new information. A new identity is being forged, one that can better cope with the current realities. The numbness that characterizes this period is a kind of anesthetic, allowing profound changes to occur inside of you, even without your being aware. The best thing to do now is to rest and let others care for you as best they can.

Little by little, shock gives way to emerging rays of clarity. Gradually, a new state of balance is attained, one that is more accepting and free of excessive fear. Virtually everyone I have spoken to who has been diagnosed with a terrible illness arrives at this inner state of equilibrium. What people don't often realize is that the changes that have occurred unconsciously have brought about an entirely new vision of life that is itself more balanced and humble. People appreciate their loved ones as never before. They awaken to small expressions of love and feel tremendous gratitude. Often they seek out the beauty and nourishing richness of nature, and find themselves marveling at seemingly ordinary events—a bird in flight, for example, or the morning sun on wet grass. Despite all the pain that they are going through, they see life with new eyes.

A shattering confrontation with death alters a person's life and character and makes the first step in the healing journey possible. Like the other six steps, the first is a transformation all its own. The change that is attempting to unfold at this stage is to move from shock to a humble, loving, and compassionate relationship with yourself, and with those around you. The step involves a kind of coming back to yourself, of reestablishing intimacy with your inner life. This step is the foundation for the entire healing journey.

We should distinguish between compassion and self-pity. Implicit within self-pity lie feelings of being a victim, anger with oneself and others, and even self-hatred. When we experience self-pity, we are experiencing our powerlessness, our inability to take corrective action, and a kind of rejection of self. Compassion, on the other hand, is characterized by love of oneself and of others, especially those who suffer. There is both nobility and honesty in compassion. And perhaps most telling of all, there is the power to take remedial action. In the end, the compassionate heart is a warrior's heart, because it seeks to make the world a better place, not only for oneself, but for others, as well.

Humility is the basis for compassion. Humility allows us to accept ourselves, to ask for help, and to receive such assistance in gratitude, which makes it all the more enriching. In humility, we experience and express genuine compassion and love for others, too. This state of humble compassion is the foundation for self-love.

Though most of us have been trained to reject feelings of humility and compassion, especially compassion for oneself, it is nonetheless the natural response whenever we experience an illness or injury. Even the common cold has the capacity to humble us, to put us flat on our backs, to make us forget the outside world and, instead, turn our attention and our care on ourselves. Turning back to ourselves when we are ill is a natural response. For those suffering from a serious illness, the challenge at this stage of the healing process is to create and sustain a compassionate relationship with yourself. That compassion springs from a recognition of your own wounded body and heart, which must now be addressed and cared for.

Creating such a relationship with yourself is not always easy, however. Indeed, many of us believe that the ideal behavior at this time is to deny our pain, to march on stoically, and to ask for as little as possible. In short, to become invisible. Others take a different approach: Their anger and regret are expressed outwardly as bitter complaining that alienates all around them. The results of such complaining are so predictable that we can only wonder if the person is actively seeking the rejection he or she inevitably receives. Is their relationship with themselves so toxic that they are secretly asking others to confirm their unworthiness of love?

In any case, neither stoic invisibility nor outward expressions of rage are the least bit healing, and they stand in the way of all that you are attempting to accomplish.

The Paradoxical Self: The Choice Between Love and Self-destruction

The stories of firefighters, police officers, and common people who risked their lives, or gave them, to save others during the September 11, 2001, attack on New York's World Trade Center will stir generations to come with awe and wonder. These were ordinary people, beset with the same concerns, fears, and complaints as the rest of us. How is it possible, we should ask, that any one of us can be desperately afraid, but with a small shift in awareness can suddenly find ourselves helping another human being because we realize that he or she is hurt, or in pain, or afraid? What is this miracle that allows us to feel compassion for those whose suffering suddenly seems more important than our own? Something lives inside of us that, when awakened, opens the heart and the gates of love. It spurs us to act in ways that can only be described as unconditional love.

This miracle is even more baffling when we consider the self-criticism, selfishness, and self-destruction of which each of us is also capable. These apparent opposite states of being, in which love and self-hatred exist side by side, reveal the paradox of the human condition. On one hand, we can be heroes and healers—on the other, small and self-destructive.

Religious traditions recognize this basic duality and have their own interpretations of it. In Buddhism, it is said that each of us possesses the Buddha nature—that is to say, the fully awakened state—and the bodhisattva, the healer and saint. At the same time, each of us also contains the worlds of hell, hunger, and animalia, the very lowest levels of humanity. It is up to each of us to choose which of our inner worlds we live in. Somewhat similar ideas exist in Christianity in which Jesus tells his disciples that the kingdom of heaven exists within them, but that evil lives inside of them, as well. Moses spoke directly to this fundamental duality, and the need to make wise choices, when he laid down the law, then told his people, "I have given you the choice between life and death. Choose life."

It's especially important now for us to recognize this fundamental duality in our nature. Healing depends on the ability to shift from the parts of us that are critical, angry, and self-wounding, to the parts of us that are loving, compassionate, and healing. As a metaphor, this change is often referred to as a shift from the head to the heart. The intellectual center is the part of us that analyzes information, creates categories and judgments, and gives us the experience of our own individuality. As positive as these characteristics are, they also give us the experience of separation from others, and even from parts of ourselves. The rational, intellectual center, for example, stresses the separation between mind and body, and between the parts of us that are ill, versus those that appear to be healthy. Once that separation is established, it's easy to see the suffering parts as bad and the parts that remain healthy as good.

Such thinking has created a distinct form of health care. Since illness is the source of danger, the intellectual center stresses actions that will eradicate the disease in any number of ways. This approach can include drug treatment, surgery, radiation therapy perhaps, or all three. Of course, all such treatments are administered by a medical doctor, who seeks to finds ways to destroy the illness. Your behaviors are not all that important, because you are not seen as a particularly powerful factor in the process of destroying the disease.

The realm of the heart gives rise to an entirely different way of thinking and behaving. The heart emphasizes the needs and characteristics that people have in common. From the heart springs compassion— the heart knows that your suffering is just like mine—and a recognition of our unity, which is the basis for love. From the heart's point of view, the parts of your body that are suffering—that is to say, the parts that are beset by illness—are calling out for love and care. The heart seeks to do this by directing you to find loving ways to treat your body and strengthen your immune and healing systems. Such practices can include healing touch, which includes therapeutic massage, acupressure (a system that uses finger pressure on acupuncture points), shiatsu (the Japanese form of acupressure), Jin Shin Jyutsu (a Japanese form of massage that applies gentle touch at precise locations on the body), and Reiki, which is a form of laying-on of hands. (See the Resource Guide at the back of the book for a description of many forms of therapeutic, healing touch.) Other heart-centered approaches are dietary change and non-strenuous forms of exercise, such as gentle stretching, yoga, and a martial art such as Tai Chi Chuan or Qigong. They also emphasize the loving care that you can provide yourself. Your love for yourself is now an essential factor in the healing process.

Truly effective treatment usually includes both the intellectual approach—in which medical practitioners isolate and attack the illness—and the heart approach, in which the body's immune and healing forces are supported. Though many doctors are loath to acknowledge heart-centered healing, it's fair to say that the intellectual approach is not complete without the heart and its related behaviors. This is especially true when medicine has run out of answers. At that point, we must turn to the consciousness of the heart and the healing methods that flow from it.

Right now, you need loving care. The heart-centered consciousness within you—and in others who may be around you now, or will show up later on your journey—is nonjudgmental, understanding, and loving. It is gentle with you, and especially with your body. Most of all, the heart is capable of responding with compassion to all your needs and fears, without compelling you to act from those fears.

The heart is prepared to wait for answers, because the heart knows intuitively that the healing journey is an organic process, a process that has just begun. Valuable forms of healing, indeed, potential answers, still lie in the future. They will appear at the right moment in time. At this moment, however, a specific type of transformation must be accomplished, which is to establish a compassionate, loving relationship with yourself and especially with your body. With such an understanding, you will be able to evaluate therapies—both medical and complementary—with a relatively calm, reflective, and intelligent mind. You will also be able to make the most of the appropriate healing tools when they arrive.

The biggest impediment to such a state of equilibrium, of course, is fear, especially because it can drive you to make rash and even fatal decisions.

Driven by Fear

Fear seeks a cure. It demands an instantaneous answer to an overwhelming problem. Unfortunately, there are no cures—that is to say, there are no medical solutions to the illness. There is only the possibility of real healing, or the process by which the body's internal conditions are radically changed so that the illness is made to wither, while health is promoted and restored. Unfortunately, for the desperate soul bent on finding an immediate escape from danger, anything that offers the slightest whiff of a cure becomes something to leap at. It's especially dangerous when the doctor himself offers the patient a "long shot"—the experimental medical treatment.

Experimental medical treatments, usually offered by the large research centers, have all the trappings of medical authority, but little, if any, of medicine's standards for efficacy. They are experiments conducted on desperate people. Many such experimental treatments have no therapeutic value at all, and they are often accompanied by terrible side effects. One man I knew, who had been diagnosed with pancreatic cancer, was told by his doctor that his condition was hopeless. Nevertheless, the doctor encouraged him to get himself enrolled in an experimental cancer trial that was being conducted by a large research facility in Boston. The man pursued the lead, only to discover that he would have to be enrolled in a preliminary protocol before he got the full treatment. Why? The scientists had to determine if the man could tolerate the severe side effects from some of the chemotherapy drugs. If he could survive the initial trial in a relatively stable condition, he could get the full drug therapy. The possibility for extending his life was emphasized by the doctors, but they did admit that death was among the side effects from the drugs.

Propelled by fear and the belief that this might be his only hope for survival, he decided to go ahead. As it turned out, he could not tolerate the drugs and soon died, but not before he suffered a ghastly array of side effects from the chemotherapy. Not only did he suffer, but so did his family, who were forced to watch him pass away in agony. His family also lamented the fact that his life had been shortened by the so-called treatment.

Among the lessons we can take from such experiences is the recognition of our own profound vulnerability, especially now. When Marlene McKenna visited the leading cancer research centers, she found that the experimental treatments being offered had no substantial therapeutic value, though each was being sold to her by the researchers who needed people in their experiments. At one point, Marlene ruefully noted that she felt like a human guinea pig. Marlene had no illusions; she was dying. But that fact did not keep her from recognizing that the experimental treatments being offered her had no real therapeutic value.

It must be said, as well, that many people adopt the same dietary approach used by Marlene McKenna and die. Indeed, every alternative approach—even those that possess valid therapeutic value—has failed people. But the point remains: It takes courage to assess therapies accurately and to make wise decisions. Courage can also give us the clarity to know in our gut that whatever choice we make, it is the right one for us. But when we make decisions on fear alone, we can easily make bad choices, which not only can cause death, but destroy the quality of our remaining days.

Finding the Mother's Compassion and Healing Love

There are mysterious healing powers that lie within us that must be identified and utilized in order to promote recovery. One of the most potent of these is the archetypal mother, who is the source of compassion, love, and healing. Every child knows this simple truth and runs to his or her mother—the earthly manifestation of the archetype—whenever he or she has been injured. In order to draw upon the healing power of the mother, we must distinguish between our biological mother and the archetype, who is known in various traditions as the goddess, the divine mother, the mother-in-perfection, or the Holy Mother.

The biological mother, of course, is the source of the human body. Indeed, we grew a body and developed our earliest psychological training inside our mothers. While we are in her womb, our mother's blood is our blood, her emotions ours. Her thoughts and emotions—especially those that concerned our own existence—shaped how we feel about ourselves and our own physical lives. Once we are born, our survival, at least in our early infancy, depends on her in a multitude of ways. And more to the point, how well we care for ourselves, and how well we survive, rests to a great extent on how our mothers cared for us, and on her attitudes toward our lives.

It's true that today many stay-at-home fathers serve as the caregivers of infants. But since the mother archetype lives in both men and women, these fathers are really manifesting the mother through their own lives. They are, in the phrase coined by author and poet Robert Bly, male-mothers.

The problem is, of course, that most of us were given mixed messages from our mothers about how we should feel about our own physical and emotional needs, including our need for healing. This sets up an array of conflicts within us about how we should feel about our needs, or treat ourselves, especially now, when we are in need of so much love.

Those conflicts can be dispelled by contacting the archetypal mother, who is the source of life, compassion, healing, and unconditional love. There is no criticism or blame from the archetypal mother. There is only love and understanding—an understanding that transcends your own. Even in the areas of your life that you might criticize yourself, she will not. Even the mistakes that you feel are obvious and perhaps warrant some form of retribution, she refuses to condemn.

What does such love and compassion look like? we want to know. How can it be channeled into your daily behaviors now? One of the clearest expressions of the archetypal mother in modern times was Mother Teresa of Calcutta. She said the following in her 1979 acceptance speech for the Nobel Peace Prize.

> One evening we went out and we picked up four people from the street. And one of them was in a most terrible condition. And I told the sisters: "You take care of the other three; I will take care of this one that looks worse." So I did for her all that my love can do. I put her in bed, and there was such a beautiful smile on her face. She took hold of my hand, as she said one word only: "thank you"—and she died.
>
> I could not help but examine my conscience before her. And I asked: "What would I say if I was in her place?" And my answer was very simple.

I would have tried to draw a little attention to myself. I would have said: "I am hungry, I am dying, I am cold, I am in pain," or something. But she gave me much more—she gave me her grateful love. And she died with a smile on her face—like that man who we picked up from the drain, half eaten with worms, and we brought him to the home—"I have lived like an animal in the street," [he said] "but I am going to die like an angel, loved and cared for." And it was so wonderful to see the greatness of that man who could speak like that, who could die like that without blaming, without cursing anybody, without comparing anything. Like an angel— this is the greatness of our people.

Mother Teresa did not ask this woman and man how they came to be in such straits. She did not blame them for their suffering, nor wonder what they may have done to create such harrowing circumstances. She didn't ask about their ethnic backgrounds, or race, or former status. All such thoughts arise from the intellectual center—they are the basis for separation—and thus are entirely foreign to the heart-centered consciousness. Acting from the heart, Mother Teresa identified with the suffering ("What would I do if I was in her place?" she asks) and gave each of them exactly what they needed in the moment: unconditional love in the form of a bath, rest, food, and loving, tender care. She embodied compassion. Indeed, she was the living version of the archetypal mother.

Many people have encountered the archetypal mother energy in a beloved relative, such as a grandmother, or aunt, or even their own mother. Many have a spiritual connection with a religious figure who embodies the archetype. Indeed, the archetypal mother has been personified as a divine being in some of the world's great religions—Mary in Christianity, Quan Yin in Taoism, Shiva in Hinduism, and Sophia in Proverbs and Greek mythology. The divine mother is the source of all regeneration. She is the mother who, after the barrenness of winter, gives rise to the renewal of spring. She is the power behind all forms of restoration and healing.

The archetypal mother, however you may see her, can be a great source of comfort, love, and healing to you now. We first must recognize that the archetypal figure lives within each of us as a function— that is to say, it is a set of psychological patterns that tell us how we should care for ourselves and especially for our bodies. At this moment, you can call upon the archetypal mother—or those capacities in you for compassion, healing, and love—or the divine mother, if that is how you see the archetype, in order to guide you in your own self-care. From this aspect of your being, you can care for yourself with love, tenderness, and forgiveness.

The archetypal or divine mother helps us make that shift, which I spoke of earlier, from the intellectual center to the heart-centered consciousness, or from the critical nature to the part of us that is capable of compassion and unconditional love. The mother, present within each of us, facilitates that shift, she makes it possible, because she intervenes in our consciousness to show us a way of being that is beyond all criticism, judgment, fear, and feelings of unworthiness. We can call upon the divine mother by asking for help and healing in prayer or meditation.

One way to feel the presence of that figure is to ask yourself: How would the archetypal or divine mother treat me now in the midst of my pain? Or, if we need a more physical example to consider, you can ask: How would Mother Teresa treat me now?

Just by asking yourself that question honestly and sincerely, you will experience a shift in your awareness. You will feel the love of the divine mother that is within you. That love can cause you to relax and settle more fully into your body, into the wisdom of your heart, and into the present moment. You can almost feel a spiritual presence that embraces you. If you sustain that feeling, even for a few minutes, you will awaken to the love that flows within you. That same inner state, which is the compassionate aspect of your being, can permeate your life if you allow it to guide your actions, especially when you need rest, or attempt to care for your body, or when you speak to someone you love.

The archetypal mother's powers flow naturally into the very best healers, both men and women. Indeed, the mother's healing abilities are what imbue the true nurse, who combines compassion, a healing touch, courage, and medical expertise. These characteristics, when they are combined in a single person, represent a rare degree of psychological integration, because such persons are able to hold within themselves the loftiest characteristics of our humanity, as well as a practical knowledge of what to do in a crisis.

Like the mother, the true healer is free of any trace of the inner critic. She does not blame you for your illness or injury. Her consciousness is rooted in the absolute now. Her only interest is in your immediate needs and how your illness can be overcome. She cares about your suffering and all your emotional needs, which are part of the struggle against your illness. It's worth asking yourself: What would my ideal healer do for me now? As much as possible, do for yourself what that healer would do for you. Also, ask others to do what they can to help you now. If you continue to act as a good healer toward yourself—that is to say, to act nonjudgmentally and noncritically—you will recognize a good healer when one shows up in your life.

Bringing the Mother's Love to Your Inner State

Many people who have overcome serious illnesses have told me that at some point in their lives, they lost track of themselves. They allowed the daily demands and hectic schedules to steal their lives away from them. That loss, they told me, contributed to the onset of their diseases. Losing ourselves to the demands of life increases our stress, because we lose track of our own limitations and needs. One of the ways we are pulled away from ourselves, and our own needs, is by constantly having to meet the demands of others. In the process, we rarely if ever take time to wonder: What do I need now? What is my body asking me for? The hurry-up of such an existence prevents us from knowing our needs and the needs of those we love the most. Somehow, the most important parts of our lives go unnourished.

The compassion and unconditional love of the archetypal mother brings you back to intimacy with yourself. Coming back to yourself is an act of self-love. It makes you more attuned to yourself, your environment, and the lives of those you love. Many Buddhist traditions call this the practice of mindfulness. It is simply being aware of yourself, your feelings, your body, and what life is presenting to you each day, without reacting to those feelings with any trace of judgment. The archetypal mother teaches us to listen without having to change anything. Instead, we are encouraged merely to be aware of what we feel and to hold those feelings with compassion.

To do this, we need time everyday to sit with our thoughts and feelings and allow them to exist without censorship or criticism. Our only assignment is to bring awareness to our physical sensations, our emotions, and our thoughts. This act requires nothing more than to sit comfortably in the sun, to stroke the cat, and be aware of what we are feeling. As fear, anger, or sadness arises, we can gently breathe soothing love into those emotions, and into the places in the body where those feelings are held. There is no work involved. You are simply allowing your own existence to become the object of your awareness. And as your life emerges into your consciousness, you are holding it in your heart. Something odd and wonderful can happen. You can experience yourself relaxing deeply and being held in a feeling of soft grace, as if a larger force within you were opening its wings and surrounding you with peace and harmony.

Practicing Awareness in the Mother's Love

Walk In Nature

Everytime we walk in a forest or by the ocean, or sit by a river or lake, we are communing with the archetypal or divine mother. Nature, the expression of the mother, overwhelms us with its gentle, healing energies. As so many of us have experienced, it's nearly impossible to sit by a river, or walk at the ocean, and maintain negative or critical thoughts. Eventually, nature overpowers our negativity and fears and replaces them with a greater degree of peace and balance.

If you can't get to a park or some natural environment, take short, gentle walks around your block or in your neighborhood. Don't power walk and don't exhaust yourself. Rather, walk with awareness of your body's needs and feelings. Walking is the ideal exercise. You may start out walking burdened by your cares and concerns, but by the time you get home, you'll experience much greater relief. You will have purged yourself of so much negative and distressing tension, which will allow your mind to clear and your compassionate nature to emerge more clearly.

Record Your Feelings and Thoughts

Writing in a diary can be a healing exercise, or a way to support the ill-ness, depending on the part of yourself from which you write. If you write from the critical voice, you will spend your time listing your fail-ures and the reasons for those failures. That kind of indulgence will only make it more difficult for you to heal. If you write from the compassion-ate voice, you will become intimate with your own suffering—that is to say, you will bring awareness to your symptoms, fears, anger, or conflicts—while at the same time holding those feelings with care and love for yourself. If you hold these feelings with a compassionate heart, you will experience them without judging yourself. You are simply being aware of your anger, sadness, and fear, for example, and experiencing the feelings fully. If you allow these feelings to emerge fully and hold them with compassion, without any self-criticism, they will pass. Like dark clouds that are finally swept away by the wind, you will be left feel-ing deeply relieved, clear, and free of inner conflict.

When you write in your journal, report how you are coping with whatever is occurring in your life. Acknowledge each positive experience as a blessing or a victory on the healing path. These experiences become the basis for gratitude, which can sometimes have the mysterious effect of multiplying the blessings and the victories, or at least enhancing your ability to see them. As your gratitude for small blessings grows, you may also recognize these positive events as subtle clues to an unseen force that may be assisting you in your efforts to heal.

Do Gentle, Healing Exercise

This same awareness and compassion can be brought to the body through the practice of gentle stretching, yoga, or the ancient Chinese exercise called Qigong, or the martial art called Tai Chi Chuan. These exercises are not done with an intention of achieving the perfect posture, but with the intention of embracing your body with intimacy, care, and love. Walking can become a meditation on your love and compassion for your body, and your entire being, as you experience your strengths and accept and appreciate your limits.

See a Healer with a Strong Motherly Nature

At this stage in the healing process, you may prefer a practitioner of some form of complementary medicine, such as a Reiki therapist, acupressurist, or Jin Shin Jyutsu practitioner who can provide gentle healing touch and support, without asking you to change your behavior. It's more important to be understood and supported than to be criticized and encouraged to change. For that, you will need a person who restricts himself or herself to providing gentle massage, or some other form of healing touch, without necessarily guiding you or encouraging you to adopt new behaviors. Seek out a healer who is understanding, compassionate, and loving, one who is capable of channeling that love through his or her touch.

Teachers will show up later on the path when you are prepared to take up new healing tools and change old patterns. But at this moment, you may feel a need to rest in someone's compassion and understanding. Healing touch and compassionate listening is more important to you than advice. (More about healers and healing touch in Chapter 4.)

Do Your Everyday Activities with Awareness and Compassion

Even the simplest acts can be done with gentle, soothing awareness. Doing your job, cleaning your house, cooking and eating your food, choosing the kind of music you will listen to, interacting with those you love—everything can be done slowly, consciously, and in a healing way. As you go through your life with this awareness, notice how each event or person affects your emotions, your thoughts, and your physical body. From that knowledge, you can choose more carefully the kinds of events you are willing to participate in and the people with whom you spend time. Such self-knowledge becomes the basis for wise choices and acts of self-love.

Pray and Meditate

Directing your prayers toward the divine mother, or using guided imagery and meditation to become aware of your feelings, can bring great peace and balance to your inner life. (Much more about prayer and meditation in Chapter 6.) One of the best ways to deal with negative emotions, such as anger and fear, is to do the following meditation, which can lead you from your fear and anger to sadness, compassion, and self-love.

A Meditative Journey to Compassion and Love

Mindfulness can help us deal very effectively with fear and anger, the two big emotions that, if allowed to, can drive us at this point. Here is a meditation that can help dissipate negative emotions, open your heart, and awaken your compassion and love for yourself.

Begin by sitting comfortably in a quiet room in your home. If possible, light a candle or two to create a feeling of intimacy and calm. Close your eyes and relax. Breathe deeply into your belly, breathing through your nose with your mouth closed. Emphasize the exhalation. Envision yourself releasing any tension that may be held in your body with each out breath. As you breath, allow yourself to become aware of your body. As you do, your mind and body will start to relax ever more deeply. When you feel deeply relaxed, proceed to the next step.

Without creating any image, or attaching yourself to any image that may emerge, allow yourself to feel your fear or anxiety. Be aware of the fear, as if you were looking at it without judging it, without repressing it, and without holding any image for very long. At first, you will notice that your fear will increase. Stay with it. Keep breathing into your belly, inhaling and exhaling deeply. If you continue to breathe, you will witness your fear steadily diminishing. You will notice that your fear is shrinking as you continue to breathe and your body and mind become more relaxed again.

Soon, you will very likely become aware that your fear is retreating. As it does, you may find it being replaced by anger. Continue to breathe deeply, emphasizing the exhalation and the release of tension. Allow the anger to well up inside of you. Feel it. (Allow yourself to express your anger, if you wish; punch a pillow, pray, direct your anger toward its source, even at God, if that's who you are angry at. Stay with your anger, keeping your eyes closed, while breathing deeply.) Hold your anger in your awareness just as you did your fear: without judgment, without holding any image in place for very long. At some point, you will start to feel trapped by your anger, as it reaches a crescendo. You will recognize that all your decisions led you to this point in your life. There was no escaping this moment. Every one of your choices cascaded into the next, which fell into the next, so that it never felt as if there were choices at all, but just an endless string of events that led you to this time. You are not to blame for being in these circumstances. Life brought you to this moment, and there was no escaping it. When you allow yourself to feel fully and perhaps express your anger, you will feel trapped. When that feeling of being trapped has reached a peak, it will naturally change into sadness—a pure and cleansing sadness that, for many, will be transformed into tears. If you are crying, allow all your tears to flow.

As you cry, your sadness will quickly give way to an overwhelming feeling of compassion for yourself. You will awaken to your tenderness toward yourself, your vulnerability, and the courage it took to walk this path in life. You have done the best you could with this life. Embrace yourself with that compassion and care. Continue to breathe. That compassion will naturally lead you into enveloping feelings of love for yourself.

That love for yourself is the basis for healing and hope.

Don't be alarmed or critical of yourself if you do not pass through every level of this meditation. Continue to practice it without judgment or any trace of self-criticism. The key to this meditation is to get to your sadness and allow yourself to release that pain as tears and compassion for yourself.

The Power of Small Blessings to Heal

Small activities that bring relief and pleasure can have a significant effect on your immune system, scientists tell us.

Researchers have found that small pleasures can have a significant effect on a person's immune system. A single pleasurable event can boost the immune system for as much as two days, according to research conducted by Dr. Arthur Stone, a psychologist at the medical school of the State University of New York at Stony Brook. Conversely, negative events, such as criticism, especially from a superior or one's employer, can depress immune function for up to twenty-four hours, thus making people more vulnerable to illnesses.

"Positive events of the day seem to have a stronger helpful impact on immune function than upsetting events do a negative one," Dr. Stone told the *New York Times* (May 11, 1994). "Having a good time on Monday still had a positive effect on the immune system by Wednesday," Dr. Stone said. "But the negative immune effect from undesirable events on Monday lasts just for that day."

The most powerful effects on immune response, Dr. Stone found, were positive events that one did alone, such as fishing or jogging. On the other hand, when study participants were criticized by an employer, suffered a difficult encounter with a coworker, were under prolonged stress at work, they experienced a diminution of their immune response for the next day.

Of course, the impact of small pleasures on the immune systems of people with already-existing illness has yet to be shown. Still, those who have overcome life-threatening disease say that they don't need a double-blind study to affirm the power of small pleasures.

Providing yourself with small pleasures is, in fact, taking action. Small actions can affect your life for the better. You realize that you have power. At that point, you will very likely want to do more to help yourself. When that awareness arises, you are ready to take the second step on your healing journey.

STEP 2

The Person Takes Responsibility for His or Her Recovery

As you practice compassion for yourself, something begins to stir within you. The love you are giving to yourself naturally creates a desire to support your body and the healing forces within you. This is the moment that your fighting spirit, or the gentle warrior within you, is starting to emerge. Like a new birth, that fighting spirit must be supported. You can do that by taking the second step on your path, which is to accept responsibility for your own healing.

The second step is made possible by honestly and courageously asking yourself: What can I do to promote my health and chances of recovery? The answer you give will form the basis for a healing program. That program will grow sophisticated and powerful as more answers come. But for now, doing what you know you can do will give you an immediate sense of personal power, control, and hope.

When a patient is told by his doctor that his situation is hopeless, he is, in essence, being pronounced dead in advance. Those words alone can crush the spirit. Regardless of the severity of the illness, they become a self-fulfilling prophecy for many. In his book, *Space, Time, and Medicine*

(Shambhala, 1982), Larry Dossey, M.D., tells the story of an old man who had no signs of disease, but was dying nonetheless after he learned that a local shaman had placed a hex on him. Upon hearing the news, the man immediately began to lose weight and wither away. When he finally turned up at the local hospital, he was emaciated and about to die. Dossey and his fellow physician, a doctor named Jim, tried every test imaginable on the man, but none revealed a single sign of illness. Finally, Jim told the man that he was dying. The old man said he knew he was dying. He also knew why: He had been hexed, he said, by a local shaman. Determined to save his patient's life, Jim conducted a midnight dehexing ceremony, complete with a candlelight ritual that involved burning a lock of the man's hair. As Dossey put it, "I now realize what I didn't know then. I was witnessing an archetypal struggle—one shaman battling another shaman—a struggle over life itself."

As it turned out, the ritual worked. The man was convinced that the doctors had succeeded in casting off the curse. The following day, the man was jovial. His appetite returned; he ate copious amounts of food; and gradually he regained his normal weight. He left the hospital seven days later in joyful spirits and, according to all his tests, in perfectly good health.

For most people today, medical doctors are modern-day shamans. They possess a power to discover illness, destroy it, and save lives. That is an awesome ability, which explains why doctors are so revered and, indeed, given titanlike status. But when that power and status are turned against a patient, as it is when a doctor says that he or she is going to die, it is often enough by itself to seal a person's fate. I have noticed many times how a robust man can shrink and wither within weeks of being told that he has a terminal illness. Did the physical changes occur because the illness was poised to overwhelm the man's defenses, or was it the bad news that weakened him and hastened his demise?

The problem for many people who have been diagnosed with a serious illness is that they must cope not only with the illness itself, but also with the overwhelming effects of the doctor's prognosis, which, for some, amounts to a hex. Both problems must be dealt with effectively if the person is to regain his or her health.

It's easy for a person to confuse these two problems and see them as one. Many people search for an authority figure—either another doctor or alternative healer—who will give them reason for hope and, in effect, remove the hex. Yes, they want an effective medicine, to be sure. But they really have no basis to evaluate the medicine, apart from what the doctor tells them. They can only believe in the medicine if the doctor himself believes in it. In effect, the doctor/healer invests his personal power and prestige in the medicine, so that the patient can believe in the remedy, too, and thus have reason for hope. This is the magic behind medicine and, indeed, behind the effectiveness of placebo. All of us know that without hope, we cannot fully engage in the struggle to survive. Hope inspires and rallies the healing forces within us.

Unfortunately, in situations like this, the hope is derived from someone else, namely the doctor or healer. We have no connection with ourselves or our own healing power, which means that if the doctor decides to give us bad news, we are lost because we were never able to derive any confidence from our own inner resources.

Under such circumstances, it's extremely difficult to make wise medical or lifestyle decisions. We can succumb to experimental treatments that have no real therapeutic value; we can also surrender to charlatans who are offering the latest version of snake oil. In either case, we can chase after the advice and support of others, but never feel truly confident in anything we hear. Why? Because they cannot give us what we are looking for, which is a strength and resilience that come from within. There is a way to find that strength within ourselves, however, but it isn't by investing our hope in others.

The way to restore your power and strength is by becoming a co-healer. That is to say, you must take responsibility for your part in the healing process. The aspect of healing that only you can contribute is your will to survive. Your willpower cannot be fully engaged until you accept the challenge, and the responsibility, to do all you can to strengthen your immune defenses and change the conditions inside of you that currently support the disease. As you do this, you inspire your will and your personal power. And in the process, you experience a new level of control over your healing process.

This act brings to life your fighting spirit, which can galvanize your own healing powers and give you reason for hope. You are no longer hanging by the hope derived from your physician or healer. These people are no longer the ones who bring the magic to the medicine. Rather, it is your own spirit that inspires the remedy with the power to heal. That's what happens when you take responsibility for your recovery: The fighter in you, with all its healing powers, awakens and engages in battle.

This is not to say that you will walk the healing path alone. No one can bring about his or her recovery without help from many other people, including doctors, teachers, counselors, guides, and loving supporters. But there is an aspect of the healing process that only you can control. And it is in fulfilling your role that you gain your power and generate real hope. This step begins by searching for answers.

It is a terrifying idea, at first, that we should have to start searching for healing solutions after a doctor has said that there are no solutions. Most of us have been indoctrinated to believe that all health solutions come exclusively from doctors and pharmaceutical agents. We find it hard to believe that something of real value could come from a complementary or alternative treatment. In times like these, it's helpful to reflect on a little medical history.

As late as the 1970s, medical science maintained that there was no cure for heart disease, which is still the leading cause of death in the Western world. Even in the early eighties, many doctors routinely told patients that coronary heart disease—caused by inflammation and cholesterol plaques that grow inside the arteries leading to the heart—were irreversible and incurable. Today, we know that that's not true. We also know that a cure was always available to anyone who adopted a low-fat, plant-based diet, which can reverse coronary heart disease. That same diet is able to reverse other serious diseases, including type 2 diabetes. But few people in the West adopted such a diet because Western science had yet to learn that it was an effective treatment. People accepted that there was no cure for heart disease because doctors and scientists said there was no cure.

That is, until Nathan Pritikin found it.

Pritikin: Pioneer, Warrior, and Healer

Nathan Pritikin was a brilliant scientist and inventor who held more than sixty patents in electronics, chemistry, and engineering. Not only did he invent new technologies, but he manufactured his inventions, as well, which made him a very successful man. Pritikin had attended only two years of college at the University of Chicago, but he used to say that he was better off for not having had a formal education. "If I had had more education, I'd be trapped into thinking like everyone else thought. Without so much training, I could explore scientific questions with a fresh view of things."

On February 11, 1958, Pritikin, who was forty-three years old at the time, underwent an electrocardiogram stress test at the Sansum Medical Clinic in Santa Barbara, California, and was diagnosed with coronary heart disease caused by cholesterol plaques clogging the arteries of his heart. Nathan's medical records show that his cholesterol level was 280 milligrams per deciliter of blood (expressed as mg./dl.). Today, we know that a cholesterol level of 280 is extremely dangerous and can cause what scientists refer to as galloping atherosclerosis—or rapidly advancing coronary heart disease.

Pritikin, who was under the care of two physicians, was prescribed Atropine, a drug that might stimulate the vagus nerve in the neck to increase blood flow to Pritikin's heart. Nathan was also ordered to limit his walking to the equivalent of four blocks per day, to take a nap every afternoon, and to eliminate all strenuous activity, including bicycle riding and tennis, two activities he had come to enjoy.

"Is this the only treatment?" Pritikin asked. "Don't you want me to change my diet or do something else to cure the illness?"

"No," his doctor told him. "Heart disease is incurable."

"What do you believe is the cause?" Pritikin wanted to know.

"Heart disease, cancer, and other degenerative illnesses are the natural consequence of aging and stress," his doctor informed him. "There's nothing that anyone can do to avoid them."

Nathan could not believe his ears. The doctor warned him that if he did not follow the recommendations, he would be risking a fatal heart attack.

None of the recommendations were easy for Pritikin to follow. Atropine caused Pritikin's eyes to dilate and forced him to wear sunglasses. Walking any distance terrified him, and he dutifully curtailed all physical activity. As for the nap, occasionally he forced himself.

Pritikin was no ordinary heart patient. He had been studying the relationship between diet and health—especially diet's relationship to heart disease—since the late 1940s, when he read that Europeans who had been occupied by the Nazis during World War II experienced a dramatic decline in coronary heart disease. The occupied countries were placed on food rationing and were forced to eat a traditional peasant diet of barley, potatoes, garden vegetables, and fruit. All the meat, eggs, cheese, and other high-fat foods went to the German soldiers.

After the war ended, European physicians and scientists discovered that during the war years, and for some time afterward, the people who had been on the peasant diet experienced a dramatic decline in deaths from heart disease. Autopsy studies showed that many people experienced a remarkable absence of atherosclerosis in the coronary arteries.

Nathan was one of the few people who saw the connection between the rationed diet and the healthy hearts, an insight that triggered a lifelong study of the relationship between diet and health. He soon learned, as well, that people around the world who ate their own version of the peasant diet—one composed mostly of whole grains, vegetables, and fruit—had very low rates of heart disease, cancer, diabetes, and other serious illnesses. Animal studies revealed that blood cholesterol might be the key. High cholesterol was associated with heart disease, while low was associated with good health. Pritikin theorized that if a person with heart disease lowered his cholesterol far enough, he might be able to cure himself of heart disease.

As passionate as he was about his ideas, Pritikin did not immediately adopt them. He ate as every other American did. He was particularly fond of ice cream, of which he ate a pint every night. But when he was diagnosed with heart disease and told to retire, he changed.

Pritikin adopted his own version of the peasant diet and eliminated all red meat, dairy products, eggs, and chicken. The only animal food he ate was fish. Pritikin's doctor, Dale Creek, was immediately alarmed by Pritikin's change in eating habits. He told Nathan that if he changed his diet, he would deprive his body of essential nutrients and would soon become sick. Creek wrote Pritikin, "Be temperate in all things— including temperance."

Pritikin was also afraid that he might bring on malnutrition, so in May 1958, he consulted a nutritionist at the University of California at

Los Angeles (UCLA) to discuss the changes he had made, and how he could prevent vitamin deficiencies.

The UCLA nutritionist thought Pritikin had lost his mind and told him flatly that lowering his cholesterol level through diet was dangerous. You cannot "cut out foods high in fat and cholesterol," the nutritionist told him, because "these are the best foods the body can eat."

"We can't help you," the nutritionist told Pritikin. "It's too dangerous. You might kill yourself."

Nevertheless, by June 1958, Pritikin became even more daring in his dietary changes. He was searching for the ideal diet and began to experiment widely, eating nothing but lentil beans for a week, then switching to brown rice for another week, then including beef for two or three meals a day.

He kept meticulous records during these experiments. Every tiny change in his eating patterns was noted. "Eating 10 dates after dinner," he wrote as one of his entries. "Start fruit at 1000 calories 55 percent total intake," he said in another. On another occasion, he noted: "Three weeks on fruit at 55 to 60 percent of total calories, 1000–1200 calories fruit." Every telltale reaction that he experienced was recorded: "22 days on dried fruit, 12 dates, 60 percent calories on dried fruit; calories 1800, was thirsty last two weeks, constant dry taste in mouth."

Nathan's peculiar behavior made his wife, Ilene, wonder if the UCLA nutritionist wasn't right about her husband. Many years later, Ilene said, "I thought, 'Who is he to challenge the medical world and go off in a very strange direction?'" As Nathan said to Dr. John McDougall, physician and author, in a videotaped interview in 1982: "My wife thought I needed a psychiatrist more than I did a medical doctor." Despite her misgivings, Ilene went along with Nathan's requests, preparing whatever strange assortment of foods he happened to be eating that particular week.

With each new experiment, he had his blood checked to discover the effects on his cholesterol level. As he expected, his cholesterol level rose and fell with his dietary changes. When he included beef and other animal foods, his cholesterol level rose. When he ate mostly plant foods, his cholesterol level fell.

Pritikin was equally diligent about his nutrient levels, undergoing regular blood tests to determine if he was experiencing nutrient deficiencies. Contrary to all that he had been warned about, he was never deficient in any vitamin or mineral.

After much experimentation, Pritikin finally arrived at a diet made up of brown rice and other whole grains, vegetables, beans, and fish. His cholesterol level stabilized at 120 mg./dl., and remained there for the rest of his life.

"It really was not that complicated," Pritikin would say many years later. "After a couple of months, I realized I was no different than any of the animal studies. The same way animals drop their cholesterol level, so do humans. I never did run into deficiencies, or have any problems at all [with getting adequate nutrition]. I was just frightened unnecessarily."

The effects of his diet on his overall health were remarkable. His energy increased dramatically, as did his mental clarity. He felt better than he had in years.

In June 1960, just a few months before his forty-fifth birthday, Pritikin's latest electrocardiogram showed that his heart was getting more blood. As his medical record notes: "Definite improvement since the tracing of December 15, 1959 . . . Normal electrocardiogram."

At that point, Pritikin was ready to push the envelope again. He knew that if he was going to recover fully, he had to start exercising. The problem was that exercise could kill him instantly. He would have to start slowly, he decided. He walked two blocks, then stopped and checked his pulse to determine if his heartbeat was consistent. It was. He did that walk three times a day for a week, then went to Cottage Hospital and had another EKG to determine if his heart had deteriorated at all. It hadn't. From there, he increased his distances to eight blocks per day, then to a quarter of a mile a day, and then two quarter-mile walks per day, until finally he was up to a mile and a half a day without stopping. Before every increase, he underwent an EKG test. All of them showed that he was well.

One day in the fall of 1961, after completing his daily walk, he went into his backyard and decided to run a short distance, just twenty steps, he calculated. He ran in street shoes and long pants, but the sheer freedom and exhilaration was an epiphany. Inside of Pritikin was a runner. The thrill and the joy of running triggered visions of going for miles, but as before, he disciplined himself and started slowly, jogging a half mile. However, during one of his early runs, his knee collapsed. He had been running laps in his backyard when a stabbing pain exploded in his knee and sent him crashing to the ground. An orthopedic surgeon in Santa Barbara examined the knee and asked if he hurt himself while playing football with his children. "No," Nathan replied. "I've been running."

"Running?" the doctor asked. "You can't run, you're forty-six years old. You'll wear out all the cartilage in your knees if you run. By the time you're fifty you'll need a cane to get around. If you want to exercise, you'll have to swim. People over forty can't run."

"Can't I change my shoes or my gait or something to make it possible to run?" he asked.

"No. People over forty can't run."

Pritikin's knee took three weeks to heal. After he was well, he decided to have one more run, a kind of farewell jog to a pastime that he had unfortunately grown too old to enjoy. Unconsciously, he kicked off his shoes and ran barefoot in the grass. He ran one lap, then two, then a third, all without pain. He ran some more and still no pain. And then it hit him: It was the shoes! Street shoes provided no support, which of course made him vulnerable to all kinds of knee, leg, and foot injuries.

"I realized that you can't run in street shoes," Pritikin would say years later. He needed a shoe that would absorb the shock of running. Of course, in 1961, there were no running shoes of the type we have today. That was not a significant problem for him. He designed his own runner's shoe and took it to a shoe manufacturer to have it made. Once the shoes were constructed, he was off and running.

"I never had a knee problem again," he recalled.

Pritikin was running long before such a thing was considered normal behavior. And, indeed, he was an odd sight to see: a man in strange shoes and long, dark pants running along the winding, tree-lined roads of Santa Barbara. The town's well-heeled, gentrified residents would see Pritikin running, pull up alongside him, and ask if he was all right. Did his car break down on the road? they would ask. Did he need a ride to a gas station or home? "No, I'm fine," he would tell them, and keep right on going.

Many people who exercise regularly find running boring and tedious, but Nathan was a born runner. "Man was made to walk," he liked to say, "but running is what gives him joy." Running reminded him of the body's wondrous grace, power, and self-healing powers.

On February 16, 1966, Pritikin underwent a treadmill stress test, which is an EKG test that is done while walking or running. This test could reveal if one or more of his coronary arteries was still blocked. Once he had the electrodes attached to his body, he ran on the treadmill for three miles, which took twenty minutes—a routine run for him. The EKG showed that his heart functioned perfectly. Much to the disbelief of his doctors, Pritikin had cured himself of coronary heart disease, a feat that doctors believed was impossible.

That was just the beginning. Ten years later, Nathan opened the Pritikin Longevity Center where he cured tens of thousands of people of coronary heart disease, diabetes, high blood pressure, claudication, blindness due to atherosclerosis of the eyes, arthritis, and many other serious illnesses. Many of these people had been told by their doctors that their illnesses were incurable, or that they could only recover through coronary bypass surgery. Yet, like Nathan himself, they found that the right behaviors could restore their health—even if their doctors said that such a thing was impossible.

Remarkably, while Pritikin was healing people by the thousands, he was being vilified by medical authorities and scientists. It wasn't until the mid-1980s that he started to receive acceptance from the medical establishment, and not until the early 1990s that he was thoroughly vindicated by the scientific evidence.

Pritikin's experience is far more common than you may realize. Chinese medicine, acupuncture, chiropractic, and many forms of massage were, at one time or another, all condemned by medical authorities as worthless and even quackery. Today, all of these disciplines have been found to offer effective remedies for a wide range of illnesses. Acupuncture, for example, can be effective in the treatment of more than sixty diseases, according to the World Health Organization. For decades, the consumption of antioxidant vitamins, and the use of many of today's most popular herbs, including echinacea, goldenseal, saw palmetto, and ginkgo biloba, was ridiculed. Now, surveys show that most cardiologists take antioxidant supplements daily to protect their own hearts, and the above-mentioned herbs have all been shown scientifically to have significant therapeutic value.

One of the lessons that we can derive from medical history is that answers to disease exist long before mainstream medical authorities finally embrace them. Indeed, many valuable methods of healing are condemned before they are celebrated. Those who recover from serious illness realize, at an early stage in the healing journey, that healing modalities exist that their doctors have either rejected or do not know about.

We cannot overestimate the importance of this seemingly small awakening. It represents a kind of weaning, first from medical authority, and second from the belief that someone else can determine how the rest of your life will unfold. With this awakening, a small flame of hope starts to grow. And from it comes a power to search for a solution. When you take that step, you can feel an almost instantaneous rise in personal power and hope. Suddenly, you are in contact with a powerful part of your being that is willing to search for answers and fight for your life.

Taking Responsibility Means Taking Back the Power

The warrior's power flows from a singular commitment: He or she takes responsibility for creating his or her future. Make no mistake: The second step on the healing journey is an act of will. When you find yourself at this step you must search for answers and adopt the healing modalities that resonate as true and efficacious. You may continue to consult your doctor at this stage—always a wise choice, for reasons I will discuss—but the relationship is different now. You seek the physician's information but not his authority. You reserve entirely to yourself the power to make medical decisions, even when your doctor says that your decision is wrong. Indeed, those who take responsibility for their healing invariably run into disagreements with doctors and even loved ones who want them to follow the conventional course, even when conventional medicine offers very long odds against recovery.

In his book, *Love, Medicine, and Miracles,* Bernie Siegel, M.D., describes what he calls "exceptional patients." These are the people, he says, who are often seen as difficult, especially for their doctors. In an interview with the *Los Angeles Times,* Dr. Siegel said that exceptional patients do not win popularity contests with doctors. They want to know why tests are done or treatments prescribed. "They're never in their hospital rooms," said Dr. Siegel. "They disrupt the system [because] they're fighting for their identities."

Exceptional patients guard the quality of their lives. Each treatment is evaluated for both its capacity to improve length of survival and its side effects. Exceptional patients often choose to avoid treatments that diminish the quality of life, while only giving a slight chance of lengthening life. Also, exceptional patients tend to determine for themselves how long they will accept a given treatment. In short, these are not passive people. They are involved in every aspect of their healing process.

"Exceptional patients often break the rules," said Dr. Siegel, by utilizing treatments according to their own judgment and intuition. They adopt alternatives and often use those alternative approaches in combination with standard medical treatment. "Exceptional patients are fighters . . ." Dr. Siegel said. "These are the people who very often beat a killer disease."

Virginia Harper, who cured herself of Crohn's disease using a macrobiotic diet, exemplifies Dr. Siegel's description of an "exceptional patient." Virginia was told by medical doctors for years that there was no answer for Crohn's disease, an illness that causes the tissues of the small intestine to become inflamed and ulcerated. Open wounds appear within the intestinal wall, causing terrible pain, diarrhea, fever, and bloody stools. These were not the only consequences of her illness, however. Doctors prescribed Prednisone, which made Virginia's body bloated and overweight. She had terrible headaches. Her eyes became sensitive to light. Her joints ached, and her feet swelled so badly that she nearly screamed when she placed them on the floor in the morning. Her intestines were a constant source of pain. She was often depressed and weepy. These and other symptoms become even more intense during the many flare-ups that she suffered. At the same time, Virginia suffered from Takayasu arteritis, an incurable autoimmune disease that causes arteries in the neck to harden and threatened to bring on a stroke.

Like everyone else with Crohn's, Virginia was told that drug treatment might slow the disease, but it inevitably progressed through the small intestine and sometimes even migrated to the large intestine, as well. For most people, surgery is needed to remove lengths of diseased intestinal tract. Eventually, so much intestine is removed that an opening must be made in the stomach wall where a bag is attached so that waste from the intestinal tract can be eliminated. The future for anyone with

Crohn's disease is grim. After many years of intense suffering, most succumb to premature death.

In January 1980, Virginia herself was scheduled to begin a new regimen of chemotherapy drugs, then undergo surgery to remove a portion of her small intestine. Just a month before, however, she decided to go on a macrobiotic diet to treat her illness. During her first few weeks on the diet, she experienced small but positive signs. In January, she told her doctor that she had begun the diet and decided to postpone the new drugs and the operation. He demanded that she stop the diet immediately. In her book, *Controlling Crohn's Disease the Natural Way* (Kensington, 2002), Virginia recalled that first conversation with her doctor about macrobiotics.

"How have you been feeling?" her doctor asked her.

"Very good," she said. "I really do feel much better."

"Oh? Well, that's great," the doctor said. "Have you experienced any changes in your condition since we last saw each other?"

"Well, that's what I want to talk to you about. I want to postpone the chemotherapy and the surgery," Virginia told him.

"Why?" he asked. Virginia could hear alarm in his voice.

"Because I have started a macrobiotic diet and I want to give it some more time to see if it could make me well," Virginia answered. "I've already experienced some small signs that it's helping me."

"You can't do that," the doctor demanded. He then got up from behind his desk and started toward Virginia, who was sitting in a chair opposite his desk. "That food is going to be too hard on you. You're going to hurt yourself. There's not one bit of scientific proof that a macrobiotic diet can do any good."

"How is it going to hurt me?" Virginia asked him.

"As your doctor I can't allow it. You are in a very delicate condition and that crazy diet can only do you harm."

"I have already been doing it and it's helping me some. I want to give it more time," Virginia responded, emotion rising in her voice now.

"You cannot go on a macrobiotic diet," the doctor asserted. "It's crazy and dangerous. I will not go on treating you if you do."

Virginia broke down in tears and told him flatly, "This is my only hope. I need you to support me. This diet makes sense. The food is going into my intestines. That's where the problem is. Look at me. If I make it to thirty years old, I'm not going to have my intestines. This is my last chance and I need you to help me."

Shocked by Virginia's reaction, the doctor relented and agreed to go on following her, but only if she saw him more often. She agreed. Over the course of the next year, Virginia accomplished something her doctors had said was impossible: she cured herself of Crohn's. She freed herself of all Crohn's-related symptoms, lost weight, weaned herself from all drugs, and regained her life. To this day, some twelve years later, Virginia experiences no evidence of Crohn's. Nor does she have any signs of Takayasu arteritis. Medical tests and her own experience have proven that she has fully recovered from both illnesses. Today, Virginia lives an extremely active and productive life teaching people how to overcome Crohn's and other inflammatory bowel disorders. Had she listened to her doctors, she no doubt would have lost much of her intestinal tract by now. She might also be dead. One of the reasons that she was able to save her own life was because she took responsibility for her own recovery, even when there was enormous pressure to succumb to the will of her doctor.

Like Nathan Pritikin, Virginia's example reveals the important distinction between accepting medical treatment because it is valuable and effective versus accepting it because the doctor imposes his authority and will on the patient. Nothing Virginia was being offered by medicine was working. On the contrary, even while being treated, she suffered ongoing symptoms and regular flare-ups, many of which forced her to be hospitalized. Her life was literally being destroyed by the disease. Her knowledge of her illness and its treatment, her study of macrobiotics, and her intuition led her to conclude that the diet was worth adopting. The question she faced was: Who is ultimately responsible for this decision, me or my doctor? The answer seems obvious, but all too many people refuse to take up the healing journey because their doctors dismiss all forms of complementary medicine as worthless and even dangerous. That would be fine if the patient found out for himself what the value of a particular approach might be, but all too many stop their search when the doctor refuses to give his permission.

Both Virginia and Nathan remained in close contact with their doctors, who performed regular diagnostic tests and were able to monitor their progress. If the diets they chose to follow had no therapeutic value, or actually made their diseases worse, the medical tests would have revealed them to be harmful. As it happened, medical tests showed that both were making steady improvement and eventually showed that both had made the right decision. Staying with the doctor as a source of medical information and advice, however, was an essential part of their healing paths. Neither had any interest in engaging in a fantasy or proving an ideological point about diet and health. Theirs were serious attempts at healing. If a particular program didn't work, both wanted to be rid of their approaches as early in the process as was possible. In both cases, the doctors were there to provide essential information and help them make wise decisions.

This approach might be called "making medicine work for you." People oftentimes say that their doctors work for them, but how many truly feel that they have hired their physician and are really in control of their medical decisions? Most people become "patients." They go to their doctor—not the other way around—then wait for the busy doctor to see them, either in the doctor's office or at the hospital. They submit to the tests the doctor orders. They accept the medications or chemotherapy that the doctor prescribes, often without question, and take such drugs for as long as the doctor recommends. They undergo the surgery that the doctor says is needed. They comply with their doctor's orders. The patient is not in control; the doctor is. Doctors are used to being in control, and they are very reluctant to give up that power. Many doctors are so used to being in charge that they become irate, as Virginia Harper's doctor did, when the patient decides to adopt a healing approach that is not included in the doctor's conventional arsenal. Conflicts such as these are not inevitable—many doctors welcome the moment when their patients become co-healers—but they are common, especially when the patients realize that it's their lives on the line, and they have every right to make their own decisions.

For many people, taking control in the healing process seems like pure hubris, but science has shown that patients who exert some control over their circumstances experience a significant improvement in immune function. On the other hand, those who experience helplessness are more likely to suffer a significant decline in immune strength.

A study done by Yale researchers William J. Sieber and Judith Rodin and published in the medical journal, *Brain, Behavior and Immunity*, compared the effects of prolonged stress in the form of noise on two groups of people, one group that could not control the noise and the other that could. The researchers found that the group that could control the noise experienced no significant declines in immune reaction. However, the group that could not control the noise suffered sharp declines in natural killer cell activity. Natural killer cells attack and destroy bacteria, viruses, and cancer cells.

Such human research has been supported consistently by animal studies. A study published in *Science* compared two groups of laboratory animals, both of which were subjected to unexpected and repeated shock. One group was able to escape the shock; the other could not. The scientists found that the group that was able to escape the shock experienced little or no impairment of their immune systems, but the animals that had no control over the stress of their circumstances experienced significant declines in immunity and greater susceptibility to disease.

Taking control of your situation, even in small ways, can have a profound impact on your outlook, hope, and immune function. As you go deeper into the healing process and find healing tools that independently strengthen your health, your feelings of control—along with the associated improvement in immune reaction—can grow even stronger.

Does Taking Responsibility Mean I am to Blame?

Several years ago, a woman asked me for advice on how she might support her own recovery from breast cancer. I suggested dietary and lifestyle changes. Weeks later, I spoke to her again and asked if she had made any progress along the lines we had discussed. "No," she said. "I decided that I could not change my way of eating because if I did that, I would be admitting that I had created my cancer. I can't do that," she said. "I don't want to feel that I'm to blame for my illness."

I couldn't help but sympathize. Many people confuse the act of taking responsibility with blaming themselves for their past actions and perceived mistakes. The truth is, no one can be blamed for becoming ill. Illness is caused by too many variables over which we have no control.

Among them, of course, are genetic weaknesses and exposure to environmental pollutants at an early age, neither of which we could have changed, even if we knew about them. In addition, all of us have been subjected to varying degrees of trauma. For many of us, those traumas gave rise to chronic fears, anxiety, and negative beliefs, all of which can impair immune function and predispose us to illness. Consider a study done in the early 1950s by Harvard University researchers who administered an extensive questionnaire to healthy Harvard undergraduates. Among the questions on the survey were: Did you experience a warm and affectionate relationship with your mother? and Did you experience a warm and loving relationship with your father?

Thirty-five years later, the same undergraduates were examined again by the Harvard team of scientists. The researchers gave these now-adult study participants detailed medical and psychological tests and thoroughly examined their medical records. What they found was that 91 percent of the study participants who, as undergraduates, had said that they did not have warm, loving relationships with their parents, especially with their mothers, were later diagnosed with serious illnesses, including heart disease, high blood pressure, ulcers, and alcoholism. Conversely, only 45 percent of the former students who had reported positive relationships with their parents, especially with their mothers, were later diagnosed with serious diseases. In other words, those who had difficult relationships with parents were twice as likely to suffer major illnesses as adults. The study, known as the Harvard Masters of Stress Study, demonstrated overwhelmingly the power of early experiences to determine health later in life.

Of course, not all those who get sick necessarily had a poor relationship with their parents, but the study does reveal just how powerful environmental factors can be when it comes to determining health. It also reveals the utter irrelevance of blame, since most environmental factors are beyond our control.

Taking Control Begins by Recognizing Your Imbalances

At this stage in the healing journey, taking responsibility and control essentially means becoming more aware and active in three different areas of your life.

1. You must have a comprehensive knowledge of your disease and its treatment. It's important to understand how the treatment works, and what the odds are that it will extend your life or bring about a cure of your illness. You must also know the potential and even likely side effects of conventional treatment. Is death among the possible side effects of the treatment? Do the side effects outweigh the potential benefits of the treatment? Are you comfortable with the risk-benefits ratio, and are you prepared to accept the risks?

2. Vary the sources of your information about your disease and treatment. Your medical doctor is only one source of information. He or she will present the conventional medical view. In a great many cases—including those involving heart disease, cancer, and digestive disorders—that conventional view may be more narrow and limited than what you need. It's important to remember that the overwhelming majority of doctors are trained to use drugs and surgery, not food, herbs, exercise, Chinese medicine, or lifestyle treatments. Many caring physicians will encourage you to expand your knowledge in these areas and will even support you by recommending qualified complementary practitioners with whom the doctor regularly cooperates. Ask your doctor for these types of referrals; this is a good place to start your wider explorations. If your doctor denies the value of complementary treatments, then seek other sources from books, newspapers, magazines, friends, business associates, church and civic leaders. There are many Internet sites that can be extremely helpful in gaining information about medical and complementary forms of treatment. You can do a medline search and get summaries or the full article

on any scientific subject by logging on to www.ncbi.nlm.nih.gov/ pubmed, or www.nlm.nih.gov, which is the National Public Library of Medicine. (The Resource Guide in the back of this book offers an extensive list of sources and Internet sites for complementary care and medicine.)

3. Honestly examine your life and determine where your imbalances lie. Ask yourself the following questions:

- Do my eating habits and lifestyle support recovery? Are there changes in my eating habits or daily patterns that could be made to strengthen my chances of recovery? What am I doing to learn more about the relationship between diet and health? Am I prepared to change my way of eating to support my recovery? (Answers on the subject of diet are provided in Chapter 3.)

- Are my stress levels too high? Much of your stress may be coming from your illness, but ask yourself: Are there stressors other than my illness that I can manage better, or even eliminate? What is my relationship with time? Am I continually short of time? If so, why? What must I do to change my life so that I have more time and less stress?

- Do I exercise enough? If not, then what can I do today to start exercising? Can I take a daily walk, even if it's only for ten minutes? The answer, for most people, obviously is yes. (More on exercise in Chapter 5.)

- Am I getting the love I need? Am I giving love to those I truly care about? What can I do now to enhance my life in both of these areas? (Guidance on this question is provided in Chapter 4.)

- Am I in conflict with the people I love or are my important relationships at peace? What are the sources of that conflict? What can I do to resolve that conflict so that I can be more at peace with myself and those I love? (More on resolving conflicts and creating forgiveness in Chapter 4.)

- Is my work helping or hindering my healing now? Is it taking too much of my time and energy? Does my intuition tell me that I should leave my job, if only temporarily?

- What is my relationship with the spiritual dimension of my life? Am I at peace with God? Are there things I could do to create a better relationship with my perception of the divine? What can I do today that will create greater spiritual peace in my life? (More on faith in Chapter 6.)

It can be illuminating and inspiring to write your answers to each of these questions in a journal or diary. As you write your answers, explore your feelings as deeply and as honestly as you can. As you make your way along the healing journey—and the pages of this book—you will find answers to each of these questions. But for the moment, it's important for you to experience your own insights and provide your own answers. This is a moment when you must take back your power by making whatever you know to be the next right step.

Appropriate changes in every one of these areas can boost your immune and cancer-fighting systems dramatically and improve your chances of recovery. Taking responsibility means acting in positive ways within all of these domains.

The Turning Point

There comes a moment in the healing journey when you may realize that you can fight for your life and, more important, that you can win. This moment of awakening is associated with a tremendous increase in energy and a burst of joy. Where that energy and joy come from is a mystery. One can argue that they arise from a rush of enthusiasm and the sudden engagement of your will to live. But perhaps there is more to this moment than the rational mind can explain. The instant you realize that you can change your behavior and regain your health something resonates inside of you. Your soul is stirred. An opportunity to evolve and to grow as a human being has suddenly been presented to you. There is a burst of energy. It's as if the soul were saying, "Let's go!"

Bob Singer was one of those who made such a leap of faith and took control of his health. In 1977, Singer, then forty-five years old, from Evergreen, Colorado, arrived at the Pritikin Longevity Center in Santa Monica, California, in a wheelchair. His cholesterol level was 350 mg./dl. He was fifty pounds overweight and had advanced coronary heart disease, high blood pressure, chronic insomnia, and severe gout. "My legs were horribly swollen," he recalled. "I felt miserable, totally miserable. I was nervous, I couldn't sleep at night, but in the morning I couldn't wake myself up."

Singer was the creator of 250 Orange Julius fast-food outlets around the country. He traveled continuously, opening new franchises and checking on old ones. All the travel, business pressures, and the fast food that he regularly consumed had left him physically ill, exhausted, and emotionally drained. His doctor didn't mince his words. "You don't have many more months to live," he told Singer flatly.

When he arrived at the Longevity Center, he was given a simple exercise regimen: walk around the block once a day. It didn't matter how long it took him. When he managed to make it once around the block the following day, he considered it "a minor miracle." The next day, he walked around the block twice. He was elated. But from that point on, he tried to increase his distance by one additional round. Meanwhile, he ate the diet that the Longevity Center served every day: whole grains, fresh vegetables, beans, and low-fat animal products that are the staple of the Pritikin diet.

What happened to Singer during his month-long stay at the Longevity Center might be characterized as slightly better than a "minor miracle." His cholesterol level fell to 225 mg./dl. and he was *jogging four miles, four times a week*. He felt reborn.

When he returned home, he maintained the Pritikin program religiously. His cholesterol level fell to 180 mg./dl., and he lost fifty pounds. When he was interviewed eighteen years later, he was still adhering to the Pritikin program. His latest cholesterol level was still 180, and he hadn't gained a pound. He was still jogging daily.

"I really do feel that Nathan Pritikin saved my life," said Singer. "I don't think there's any question that if I hadn't gotten on the program, I wouldn't be here today."

STEP 3

Adopt a Healing Diet— The Most Powerful Self-Help Tool Available to You

David Miller, a forty-nine-year-old environmental engineer, suffered from high blood pressure, adult-onset diabetes, and overweight. He also had a cholesterol level that fluctuated between 280 and 300 milligrams per deciliter of blood (mg./dl.). He had been on medication for high blood pressure for three years, and for diabetes for the past eight years. The diabetes drug, Micronase, was no longer having the desired effect, his doctor informed him. If David didn't lose weight, he'd have to start taking insulin. David and his wife, Rosie, went to Dr. John Mc-Dougall's health clinic in Santa Rosa, California, where they adopted McDougall's diet, made up exclusively of plant foods, such as cooked whole grains, fresh vegetables, beans, and fruit. In two weeks, David's cholesterol level fell from 287 mg./dl. to 169 mg./dl. Both his blood pressure and blood sugar normalized, and he was taken off all medications for hypertension and diabetes. Within two months, he lost twenty pounds. He remains on the McDougall diet, saying that he enjoys feasting on holidays, when he eats turkey or ham, but between these feasts he has no trouble adhering to the McDougall program.

Ray N. McKinley, a dentist, heard John McDougall speak in Grand Rapids, Michigan. After the lecture, he spoke to Dr. McDougall about his seriously ill son, Bryan, who suffered intense and terrible pain from severe juvenile rheumatoid arthritis and other related problems. In a letter to Dr. McDougall, Dr. McKinley wrote, "Bryan was on 35 mg. of Prednisone and 1200 mg. of Advil daily. He was in so much pain he screamed and cried day and night. In one year he lost weight and did not grow one inch. His blood work reflected a SED rate of over 40." (An erythrocyte sedimentation rate test, or SED test, gives a general indication of health. It measures how quickly red blood cells settle into the bottom of a test tube in an hour. In health, they are kept in suspension by the blood's electrical current, but severe inflammation and other disease-related factors cause them to fall much more rapidly to the bottom of a tube. A normal SED rate is anywhere from 0 to 20 mm/hour; the higher the number the more likely is the presence of disease. At 40-plus, Bryan's SED rate was serious cause for concern.)

None of the medications Bryan was taking were having any positive effect on his illness. Meanwhile, Dr. McKinley and his wife, Lynn, were terrified of what lay ahead for their son.

McDougall and McKinley talked at length that day, and McDougall recommended that McKinley take his son off all animal foods and put him on the McDougall diet. McKinley went home, bought one of McDougall's books, and followed the advice to the letter. The results were nothing short of miraculous.

"Within six months, we had Bryan off all his medication," McKinley later wrote to McDougall. "He was free of pain, gaining weight, and growing again. His last blood work was superb with a SED rate of 1— can you believe it!"

Patricia Paris, who in 1993 was fifty-four, suffered from chronic and severe headaches, joint and back pain, stomach disorders, swelling in her knees, overweight, and chronic depression. "I would go through a bottle of pain pills a month," she later wrote in a letter to Dr. McDougall. "I used to be depressed all the time. I was in so much pain . . . I felt lousy and tired, and my stomach bothered me all the time." She bought a book by Dr. McDougall entitled *The McDougall Program: Twelve Days to Dynamic Health,* read the author's claims, but couldn't believe them. "But I thought, what do I have to lose?"

Her skepticism didn't last long. "After the fourth day [on the diet], the swelling I had in my knees disappeared and after the eighth day all the pain was gone. I felt so good that to continue following your plan was easy," she wrote to Dr. McDougall. "After awhile [sic], I didn't miss the meat and dairy. I actually prefer vegetables to my old way of eating and everything you said was amazingly true . . . I haven't had a headache in over three years . . . Now I have more energy than I had ten years ago, and I feel fantastic . . . My depression is gone and my whole life has changed . . . By the way, I also lost forty pounds."

For those who take responsibility for their health, the next step on the healing path is a change of diet. The reason is simple. The standard American diet, high in fat and processed foods, creates the internal conditions that promote disease and allow it to flourish. By changing the internal environment, the very soil within us, we can drastically reduce the conditions that support the illness and replace them with the biochemistry that creates health.

The important questions that we must answer are: Can an appropriate diet help people who have already been diagnosed with a serious or life-threatening disease, and if so, how? The answer to the first part of that question is an unequivocal yes. Appropriate diet not only can extend the lives of many people with life-threatening diseases, but it can also reverse the disease process for a significant number. That diet is composed of the following foods: whole grains, such as amaranth, barley, brown rice, millet, oats, and quinoa; a wide variety of fresh vegetables; beans and bean products, such as miso, tamari, and shoyu; fish, including whitefish and salmon; and fruit.

In order to understand the kinds of dietary changes that will support recovery, we must focus first on how and why diet heals.

To do that, we must understand three fundamental points about diet, health, and healing.

1. Diet can dramatically reduce two of the most powerful driving forces behind the most serious illnesses we face today, namely inflammation and oxidation.

Inflammation is an immune reaction that is triggered by the presence of disease-causing substances, including many diet-based substances, such as saturated fat, trans fatty acids, processed foods, sugar, and an amino acid called homocysteine that becomes elevated when we consume too much animal protein and not enough vegetables and fruits. Your immune system attempts to rid your body of the effects from these substances. However, when these and other disease-causing agents become too numerous, they can overwhelm your immune system and create the conditions for many life-threatening illnesses.

Scientists now recognize that among the many illnesses caused by inflammatory conditions are coronary heart disease, diabetes, many of the common cancers, high blood pressure, arthritis, asthma, gout, tendonitis, Alzheimer's and Parkinson's diseases, just to name a handful.

"The current theory is that low grade, sub-acute inflammation—that is to say, inflammation that does not manifest overt symptoms—can lead to an increased risk of heart disease, cancer, diabetes, obesity and other illnesses," said Michael Wargovich, Ph.D., one of the nation's top cancer researchers, formerly of M.D. Anderson Cancer Center and now at the South Carolina Cancer Center in Columbia, South Carolina. "Among the causes of inflammation is our culture's diet, which contains many pro-inflammatory foods."

"Suddenly, inflammation has become one of the hottest areas of medical research," reported *Time* magazine in its February 23, 2004, cover story. "Hardly a week goes by without the publication of yet another study uncovering a new way that chronic inflammation does harm to the body. It destabilizes cholesterol deposits in the coronary arteries, leading to heart attacks and potentially even strokes. It chews up nerve cells in the brains of Alzheimer's victims. It may even foster the proliferation of abnormal cells and facilitate their transformation into cancer. In other words, chronic inflammation may be the engine that drives many of the most feared illnesses of middle and old age."

A diet rich in vegetables, fruits, and whole grains, and low in fat, processed foods, and animal proteins, can reverse many inflammatory conditions. Two proven examples are coronary heart disease and type 2 diabetes, both inflammatory diseases that, in many cases, can be fully eliminated from the body with diet and lifestyle changes alone. Studies have shown that plant-based diets can also eliminate the symptoms of arthritis. Research has also shown that some people already diagnosed with cancer who adopt plant-based diets live longer, as well. (About which, much more below.)

In addition to inflammation is overexposure to substances known as oxidants, or free radicals, which are highly reactive oxygen molecules that break down cells and tissues. Scientists have known for decades that oxidants are the root cause of more than sixty major illnesses, including heart disease, the common cancers, diabetes, and other life-threatening disorders. Though free radicals are created by inflammation, they can also arise from other causes and thus play an independent role in both the creation and support of major illness. The primary dietary sources of oxidants are fat, processed foods, and homocysteine. The antidote to oxidants are *anti*oxidants, whose primary source are plant foods.

The research on inflammation and oxidation reveals the importance of prevention studies for those who are already ill. Inflammation and oxidation fuel the underlying disease process. Reducing them deprives the illness of what it needs to survive. If this is done before an illness manifests, it's called prevention. If it's done after a disease manifests, it's called treatment. And indeed, studies have shown that the diet that prevents heart disease and diabetes, for example, can also effectively treat it.

2. By eliminating the toxins that support disease, a plant-based diet takes an enormous burden off the immune and antioxidant systems within the body, and thus allows these healing functions to turn their attention to the disease itself.

3. A plant-based diet is rich in substances that either directly fight disease, or help the body overcome it.

In the pages that follow, I have tried to show the underlying causes of the major illnesses. I have then provided research to show that when people who have already been diagnosed with serious illness eliminate the causes of disease, many either live longer or overcome their illnesses entirely.

In this chapter, I have dealt exclusively with diet. Exercise—an important factor in fighting inflammation and disease—is discussed in Chapter 5. Other behaviors, such as positive thinking and meditation, which can boost immune function, are discussed in Chapters 6 and 7. It must be said, however, that dietary change is perhaps the most powerful healing tool available to us, as the scientific research clearly shows.

Let's begin our exploration of diet by examining the three points I listed above, starting with a closer look at inflammation and its links to major illness.

When Inflammation Becomes Excessive, Life Is Threatened

The ancient Greeks coined the term *inflammation,* meaning a fire within, to describe the redness, swelling, heat, pain, and fever that we all have experienced when we suffer a cut, or an infection, or when we become ill. These physical changes are symptoms of the immune system's attack on an invading organism or some other disease-causing agent.

Inflammation, of itself, is not a bad thing. In fact, our ability to recognize threats to health and mount an immune response—one that includes the release of oxidants by immune cells—is one reason we have survived as a species. The problem arises when toxic substances become excessive. At that point, the immune system must mount an attack that is equal to the size of the threat. Unfortunately, the consequences can be deadly.

Among the greatest sources of inflammation and oxidation in our lives today is our daily diet. Within that diet, the following are the most inflammatory and pro-oxidative substances.

- Excess consumption of dietary fat, especially saturated fat and trans fatty acids.
- Excess consumption of animal protein.

- Excess consumption of processed foods, such as refined sugar, bagels, bread, doughnuts, muffins, pastries, rolls, synthetic ingredients (including artificial colors, flavors, preservatives, pesticides, and herbicides), and artificial sweeteners. These foods lead to overweight and obesity, which in turn form the basis for many life-threatening diseases.
- Excess consumption of dairy products, such as cow's milk, cheese, and yogurt.

Let's look at each of these categories and examine the science linking them to illness and health.

Fat: Deforming Cells to Create Heart Disease

There is nothing inherently wrong with the three naturally occurring forms of fat, namely saturated, polyunsaturated, and monounsaturated fats. For many thousands of years, nature, like a great parent, limited the amount of fat we could consume. Today, we have to do that ourselves. Unfortunately, most of us are doing it badly.

The most dangerous naturally occurring fat is saturated fat, which is solid at room temperature, as compared to polyunsaturated and monounsaturated fats, which are liquid at room temperature. Saturated fat is found mostly in beef, ham, pork, chicken, dairy products, and eggs. Fish contains fat, but only a tiny fraction—in many cases less than 1 percent—comes from saturated sources. The rest comes in the form of polyunsaturated oils, which, in moderate amounts, can be health-promoting.

Saturated fats raise blood cholesterol, especially a type of cholesterol known as low-density lipoproteins, or LDL cholesterol. Once in your bloodstream, LDL particles infiltrate your arteries and tissues. Once there, they oxidize, or decay. These decaying LDL particles are seen by your immune system as a threat to health. Immune cells known as macrophages come bounding down on the LDL and literally gobble up these decaying particles. Unfortunately, the immune cells themselves become bloated and sick with LDL poisoning. This triggers an even bigger immune reaction that also takes place within your artery walls. Soon, the artery walls become thick, hard, and swollen with immune cells that are bloated with LDL. Eventually, the swelling turns into a bulbous mass that causes boils to emerge inside the pathway of your artery. This condition is known as atherosclerosis.

These boils are highly unstable and prone to rupture. When they do erupt, they cause an open wound to form inside the artery wall. Clotting proteins arrive and form a scablike clot, or thrombus, over the wound. Those clots tend to be even bigger and more dangerous for people who eat a high-fat diet. In fact, the clot can get so big inside the passageway of the artery that it can cut off blood supply to the heart or brain, thus causing a heart attack or stroke.

"The research has . . . established a key role for inflammation in atherosclerosis," wrote Peter Libby in the May 2002, issue of *Scientific American*. "This process—the same one that causes infected cuts to become red, swollen, hot and painful—underlies all phases of the disorder, from the creation of plaques to their growth and rupture . . ."

Excess Animal Protein Only Makes It Worse

As you know, saturated fat is not eaten alone, but as part of animal foods, such as red meat, bacon, sausage, eggs, or milk products, which means that saturated fat nearly always comes with protein—and lots of it. When both are eaten excessively, the combination can be dangerous to your health for the simple reason that both are highly inflammatory and oxidative.

Once in the bloodstream, animal proteins raise blood levels of an amino acid called methionine, which in turn is converted to another amino acid called homocysteine. Homocysteine joins with LDL cholesterol to form LDL-complex. Together, the two enter the artery wall and oxidize, thus forming a toxic duet that is consumed by your immune cells, which in turn triggers an inflammatory process that leads to atherosclerosis and an abundance of oxidants.

Homocysteine injures arteries in other ways, as well. It acts like battery acid on the walls of the arteries, causing open wounds to form in the artery tissue, which in turn triggers more inflammation. As if that were not enough, homocysteine also increases the blood's tendency to form clots, thus elevating a person's risk of heart attack and stroke.

The body attempts to protect itself from all of these events by using folic acid and vitamin B6 to convert homocysteine into a harmless substance. Folic acid and B6 come from plant foods, especially green vegetables and beans. People who eat lots of protein and low amounts of plant foods, however, tend to be low in B6 and folic acid. They also suffer from higher levels of homocysteine, which in turn means higher risk of heart disease.

Numerous studies have shown that diets low in animal foods and rich in vegetables and fruits lower inflammation and homocysteine levels and protect people against heart disease. Among the most recent was a study done by researchers at Tufts University and published in the *Journal of Nutrition* (April 2004). Researchers followed a group of 445 Hispanic elders and another 154 white elders, monitoring their diets and blood levels of homocysteine and a substance in their blood known as C-reactive protein (CRP). A CRP test reveals the level of inflammation in a person's body. The researchers found that "Greater frequency of fruit and vegetable intake was associated with significantly lower plasma [blood] CRP and Hcy [homocysteine] concentrations. Because both of these metabolites are known risk factors for CVD [cardiovascular disease], these findings contribute the evidence that a higher intake of fruit and vegetables may reduce the risk of CVD."

Other research has arrived at the same conclusions. "In the Physicians Health Study, high homocysteine levels tripled the chances of having a heart attack," reported Walter Willett, M.D., Ph.D., dean of the Department of Nutrition at the Harvard Medical School and author of the book, *Eat, Drink, and Be Healthy* (Simon & Schuster, 2001). "In the Nurses Study, we have shown that women with the highest intakes of B6 and folic acid were almost half as likely to have heart attacks or die from heart disease as women with the lowest intakes."

High B6 and folic acid, of course, translate into low levels of homocysteine, low inflammation, and lower rates of disease.

Reversing Heart Disease

Reducing inflammation, LDL cholesterol, and homocysteine doesn't just prevent heart disease, however. It can also reverse it. Dean Ornish, M.D., and his colleagues, showed reversal of atherosclerotic plaque in the coronary arteries in patients with heart disease who followed a vegan diet.

More recently, Richard Fleming, M.D., showed reversal of atherosclerosis in patients who also followed a low-fat, plant-based diet. Fleming, whose study was published in the medical journal *Angiology* (October, 2000), compared the effects two different diets—a plant-based diet low in fat, versus a high-protein diet—on blood flow to the heart. After one year, the people on the plant-based diet experienced reversal of the plaques in their coronary arteries, while those on the high-protein diet experienced a progression of their heart disease, with diminished blood flow to their hearts.

It should be emphasized that appropriate diet *eliminates* the underlying cause of coronary heart disease, which is cholesterol plaques, or atherosclerosis, that block blood flow to the heart. A low-fat, high-plant diet, combined with regular exercise, can also lower blood pressure, restore many people to normal blood pressure, and eliminate the need for blood pressure medication.

Fat, Inflammation, Oxidation, and Cancer

The more inflamed your system, the more oxidants attack your cells. These oxidants can bombard and deform your DNA, the brain center of every cell. Most cells die as a consequence, but under the constant barrage, many cells mutate, and some become cancerous.

Since saturated fat is a big producer of both inflammation and oxidation, it's not surprising that excess consumption of saturated fat is associated with high levels of cancer.

In a recent study done by the Harvard Medical School and published in the *Journal of the National Cancer Institute* (July 2003), scientists examined the diets, lifestyles, and disease patterns of 90,655 premenopausal women, all between the ages of twenty-six and forty-six. The researchers followed the women for eight years, all the while documenting their dietary patterns. Those whose diets were composed of the most animal foods—especially animal fats—had the highest levels of cancer. The lead researcher, epidemiologist Euryoung Cho, Sc.D., was quoted as saying, "Cooked red meat contains carcinogens, and high-fat dairy products contain fat-soluble hormones that may increase risk" of breast cancer.

When asked by WebMD about the Harvard study, Otis Brawley, M.D., associate director of Winship Cancer Institute at Emory University School of Medicine in Atlanta, said, "Believe it." Consumption of animal fat "makes enough difference that it matters. This study is not definitive, it is highly, highly suggestive that it's best to stay away from animal fat."

High Fat, Hormonal Imbalance, and Increased Risk of Breast Cancer

When consumed in excess, fat elevates certain reproductive hormones, which in turn overstimulate the hormone-sensitive organs—in men, the prostate and testes, in women, the breast, uterus, and ovaries. When these organs become overstimulated and inflamed, cells can become deformed and cancerous.

In overweight women, fat cells act like factories converting other hormones into additional estrogen. The more fat a woman consumes, the more estrogen in her system. As estrogen levels go up, the breasts are overstimulated, making them inflamed, tender, and sometimes painful.

Women on high-fat diets suffer much more intense premenstrual syndrome (PMS), including more painful cramps, heavier bleeding, headaches, swelling, bloating, fatigue, and emotional disturbances. The more estrogen in a woman's body, the more her uterus is stimulated, causing more blood to gather in the endometrial tissue. Animal fats, especially, have been shown to increase blood clotting in the menses, pain, and excessive bleeding.

As estrogen levels reach higher and higher peaks each month, they overstimulate the breast tissue, causing swelling, tenderness, and the creation of fibrocystic breast disease. With repeated stimulation, and the resulting inflammation, scar tissue forms, blocking milk ducts and forming the basis for cysts and tumors. And not surprisingly, women with fibrocystic breast disease have a higher risk of breast cancer.

Once a cancer manifests, these same conditions actually promote its growth. An estrogen- and oxidant-rich environment is the perfect host for cancer. Under these conditions, a few mutated cells can turn into a forest fire, as it were.

High estrogen is the fundamental cause of breast cancer, says Malcolm C. Pike, professor and chair of preventive medicine at the University of Southern California School of Medicine, Los Angeles. "Women need to be told that there is something they can do now to reduce their risk enormously," Dr. Pike told *Internal Medicine and Cardiology News.* The thing we must do, Dr. Pike and others maintain, is reduce estrogen levels.

Remarkably, high-fiber diets cause a dramatic drop in estrogen levels and offer significant protection against breast cancer. Fiber binds with cholesterol, fat, hormones, and other harmful substances and helps eliminate them through the feces. Vegetarian women eliminate two to three times more estrogen in their feces than nonvegetarians, according to a study published in *The New England Journal of Medicine.*

In fact, fiber's ability to lower blood levels of estrogen is truly astounding. One study showed that a high-fiber, low-fat diet reduced the estrogen levels in a group of postmenopausal women by 50 percent! A 17 percent reduction of estrogen has been shown to reduce the risk of breast cancer fourfold to fivefold. Plant-based, high-fiber, low-fat diets have been shown to lower estrogen levels by as much as 40 percent.

Women With Breast Cancer Who Reduce the Causes of Inflammation Live Longer

All of this information begs the question: What happens when women with breast cancer adopt a low-fat diet, as compared to women who don't make such changes? The answer is that those who change their ways of eating tend to live longer.

Dr. James Hebert and his colleagues at the University of Massachusetts (UMASS) Medical School in Worcester, Massachusetts, reported that the composition of the diet of women with breast cancer can determine whether the disease returns, or recurs, once it has been pushed into remission. Recurrence plays a pivotal role in survival. Once a cancer recurs, it is often extremely difficult, if not impossible, to force it back into remission.

Dr. Hebert and his colleagues found that high-fat foods, including dairy products, were associated with shorter survival among women with breast cancer, while the consumption of plant foods and antioxidants were associated with longer life. Premenopausal women with breast cancer who regularly ate butter, margarine, and lard, had a 67 percent greater chance of recurrence of the cancer than women who avoided these foods. The study, published in the medical journal *Breast Cancer Treatment* (September 1998), reported the following:

- Women who ate beef, liver, and bacon had a much higher rate of recurrence of breast cancer than women who abstained from these foods.
- Postmenopausal women with breast cancer who ate additional servings of vegetables each day had much lower rates of recurrence than those who ate few if any vegetables. The researchers found that for each additional serving of vegetables that was eaten each day, the women experienced a 53 percent *reduction* in risk of recurrence.
- The more vegetables, the longer the survival. Postmenopausal women who ate vitamin C-rich foods—such as broccoli, collard greens, kale, and citrus fruits—had a much lower rate of recurrence, and lived longer, than women who abstained from these foods. The

researchers determined that each additional 100 mg. of vitamin C—over the amount eaten from the standard diet—reduced the risk of recurrence by 43 percent.

The Importance of Low Weight to Survival

Once a person becomes ill, body weight becomes a pivotal factor in survival. Those who remain overweight, or who gain weight, experience much shorter survival than those who adopt a plant-based, nutrient-rich diet that causes weight loss. This is true for all major illnesses, including cancer, heart disease, and diabetes.

When it comes to body weight, the foods to be most concerned about are processed foods and those rich in fat. Fat is the most calorically dense substance in the food supply, providing nine calories per gram, as opposed to the four calories per gram found in carbohydrates and protein. A calorie is a measuring unit for energy. Calories that you don't burn are stored in your tissues as fat. Ounce for ounce, fat is much more likely to add weight to your body than carbohydrates or protein.

Processed foods, of course, are the most common foods in the Western diet. Go into any supermarket and you will see shelves and shelves of processed foods—bread, candy, cereals, cookies, crackers, dehydrated foods, flour, fruit juice, muffins, pancake mixes, pastries, puddings, rolls, soda pop, waffles, sugar, syrups, and many forms of meat (hot dogs, pepperoni, sausage, and Spam, for example).

Food processing is essentially the act of taking a great quantity of natural food and turning it into a smaller volume that is highly concentrated in calories. As Robert Pritikin points out in his book, *The Pritikin Principle: The Calorie Density Solution* (Time-Life Books, 2000), a pound of corn provides 390 calories, not much by any standard. But a pound of cornflakes gives 1,770 calories. What happened? Food manufacturers took many pounds of corn kernels and reduced them to a single pound of cornflakes. In the process, all the calories that were in those pounds of whole corn were concentrated into a single pound of food.

Very often, food manufacturers add fat to a processed food, which drives up the calories even further. For example, a large potato provides about 200 calories. A pound of potatoes contains only 490 calories. But if you take many pounds of potatoes, remove their water and fiber, distill their carbohydrates, and add fat, you wind up with potato chips, which provide 2,400 calories per pound. You probably could not eat a pound of cooked potatoes, at least not at a single meal, but you very likely could eat a whole bag of chips. (Lots of people do it all the time.)

The following chart will demonstrate the incredible difference in calorie content between a food in its natural state, such as brown rice, oatmeal, and many vegetables, versus common processed foods.

Unprocessed, Whole Foods	Calories per pound[1]
Broccoli	130
Strawberries	140
Apple	270
Oatmeal, plain	280
Potato, baked	490
Brown rice, boiled	500
Yam, baked	525
Pasta	560
Black beans, cooked	600

Animal Foods	Calories per pound
Halibut, poached	520
Salmon, poached	660
Butter	3250
American cheese	1700
Cheddar cheese	1820
Cream cheese, Philadelphia	990
Swiss cheese, regular	1700
Swiss, Kraft ⅓ less fat	1080

1. Calorie densities of foods from *The Pritikin Principle,* available on-line at www. pritikin.com. Reprinted with permission from the Pritikin Organization, LLC, and the Pritikin Longevity Center, Aventura, Florida.

Animal Foods	Calories per pound
Beef brisket	1550
Corned beef	1140
Ground beef, lean, broiled medium	1235
Porterhouse steak	1390
Spareribs	1790
Bacon	2170

The following chart compares the calorie content of whole, natural foods and the processed foods from which they are derived.

CALORIE CONTENT OF COMMON PROCESSED FOODS

1 Lb. Whole Food	Calorie Content	1 Lb. Processed Food	Calorie Content
Potatoes	490 calories	Potato chips	2400 calories
		French fries	1500
Corn	390	Cornflakes	1770
		Corn chips	2450
		Popcorn, plain	1730
		Popcorn, w/oil	2270
Wheat berries	230	Whole wheat bread	1280
		Shredded Wheat	1610
		Chocolate chip cookies	2140
		Dietetic cookies	2180
		Oreo cookies	2200
		Entenmann's fat-free cookies	1510
		Fat-Free WW crackers	1620

To give this list some perspective, consider that you need ten calories per day to maintain one pound of body weight. A person who weighs 200 pounds needs to eat 2,000 calories to maintain that weight. If he or she loses, say, 300 calories per day, and sustains that 1,700 calories per day over time, that person's weight will fall to 170 pounds. A person who weighs 150 pounds, but wants to weigh 120, will have to drop his or her calorie consumption from 1,500 calories per day to 1,200 and sustain that diet, which will eventually cause his or her weight to fall to 120.

A diet rich in both fat and processed foods is a formula for overweight. Very few people can burn all those calories and remain lean, which is why so many Americans today are overweight. Unfortunately, weight gain leads to life-threatening illness and, very often, a shorter lifespan.

A study published in the *Archives of Internal Medicine* found that people who are overweight at the age of forty die three years younger, on average, than those who are at or below their ideal weight at the age of forty.

The link between overweight and cancer was essentially proven after a new study, published in the April 2003, edition of the *New England Journal of Medicine,* showed that overweight dramatically increases the risk of most common cancers, including those of the breast, prostate, uterus, ovaries, cervix, colon, rectum, kidneys, esophagus, liver, gallbladder, pancreas, stomach, and those of the lymph system (non-Hodgkins lymphoma). Another study, published in the *Journal of the National Cancer Institute,* reported that overweight and obese women have twice the risk of contracting breast cancer than women who are at their ideal weight or lower.

Among the reasons for this striking rise in disease is the fact that processed foods contain the most dangerous form of fat—trans fats, or what are commonly referred to as "partially hydrogenated oils." Trans fats are used to make margarines, pastries, muffins, and other processed foods.

Scientists at Harvard School of Public Health have been monitoring the health and health habits of more than 80,000 female nurses since 1980, one of biggest and most extensive studies ever undertaken. The study, called the Harvard University's Nurses Health Study, has found, among other things, that each 2 percent increase in trans fats raises a woman's risk of coronary disease by 93 percent. By comparison, the researchers have found that for every 5 percent increase in saturated fat, a woman's chances of having heart disease increases 17 percent.

A review of the literature, published in the September 2002, issue of the *Journal of Nutrition,* showed that both population and clinical studies have shown that trans fats increase insulin resistance, inflammation, overweight, and the risk of both diabetes and heart disease.

For Those Who are Ill, Low Weight Can Mean Longer Survival

Weight is not only associated with higher rates of illness, but it's also a big factor in determining whether or not a person with major illness will survive.

Researchers at the University of Massachusetts Medical School interviewed 149 women with breast cancer to learn in detail their dietary practices and other lifestyle habits. The interviews took place around the time of their diagnosis, after which the scientists followed the women for at least five years. The study, published in the medical journal *Breast Cancer Treatment* (February 1999), reported the following:

- Those who ate more calories experienced higher rates of recurrence. For every 1000 additional calories consumed, there was an 84 percent increased risk of recurrence. The researchers found that among those women who ate more calories, most of those calories came from fat. Just eating an additional 100 calories per day over the standard 1,200 calorie diet increased the risk of recurrence by 5 percent.
- In late-stage breast cancers, the risk of death increased by 57 percent for each additional 1000 grams per day.

The bottom line is this: Weight loss is an essential part of the healing process.

Remarkably, weight loss is easy on a diet composed of unprocessed foods, such as whole grains (amaranth, brown rice, barley, millet, oats, and quinoa), beans, fresh vegetables, and fruit. These foods are all low in calories, but rich in water and fiber, which fills you up without increasing weight. Indeed, people can eat until they are full and still lose excess weight.

This was demonstrated in a study published in the *Archives of Internal Medicine* (January 26, 2004), which showed that people on a high-carbohydrate, low-fat diet could eat as much food as they wanted but still lose a pound a week. The diet was made up primarily of whole grains—as opposed to processed foods, such as bread and pastries—vegetables, and fruit. They did not exercise, yet they lost a pound a week, on average.

"It's not excess carbs that translate into body weight, it's excess calories—no matter where they come from," said Alice H. Lichtenstein, DSc., professor of nutrition at Tufts University in Boston. Others point out that Americans have been duped into believing that all carbs cause weight gain. In fact, the carbs that cause the most weight gain are the processed kind, which are extremely high in calories. Complex carbohydrates, found in whole grains, fresh vegetables, beans, and fruit, cause weight loss—even when you eat till you are full.

After more than two decades of writing about people who have overcome serious illnesses, I have found that those who adopt a plant-based diet inevitably lose weight. The most common experience among these people was that the weight loss eventually stopped; weight leveled off and returned to their optimal levels. Excess weight was kept off as long as the person remained on the plant-based diet.

One of the reasons that weight loss is associated with improved life expectancy, especially among cancer patients, is that weight loss removes visceral fat, or the fat that surrounds organs. Scientists now believe that visceral fat fuels cancer by increasing free radicals around tumors. Free radicals actually serve as a kind of gasoline, stoking the fires of cancer cells and tumors.

Insulin: Essential for Life but Dangerous at High Levels

Another key to both the prevention and treatment of illness is insulin levels. Insulin is produced by the pancreas and allows blood sugar, or glucose, to enter cells and be used as fuel. It's essential for life. The problem is that when insulin becomes high, it triggers inflammation that eventually can destroy your body.

Processed foods provide an abundance of simple sugars—or calories—that are rapidly absorbed into your bloodstream. High blood sugar is seen by your body as a potentially diabetic condition and a threat to your health. When this happens, the brain tells the pancreas to produce lots of insulin so that the sugar in your blood can be burned as rapidly as possible. Not all the sugar can be burned, however. The unused sugar is converted into fat and stored in your tissues. All of which means that the more processed foods you eat, the fatter you get.

Overweight, of course, increases the risk of type 2 diabetes, also known as adult-onset diabetes. However, studies have shown that when people with type 2 diabetes adopt a plant-based diet, lose weight, and exercise regularly, many are able to free themselves from all diabetic medication. Research done on people with type 2 diabetes who adopted the Pritikin diet showed that after four weeks on the program, 70 percent were free of all diabetic medication.

Improving the Chances of Survival in Men with Prostate Cancer

High insulin levels are associated not only with weight gain and diabetes, but also with cancer. People with high insulin, overweight, high blood fats (or triglycerides), and high cholesterol—a condition referred to as syndrome x—have been shown to be at greater risk of both breast and prostate cancers. However, when men with prostate cancer adopt a plant-based diet and perform regular exercise, their insulin levels fall, and their chances of survival increase.

A recent study done by UCLA scientists and published in *Obesity Reviews* (2002: 3, 303–308) showed that men with prostate cancer improve their chances of survival by adopting an insulin-lowering, low-fat diet. Researcher James Barnard, Ph.D., and his colleagues found that men with prostate cancer who followed a low-fat diet, rich in whole grains and vegetables, and who exercised regularly experienced a dramatic drop in insulin levels. At the same time, these men produced more of a substance that binds with insulin and helps eliminate it from the body. Remarkably, the researchers found that the cancer cells in the men on the low-fat diet started to die, a process known as apoptosis. As long as they are given the conditions to support their life, cancer cells are virtually immortal. They also become increasingly resistant to treatment. Scientists have long been searching for ways to induce apoptosis, or programmed cancer cell death. Barnard's study suggested that the diet and exercise program may have created an internal environment that was highly antagonistic to the cancer. All of these conditions helped improve the chances of survival among these men.

Plant-Based Nutrition: What Your Body Needs to Survive and to Heal

Vegetables, fruits, and whole grains fight inflammation in many different ways. One way is by triggering an anti-inflammatory enzyme series in your cells known as the cyclooxygenase enzymes, also known as COX-1. Many plant compounds, especially substances called polyphenols (found in vegetables, fruits, tea, and red wine), as well as omega-3 fatty acids (commonly found in flax seeds, some nuts, and coldwater fish, such as whitefish, salmon, and tuna), all trigger the COX-1 enzymes and inhibit inflammation, according to a study published in *Current Atherosclerosis Reports* (January 2004). There are two COX enzyme pathways. The second is designated COX-2 and triggers inflammation. Red meat, dairy products, and saturated fat all trigger the COX-2 pathway and promote inflammation.

Certain plant chemicals are especially important in the fight against inflammation and oxidation. The first of these, of course, are the antioxidants. Antioxidants reduce and sometimes even stop oxidation, including oxidation of LDL cholesterol, which means they prevent atherosclerosis. Researchers have found that antioxidants boost the number and aggressiveness of virtually all immune cells, including natural killer cells, among the most important weapons the immune system has to fight cancer. Scientists have also found that when the tissues contain reserves of antioxidants—a kind of nutrient bank account—immune cells are more aggressive and effective against all forms of illness.

The ongoing Harvard University's Nurses Health Study has found that women who ate five or more servings of carrots per week had 68 percent fewer strokes than those who ate carrots only once a month. Women who ate antioxidant-rich foods also suffer significantly fewer heart attacks, the researchers report.

Cornell University researchers found that the Chinese, who eat their traditional grain and vegetable diets, have the highest blood levels of antioxidants and the lowest cancer rates. The Cornell researchers found that the antioxidants have a particularly strong effect on natural killer cells and their ability to destroy cancer cells and tumors.

The antioxidants that we hear most about are vitamins C, E, and beta carotene, the vegetable source of vitamin A. But there are many more, including vitamin B6, glutathione, flavonoids (a group of compounds found in vegetable foods); several minerals including selenium, zinc, copper, and manganese; and an amino acid called L-cysteine. In fact, many plant chemicals referred to as carotenoids and phytochemicals act as antioxidants, which means that with every vegetable, piece of fruit, and bowl of grain you eat, you get hundreds—and sometimes thousands—of antioxidants.

Plants are the only real source of antioxidants. Animal foods contain no beta carotene or vitamin C. Neither do they provide carotenoids or phytochemicals.

Scientists advise us to eat at least five servings of whole grains, vegetables, and fruits per day to get adequate antioxidants.

People who eat fewer than five servings of antioxidant-rich foods each day experience twice the risk of developing cancer than those who get those five servings, says Bruce Ames, Ph.D., professor of biochemistry and molecular biology at the University of California, Berkeley, and a longtime researcher.

One recent study, published in _Nutrition and Cancer_ (2003; 46[1]: 5–22) showed that women with breast cancer who took vitamin C and E supplements experienced fewer recurrences and lived longer than women who did not take these antioxidant vitamins.

According to Dr. Wargovich, plant chemicals, such as polyphenols, are often many times more powerful antioxidants than simple vitamins, such as C and E. Not only do these polyphenols act as antioxidants, but

The following charts provide a short comparison between the antioxidant content of animal foods versus that of plant foods.

❖

AMOUNTS OF VITAMIN C AND BETA CAROTENE

Food	Serving Size	Amount/mg.	% of RDA
Eggs	n/a	0	0
Dairy foods	n/a	0	0
Red meat	n/a	0	0
Ham	n/a	0	0
Poultry	n/a	0	0

BETA CAROTENE

No established RDA; scientists recommend between 10 and 30 mg. per day.

Food	Serving Size	Amount/mg.	% of RDA
Brussels sprouts	½ cup	3.4	11
Carrots	½ cup	12.2	41
Kale	½ cup	8.2	27
Mustard greens	½ cup	7.3	24
Spinach	½ cup	4.4	15
Squash	½ cup	16.1	54
Sweet potato	1 medium	2.9	10

they also induce apoptosis, or programmed cell death in cancer cells. Cancer cells replicate endlessly and are essentially immortal—that is, as long as the host survives. However, many plant chemicals cause cancer cells to die, said Dr. Wargovich.

VITAMIN C

RDA: 60 mg.

Food	Serving Size	Amount/mg.	% of RDA
Broccoli	½ cup	49	82
Cabbage	½ cup	17	28
Cauliflower	½ cup	34	57
Chili pepper	½ cup	109	182
Green bell pepper	1 medium	95	158
Kale	½ cup	51	85
Potato (baked)	1 med.	26	43
Cantaloupe	½ med.	113	188
Grapefruit	½ med.	41	68
Oranges	1 med.	70	117
Papaya	1 med.	188	313
Strawberries	1 cup	85	142

VITAMIN E

RDA: 10 mg.

Food	Serving Size	Amount/mg.	% of RDA
Cod	3 oz.	0.8	8
Mackerel	3 oz.	1.5	15
Salmon	3 oz.	1.6–1.8	16–18
Shrimp	3 oz.	0.6–3.5	6–35
Brown rice	½ cup	1.2	12
Wheat	1 cup	0.3	3
Wheat germ	1 cup	20.5	205
Seven grain bread	1 slice	0.3	3

Food	Serving Size	Amount/mg.	% of RDA
Wild rice	½ cup	1.8	18
Almonds	1 oz.	7.0	70
Peanuts	1 oz.	3.1	31
Sunflower seeds	1 oz.	14.8	148
Asparagus	½ cup	1.8	18
Kidney beans	½ cup	4.4	44
Pinto beans	½ cup	4.1	41
Sweet potato	1 med.	5.5	55
Apple	1 med.	0.4	4
Mango	1 med.	2.7	27

Carotenoids and Phytochemicals: Mysterious Medicine

One of the newest and most exciting frontiers in nutrition science is the subject of carotenoids and phytochemicals (a word that means plant chemicals). These substances are found only in plant foods. Carotenoids, of which there are hundreds, give color to vegetables and fruits. There are many thousands of phytochemicals. These substances have myriad functions in the body, including boosting the immune system and fighting diseases such as cancer and heart disease. Here are a handful of the most common phytochemicals and some of their health-enhancing effects.

- Flavonoids suppress tumor growth, prevent blood clots, reduce inflammation, and induce apoptosis. They are abundant in apples, celery, cherries, cranberries, kale, onions, black and green teas, red wine, parsley, soybeans, tomatoes, and thyme.
- Indoles convert cancer-causing estrogens into their more benign forms and thereby prevent breast cancer. The cruciferous vegetables, such as bok choy, broccoli, brussels sprouts, cauliflower, cabbage,

collard greens, kale, mustard greens, rutabaga, sauerkraut, and turnips, are all rich in indoles. These vegetables are especially powerful against various types of cancers, including prostate cancer.

"And when we compared relative potency, vegetables from the cruciferous family, like broccoli and cabbage, reduced the risk even further," said Dr. Alan Kristal, who studied the effects of crucifers on prostate cancer rates. The scientists rigorously examined the eating habits of 1,230 men in the Seattle area between the ages of forty and sixty-four. Overall vegetable consumption provided strong protection against prostate cancer, but the cruciferous vegetables were the strongest.

"At any given level of total vegetable consumption, as the percent of cruciferous vegetables increased, the prostate cancer risk decreased," Dr. Kristal told Reuters news service.

- Saponins, found in whole grains and soy products, neutralize enzymes in the intestines that cause colon cancer, while chemicals called sterols, found mostly in vegetables, lower blood cholesterol levels.
- Isoflavones, which act as mild estrogens, are among the most celebrated of the phytochemicals. They block tumor formation, starve tumors for blood and oxygen, and act as antioxidants. They also prevent bone loss, lower blood cholesterol level, and reduce the enzymes that stimulate breast cancer. Foods rich in phytoestrogens include soy products, whole grains, berries, fruit, vegetables, and flax seeds.

Among the most celebrated of the isoflavones is genistein, found primarily in beans, especially in soybeans and soybean products. Genistein is especially abundant in the traditional Japanese soybean products, such as miso, a fermented soybean paste used in soups and stews; shoyu, naturally aged and fermented soy sauce; tamari, the liquid drawn from aged and fermented miso; tempeh, whole soybeans aged and fermented and made into a patty; edamame, boiled or steamed whole soybeans; and natto, whole, fermented soybeans, used as a condiment on grain and noodle dishes.

Numerous studies, including one in *Proceedings of the National Academy of Sciences* (April 1993) and another in *Cancer Investigations* (2003; 21(5); 744–57), have shown that genistein blocks blood vessels from attaching to tumors, thereby preventing the tumor from getting adequate oxygen and the nutrition it needs to survive. This ability, known as anti-angiogenesis, is but one of many cancer-fighting properties of genistein. It also acts as an antioxidant and fights inflammation.

Scientists now believe that the abundance of isoflavones, including genistein, in the blood of Asians may be one reason why they do not have the high rates of breast and prostate cancers that Westerners experience. These high levels of isoflavones may also explain why Asians who do contract these diseases have better survival rates than Westerners who contract breast or prostate cancer.

Vegetables Are Associated with Better Prognosis

People who already have been diagnosed with cancer tend to live longer when they adopt a plant-based diet. Women with lung cancer who ate greater amounts of vegetables and fruits experienced longer survival than those who ate vegetables infrequently, according to a study done by Dr. Marc Goodman of the Cancer Research Center at the University of Hawaii. Consumption of broccoli and other foods rich in vitamin C was consistently associated with longer survival time.

Dr. James Carter and his colleagues at the Tulane School of Public Health in New Orleans reported that men with prostate cancer who followed a macrobiotic diet lived longer than men who received standard medical treatment.

Dr. Carter also found that people with pancreatic cancer who followed a macrobiotic diet lived substantially longer than those who were treated with standard medical care, according to a study published in the *Journal of the American College of Nutrition.* Carter followed patients with pancreatic cancer for one year and found that 54.2 percent of those who adopted a macrobiotic diet were still alive one year after diagnosis, while only 10 percent of those who underwent standard medical care were still alive.

Scientists have become increasingly interested in the use of a macrobiotic diet in the treatment of cancer, especially given that so many people with carefully documented case histories have overcome cancer with the use of the macrobiotic diet. That interest came to a head on February 25, 2002, when the National Cancer Institute's Cancer Advisor Panel for Complementary and Alternative Medicine (CAPCAM) voted unanimously to fund research on the macrobiotic diet as a therapeutic approach to cancer. The fifteen-member panel, which was made up of scientists from many different medical fields, decided that there was sufficient medical support for the macrobiotic approach to warrant serious study of the diet and lifestyle as a possible means of treating cancer. The panel members were presented with six meticulously documented case histories of people who had been diagnosed with end-stage cancer. All six used the macrobiotic diet and lifestyle to treat their cancers after conventional treatment had failed. All six are still alive, some of them more than two decades after diagnosis.

Ralph Moss, Ph.D., a longtime cancer investigator and best-selling author, is a member of the NCI's CAPCAM panel that reviewed the macrobiotic presentation. After examining the evidence and macrobiotic case histories, Moss wrote the following:

> This session [of the CAPCAM panel] brought forth strong testimony that sometimes the adoption of a macrobiotic diet is followed by the dramatic regression of advanced cancers. A nurse told how, in 1995, she was diagnosed with lung cancer that had spread all over her body. She received no effective conventional therapy, and reluctantly went on the macrobiotic diet . . . What makes this case so extraordinary is that her progress was monitored weekly by a sympathetic physician colleague. The shrinkage, and finally the disappearance, of her tumors was documented millimeter by millimeter! She has now been disease-free for over five years.

A scientific study of the macrobiotic diet as a treatment for cancer is now being planned and will likely begin sometime in 2005.

The overwhelming abundance of research shows that diets rich in whole grains, fresh vegetables, beans, bean products, fruit, and fish can heal. Indeed, science is learning that plant-based diets can serve as adjunct forms of therapy for many people who are already ill and searching for powerful ways to help themselves.

The same cannot be said for high-protein diets, however.

High-Protein Diets Do Not Heal

Much is being made today of high-protein diets, which are adopted by millions of Americans in order to lose weight. Although there is no research to show that high-protein diets can be effective in the treatment of any illness, proponents of such programs point to a recent study published in *The New England Journal of Medicine* (May 2003) to support their claims of weight loss, and perhaps of improvement in blood cholesterol and triglycerides (blood fats). *The New England Journal of Medicine* study compared two groups, one that followed a "low-carbohydrate, high-protein, high-fat diet," similar to the Atkins diet, versus a "low-calorie, high-carbohydrate, low-fat (conventional) diet," similar to the American Heart Association diet. The researchers found that after three months, "no significant differences were found in total or low-density lipoprotein [LDL] cholesterol concentrations." However, the group on the high-protein diet experienced an increase in HDL levels, the good cholesterol, and a decrease in triglycerides, or blood fats, which are a risk factor for heart disease. After six months on the respective diets, the group on the high-protein diet experienced slightly better weight loss (the difference in weight loss between the two groups was only 4 percent), "but the differences were not significant at one year," reported the scientists, who were led by Dr. Gary Foster, of the University of Pennsylvania School of Medicine. The researchers noted that adherence was poor for both groups.

Though none of these findings are particularly inspiring, they are nonetheless celebrated in the popular media and by proponents of high-protein diets. They also have been used to justify eating a diet that is made up largely of steak, bacon, cheese, eggs, and heavy cream, with very limited amounts of vegetables. Proponents claim that this diet will not only cause weight loss, but is good for your overall health.

Other research has contradicted such claims, however.

Richard Fleming, M.D., did a yearlong study in which he randomized 100 patients who followed four different diets:

- Diet #1, which was composed entirely of vegetables and fruits, or what Fleming called his Phase 1 diet;

- Diet #2, composed of whole grains, vegetables, fruits, and small amounts of animal foods, which Fleming referred to as his Phase 2 diet;
- Diet #3, essentially the American Heart Association diet, which allowed between 20 and 30 percent of its calories from fat from any source;
- Diet #4, which was a high-protein, low-carbohydrate, high-fat diet.

The high-protein diet contained between 1,400 and 1,500 calories, which is a standard calorie content for the most popular high-protein diets. This calorie content, it should be pointed out, will cause weight loss in anyone who weighs more than 150 pounds.

Fleming's study, which was published in the September 2002, edition of *The Journal of Preventive Cardiology* (5(3): 110–118, 2002), showed that diets 1 and 2 provided, by far, the best results in all of the health-related categories he examined, including weight loss. After one year on the respective diets, Fleming's study participants experienced the following results.

Weight Loss

Diet #1 caused people to lose, on average, 18 percent of their body weight—nearly one-fifth of their total weight. An overweight person of 200 pounds lost, on average, about 40 pounds in one year. Anyone of 300 pounds lost about 60 pounds after one year. These were average weight losses, which meant that some lost less, while others lost more.

Diet #2 caused people to lose 12 percent of their body weight. Those who were overweight and weighed 200 pounds lost about 24 pounds. People who were 300 pounds lost, on average, about 39 pounds.

Diet #3. Only those people who weighed more than 200 pounds could lose weight on the AHA diet, because the diet contains 2,000 calories, which will sustain at least 200 pounds of body weight. Those who weighed more than 200 pounds lost weight, depending on how much above 200 pounds they were when they started the diet.

Diet #4. People on the high-protein diet lost, on average, about 13 percent of their body weight, which is consistent with other studies.

People who weighed 200 pounds and were overweight lost, on average, approximately 26 pounds. An overweight person of 300 pounds would lose 36 pounds.

Total Cholesterol

Total blood cholesterol includes both LDL and HDL cholesterol. Research has shown that cholesterol levels above 180 mg./dl. are associated with an increased risk of heart disease. That risk jumps dramatically when the number rises above 200 mg./dl.

Fleming found the following:

Diet #1, composed entirely of vegetables and fruits, caused total cholesterol levels to drop 39.1 percent. Someone with a cholesterol level of 200 mg./dl. would see their level drop nearly 80 milligrams, to about 120 mg./dl.

Diet #2, the whole grain, vegetables, fruit, and limited-fat diet, caused a drop of 30.4 percent in total cholesterol.

Diet #3, the AHA diet, caused a drop of 5 percent.

Diet #4, the high-protein diet, caused an increase in total cholesterol of 4.3 percent.

LDL Cholesterol (the "bad" cholesterol)

Diet #1, the all-plant diet, caused LDL to fall 52 percent.

Diet #2, the plants-and-low-fat diet, caused LDL to fall 38.8 percent. Diet #3, the AHA diet, caused a 6.1 percent drop in LDL.

Diet #4, the high-protein diet, caused a 6 percent increase in LDL levels.

HDL Cholesterol (the "good" cholesterol)

Diet #1 caused a 9 percent increase in HDL cholesterol.

Diet #2 caused a 3.6 percent increase in HDL.

Diet #3 brought about a 1.5 percent decrease in HDL.

Diet #4 caused a 5.8 percent decrease in HDL.

Triglycerides

Diet #1, the plant-based diet, caused a 37.3 percent drop in triglycerides.

Diet #2, the plants-and-low-fat diet, caused a 36.9 percent fall in triglycerides.

Diet #3, the AHA diet, brought about a 1 percent increase in triglycerides.

Diet #4, the high-protein diet, caused an initial drop in triglycerides of 3.5 percent after four months on the diet. After the eighth month on the diet, however, triglycerides rose 3.3 percent. By the twelfth month of the study, triglycerides were up among the high-protein group by 5.5 percent.

Homocysteine Levels

Diet #1, the all-plant diet, caused a drop in homocysteine of 13.6 percent.

Diet #2 caused homocysteine to fall 14.6 percent.

Diet #3 caused a 9 percent rise in homocysteine.

Diet #4, the high-protein diet, caused a 12.4 percent increase in homocysteine levels.

Fibrinogen Levels

When elevated, fibrinogen causes the blood to become more thick, or viscous, and to increase the blood's tendency to form clots. High fibrinogen, therefore, is associated with a greater risk of heart attack and stroke.

Diet #1, the vegetable and fruit regimen, caused an 11 percent drop in fibrinogen levels.

Diet #2, the whole grains, vegetables, and low-fat diet, caused fibrinogen levels to fall by 6.3 percent.

Diet #3, the AHA diet, caused a 0.6 percent drop in fibrinogen.

Diet #4, the high-protein program, caused fibrinogen levels to rise 11.9 percent.

. . .

I have already mentioned an earlier study done by Fleming and published in the journal *Angiology* that showed that a high-protein diet caused a decrease in blood flow to the heart, and increased the risk of heart attack.

In addition to the Fleming research, other studies have shown that high-protein intake can lead to calcium loss and osteoporosis, or the thinning of bones, according to a report published in the May 2001, edition of the professional journal, *Dietitian's Edge*.

In order to protect the body's delicate acid-alkaline balance, the brain signals the bones to release phosphorus and calcium whenever acid levels become too high. Phosphorus is the body's natural alkalizer. But as phosphorus is released, calcium is lost, as well, resulting in weaker bones. "We know that dietary protein intake influences urinary calcium losses with each gram of dietary protein, increasing urinary calcium losses by 1–1.5 mg.," wrote Belinda S. O'Connell, M.S., R.D., L.D. "This means that a person who is consuming a high-protein diet requires more calcium in his or her diet to maintain calcium balance than someone who eats less protein. In situations where dietary calcium intake or absorption is sub-optimal, a high-protein diet may further worsen calcium imbalances and increase the risk of osteoporosis."

These and other studies reflect a dramatic decrease in health by those who followed the high-protein diet. The claims made by proponents of the high-protein diets caused scientists at the Harvard Medical School to review all the evidence on high-protein diets and to publish their analysis in the January 2003, *Harvard Health Letter*. They concluded that:

- "The diet is very high in saturated fat." The scientists point out that the research shows that high intake of saturated fat is associated with "an increased risk of heart disease," stroke, and cancer. "And men have an extra concern," the Harvard group stated, "since studies from Harvard and elsewhere strongly suggest that saturated fat is an important risk factor for prostate cancer."
- "The diet is very low in fiber," which increases the risk of numerous disorders, including "heart disease, diabetes," and others.
- "The diet is very low in fruits and vegetables. Many studies link a high intake of fruits and vegetables with reduced risk of heart disease, strokes, dementia (advanced memory loss), and certain cancers."

- "The diet is very high in protein." The researchers point out that there is no evidence to show that humans need such high levels of protein. At the same time, there is research to suggest that it could be harmful to health. Animal studies have shown that "large amounts of protein accelerate the aging of the kidneys, and high-protein diets are harmful for some people with kidney disease," the scientists stated. "In addition, a high intake of protein does cause calcium loss that may increase the risk of osteoporosis ('thin bones') and kidney stones. In fact, a 2002 study found that a high-protein, low-carbohydrate diet produced a sharp increase in urinary calcium loss in just six weeks."
- Finally, the researchers pointed out that high-protein diets contain high levels of sodium, which increase the risk of high blood pressure and strokes. The absence of potassium, found in whole grains, fresh vegetables, and fruits, make it all the more likely to promote high blood pressure and strokes.

It's Not a Healing Diet

High-protein diets do cause weight loss, at least during the initial period one follows the program. Moreover, proponents of high-protein diets deserve credit for pointing out the dangers of processed foods and high insulin levels, which are highly inflammatory and associated with many illnesses, including heart disease, diabetes, and cancer. But there are far healthier ways of eliminating processed foods from your diet and lowering your insulin levels.

In fact, the Fleming studies, and all the evidence accumulated by the Harvard researchers, suggest that, in the end, high-protein diets may do more harm than good. The increases in total cholesterol, LDL cholesterol, homocysteine, and fibrinogen all create the conditions for high levels of inflammation—which is exactly the opposite of what you want to create in order to restore health, especially after you have been diagnosed with a life-threatening illness.

Staying Away From Milk Does a Body Good

Thanks to the overwhelming success of ad campaigns conducted by the National Dairy Association, milk is widely believed to be essential to health, particularly the strength of bones and teeth. But scientific studies have consistently contradicted that assertion.

There are numerous problems with dairy products, which, for people who have been diagnosed with a serious illness, could tip the balance in favor of the disease.

The first is that whole milk, whole milk cheeses, and ice creams are high in saturated fat, which, as we have seen, promotes heart disease and cancer.

Milk, cheese, and yogurt increase blood levels of a compound known as insulin-like growth factor (IGF-1), which has been shown to promote the onset and growth of cancer, especially cancers of the breast and prostate. A study published in a 1998 edition of *Science* showed that men with the highest levels of IGF-1 had four times the risk of prostate cancer than men with the lowest levels of IGF-1. Women with high levels of IGF-1 have a higher rate of breast cancer.

In *Eat, Drink, and Be Healthy,* Dr. Willett reports that men who drink milk are particularly at risk of prostate cancer.

"In nine separate studies, the strongest and most consistent dietary factor linked with prostate cancer was high consumption of milk or dairy products," Dr. Willett writes. "In the largest of these, the Health Professionals Follow-up Study, men who drank two or more glasses of milk a day were almost twice as likely to develop advanced or metastatic (spreading) prostate cancer as those who didn't drink milk at all." Saturated fat, as I showed earlier, is highly inflammatory and oxidative, thus supporting any existing illness.

Concerns have been raised about milk's possible link to other types of cancers, as well. Willett pointed to earlier research done at Harvard University by Daniel Cramer, M.D., and reported in the medical journal,

The Lancet. Cramer found that, once consumed, the sugar in dairy products, known as lactose, is converted to another form of sugar called galactose. Galactose is broken down by enzymes produced by the liver. However, when the body's ability to break down galactose is exceeded, the sugars build up in the body and affect a woman's ovaries. Women who have low levels of the enzyme needed to break down galactose have three times the rates of ovarian cancer than other women.

Milk, like all animal proteins, is high in the sulfur amino acids, which increase the acid levels in the blood and cause calcium losses. This promotes bone loss and increases the risk of osteoporosis, a disease that results in the thinning of bones and sometimes fatal fractures. In fact, studies have associated milk consumption with higher rates of osteoporosis. The Harvard Nurses Study showed that women who consistently drink milk have much higher rates of bone fractures than women who eat very few dairy products or avoid them altogether.

Studies have shown that the countries that consume milk products have the highest rates of osteoporosis. On the other hand, populations such as the Chinese that avoid milk experience low rates of osteoporosis. Not only do the Chinese avoid milk, but they also eat relatively low levels of animal protein. On average, the Chinese consume 64.1 grams of protein per day, 60 of which is from plant sources. Americans, on average, eat between 90 and 120 grams of protein, of which only 27 grams come from plant sources. The average Chinese person consumes 544 mg. of calcium per day. Yet, the Chinese have exceedingly low rates of osteoporosis. We, on the other hand, are experiencing an epidemic of osteoporosis.

"There's no solid evidence that merely increasing the amount of milk in your diet will protect you from breaking a hip or wrist or crushing a backbone in later years," writes Dr. Willett, in *Eat, Drink, and Be Healthy*.

Milk is touted as the ultimate source of calcium, but there are many other good sources that do not pose the same health risks, especially to people who are already suffering from serious illness. A cup of milk contains 300 mg. of calcium. A cup of cooked collard greens contains 360 mg.; a cup of kale contains 210 mg.; a cup of cooked bok choy, 250. Many other green and leafy vegetables are rich sources of calcium, as are many fish. A three-and-a-half-ounce serving of salmon contains 290 mg.; the same size serving of mackerel, 300. A tin of sardines contains 480 mg. of calcium.

Willett points out in *Eat, Drink, and Be Healthy* that about 75 percent of the world's adult population cannot digest milk sugar, or lactose, including some 50 million Americans. People who are lactose intolerant suffer from a variety of digestive disorders when they consume milk, including cramping, diarrhea, nausea, and bloating.

Citing the tendency of milk to create constipation, iron deficiency, and allergies in infants, the American Academy of Pediatrics has recommended that parents avoid giving their infants any cow's milk products before the age of one year.

Researchers are increasingly concerned about chemicals and allergens found in milk. Many milk products are often contaminated with bovine growth hormone, antibiotics, and pesticides, among other drugs. No one knows as yet what the effects of these substances are on human health, but many health authorities have already expressed concern that they may adversely affect the immune system.

A 1992 study published in *The New England Journal of Medicine,* and since repeated in more recent research, including a study published in *Diabetes Metabolism Research Reviews* (January–Feburary 2001), showed that dairy protein triggered an autoimmune response in sensitive children that caused immune cells to attack and destroy the insulin-producing cells of the pancreas, thus triggering the onset of juvenile (type 1) diabetes. Population studies have shown an association throughout the world between milk consumption and higher rates of insulin-dependent diabetes.

"How dairy foods came to be considered *essential* despite their high content of fat, saturated fat, and lactose is a topic of considerable historical interest," wrote Marion Nestle, Ph.D., professor and chair of the Department of Nutrition and Food Studies at New York University, author of the book, *Food Politics, How the Food Industry Influences Nutrition and Health* (University of California Press, 2002). "As it turns out, nutritionists have collaborated with dairy lobbies to promote the nutritional value of dairy products since the early years of the twentieth century. Recently, however, some scientists have raised doubts about whether dairy foods confer special health benefits. In addition to concerns about lactose intolerance, some question the conventional wisdom that dairy foods protect against osteoporosis or, for that matter, accomplish *any* public health goals. Others suggest that the hormones, growth factors, and al-

lergenic proteins in dairy foods end up doing more harm than good."
[Emphasis, Dr. Nestle's.]

For those with a serious illness, milk presents too many assaults on the body—and especially to the immune system—to be considered part of a healing diet. Indeed, two of the healing diets that I have already cited—macrobiotics and the McDougall Program—recommend that you avoid milk and milk products entirely. The Pritikin Program allows small amounts of skim milk, but Nathan Pritikin himself avoided all dairy products and urged people to do the same. He allowed small amounts of dairy to be consumed because he believed that it would make his diet more acceptable to Americans. But Nathan recognized the dangers posed by milk and believed that it was inappropriate for adult consumption.

A Healing Diet, by Any Name You Call It

All of the research, coupled with the experiences of people who have utilized diet to heal themselves, points to the same conclusion: a plant-based diet is the basis for a recovery of health.

So far, I have cited three healing versions of this diet—the macrobiotic, Pritikin, and McDougall diets. These three programs, though different in many small but important details, have much in common. All three programs share the same five core food groups, which are:

1. All three are centered on plant foods, namely vegetables, whole grains, beans, and fruit.
2. All three approaches are based on the consumption of whole, unprocessed grains, such as brown rice, barley, millet, buckwheat, amaranth, quinoa, and millet. All three discourage the use of processed foods for their richness in calories and trans fats.
3. All three utilize beans as a primary source of protein. In addition to providing easily assimilated proteins, beans contain phytochemicals that lower cholesterol, boost immunity, and suppress cancers. Macrobiotics stresses beans and bean products, especially soybean foods that are rich in phytochemicals, especially genistein.
4. All three are low in fat, especially saturated and trans fats. The

reason, very simply, is that they all restrict the amount of animal and processed foods. In the case of the McDougall diet, no animal foods are eaten at all. Macrobiotics allows fish, but recommends that people avoid all beef, pork, chicken, and eggs. The Pritikin Program permits a three-and-a-half-ounce serving of lean animal foods, including beef, each day.

5. All three restrict consumption of dairy products, including cow's milk, yogurt, and cheese. The macrobiotic regimen includes many immune-boosting and cancer-fighting specialty foods that are native to Asian and other cultures. These foods include sea vegetables, which are extremely rich in minerals, antioxidants, and phytochemicals, and many soy-based, fermented foods, such as miso, tamari, and shoyu, all of which are abundant in health-promoting flora and cancer-fighting phytochemicals.

Clearly, the healing effects of these three programs begin with their overwhelming reliance on plant foods.

What to Eat

Chapter 9 provides a complete description of the healing diet and a twenty-one day menu plan. Recipes are also provided for all the foods listed in the menu plan. The healing diet is composed essentially of the following groups of foods.

- Whole, unprocessed, cooked grains, including amaranth, barley, brown rice, buckwheat, millet, oats, and wheat.
- A variety of whole grain pastas.
- Green and leafy vegetables, including broccoli, collard greens, kale, mustard greens, and watercress.
- Round and sweet vegetables, including squash (such as acorn, butternut, buttercup, hubbard, Hokkaido pumpkin, and kabocha), mushrooms (such as shiitake), onions, parsnips, sweet potatoes, and yams.
- Roots, including burdock, carrots, lotus root, rutabaga, and turnips.
- Beans, including aduki, black beans, chickpeas, kidney beans, lentils, limas, navy beans, and soybeans.

- Sea vegetables, including arame, kombu, nori, and wakame.
- Fruit.
- Fish.
- A wide variety of condiments, natural sweeteners, snacks, and desserts.

This diet is not only healing, but delicious, especially when you learn to prepare the foods. Once you have your diet in place, however, it's time to look at other aspects of your life to promote your healing. The next big step in healing is to start bringing more love into your life.

Create a Health-Supporting Community

So far, the healing journey has forced you to focus on what you can do for yourself, but when you arrive at the fourth step, you encounter a larger message, one that seems to be spoken by a wise old man or woman who says: "You can go no further on your own. You need others now to help you heal."

For the person who is coping with a serious illness, the notion that you—or anyone else—can get well by working alone is a dangerous illusion. To borrow a well-worn phrase, it takes a village to heal a person of a serious disease. Those who get well do so, in part, by creating a supportive and life-enhancing community. The healing path unfolds before you as a growing web of connections to people and to new forms of knowledge. As you make these connections, and benefit from the intimacy, knowledge, and support you receive, you realize that the essence of the healing journey is expanding love—love that you give and receive from those closest to you, as well as from those you meet along the way.

Like a rich bouquet of flowers, love comes in many forms. One type, of course, is the love from a spouse or partner. Others include the love from family and friends, from healers and teachers, from support groups and social organizations, from clergy or spiritual leaders. Opening your-self to the many forms of love, and receiving them with gratitude, is an act of self-love and, indeed, of self-healing.

At the fourth step, you are challenged to create a network of healing relationships. In order to do this, you must humbly ask for, and accept, the help of others. Very often, the fourth step also requires that you heal old conflicts that exist in your most important relationships. Forgiveness of others, being forgiven, and forgiveness of self are central challenges on the healing journey. A pivotal place has been reached, a place where we realize that in order to heal the body, we must act from the heart.

How Does Love Heal?

Perhaps the first and most obvious way that love heals is by serving as an antidote to fear, which is the basis for all forms of distress. As St. John wrote two thousand years ago, "There is no fear in love, but perfect love casts out fear, because fear involves punishment and the one who fears is not perfected in love." (First Epistle of John, 4:18)

Fear, which is often referred to as stress, weakens the immune sys-tem, creates hormonal imbalances, and eventually destroys the body. Fear opposes life; it is antilife and, when maintained long enough, causes death.

Fear arises from the experience of separation—separation from self; from those we love and want to protect; from those who love and pro-tect us; from the resources we need; from belonging; and from our sense of a connection with the divine. The experience of separation is strangely connected to oblivion. Indeed, the more separated we are from others, the less our lives seem to matter. Conversely, we experi-ence our lives as important and meaningful through our connection with others.

The first big study to demonstrate the destructive effects of separa-tion has come to be known as the Alameda County study. In 1965, re-searchers began to track the health and mortality rates of 10,000 randomly selected residents of Alameda County, near San Francisco, California. The scientists found that those people who regularly attended church, belonged to civic organizations, and were married and had close friendships lived far longer and were far healthier than those who did not participate in social or religious community, or were not married and had few long-term relationships. In fact, people who were well con-nected within their communities were far healthier and, on average, lived twice as long as those who were isolated, even if they lived on ham-burgers, hot dogs, and nachos.

The Alameda County study has been replicated many times through-out the world. In fact, some studies have shown that people who say they feel isolated have three to five times the mortality rates as those who feel connected within their community. Remarkably, some studies have found that isolation is a more important predictor of health and mortal-ity than blood pressure, cholesterol level, and cigarette smoking.

All of this suggests that separation from the social body somehow creates dysfunction in the physical body. And indeed, degenerative illness can be seen as a consequence of separation within the body. Heart dis-ease arises when the heart is separated from adequate quantities of blood and oxygen. Cancer cells and tumors act independently—or separately—from the rest of the body and, indeed, from the greater good of the body. Disease itself can be understood as a divided physical condition in which parts of the body are no longer acting in concert, or harmony, with the overall forces that would sustain optimal function and even life itself.

Love is the antidote to separation. Love is the bridge builder between human beings and, indeed, between the human heart and the divine. Love gives us the experience of reunion, which in turn reanimates life and gives rebirth. Though there are many definitions of love, I define it as the giving of energy that nourishes and promotes life. This life-enhancing energy can flow through many mediums. It passes through a person's touch. It is in the caring eyes of someone who gives you undivided atten-tion. It's in music that soothes, relaxes, and inspires you. It's in healing words, understanding, insight, forgiveness, and celebration. It's in danc-ing, sports, and lovemaking. Love is present in every expression of joy.

Supportive and loving relationships promote healing by encouraging self-acceptance, a sense of belonging, and enduring love. Sometimes these alone are enough to overcome harmful health habits. That was demonstrated by the research done on a small village in eastern Pennsylvania, known as Roseto. In the 1960s, two scientists, Steward Wolf, M.D., and John G. Bruhn, M.D., began studying the unlikely fact that the people of Roseto experienced much lower rates of senile dementia and lower mortality from heart disease and stroke than neighboring communities, despite their high-fat diets and sedentary lifestyles. It appeared, at least on the surface, that the Roseto residents were doing everything wrong, yet they were somehow healthier than their neighbors. Why? the scientists wanted to know.

After much investigation and close scrutiny of the Rosetoans' lifestyles, the researchers concluded that the good health the residents enjoyed flowed from a single factor: their close-knit community. The people of Roseto were Italian immigrants, a group that has come to be known by sociologists as "urban villagers," so named because they retained their traditional living arrangements even after they came to America. True to the urban villager label, the Rosetoans tended to marry other Italians within their community, and their households were commonly made up of three generations of family members. They were religious people. They also participated in church and social organizations. The researchers found that Rosetoans were highly supportive of each other, especially when a member of the community experienced crisis. They provided love, care, and feelings of security, all of which translated, for many, into a positive outlook on life. The researchers showed that the Rosetoans' relaxed ways of living and their lower-than-average stress levels were the reasons for their good health and low mortality levels.

These conclusions were reinforced when the Rosetoans turned away from their traditional ways of living in the latter stages of the twentieth century and experienced a sharp increase in their disease and death rates. As Dr. Wolf observed in his book, *The Power of the Clan: The Influence of Relationships on Heart Disease* (Transaction Publications, 1993), the Rosetoans gradually became more materialistic and less socially cohesive. They became more enamored with expensive cars, for example; they bought bigger houses that were either outside Roseto, or on the outskirts of their little hamlet. Their church attendance dropped dramatically; they began to marry outside their ethnic group, and many moved away. Soon, their rates of heart disease and other illnesses were as high, or higher, than those of the average American.

Love Grows People and Heals Them

Love doesn't just bring together that which has been separated, however. It also nourishes. If you love your plants, you give them all they need to thrive: rich soil, water, sunlight, and many other environmental conditions that would support their lives. Plants do not grow when exposed to harsh or antagonistic conditions. On the contrary, the harsher the conditions, the more likely they are to die. The same thing happens to people. Above all else, each of us needs to be seen for the good that we possess and, like plants, have that good encouraged. That requires more praise than criticism, more tenderness than discipline, more understanding than intolerance. The person who genuinely sees the good in others, then promotes that good is giving love that nourishes. He or she is enhancing the lives of others.

There are a multitude of ways to promote the good in another. It can be done with simple words of appreciation—such as "You do that well," or "That took tremendous courage," or "I needed you and you were there"—or through simple acts, such as finding ways to lift a lover's burden, however small, so that his or her life is a little less fettered. In each case, the words and actions flow from your love, appreciation, and desire to make someone's life better. The impact of your words and actions, if they are imbued with genuine love and appreciation, transform the recipient and the relationship itself. Two people are no longer struggling to survive the onslaught of the other's criticism. They are no longer armored against the other's insults. And more important, they are no longer confined to their own small selves, and their own intense self-doubt, which arises when their mistakes are emphasized.

Every great coach who has worked with an individual athlete has practiced the basics of love to bring out the best in his or her player. Among the preeminent practitioners of this approach was Angelo Dundee, the trainer for the great Mohammed Ali. Dundee realized early on that Ali responded badly to all forms of criticism. So whenever he wanted Ali to throw more jabs or uppercuts, or to throw a punch in a particular way, he wouldn't instruct him, but rather would praise Ali for doing something exactly how Dundee wanted it done. "I love the way you throw that jab just like this, champ," Dundee would tell Ali, as he mimed what he wanted done. Ali would get the message and follow suit.

Love, like sunlight, is a nurturing and healing force. It has a way of getting inside of us and promoting the life energies. We are somehow stronger, more resilient, and better able to heal. A study done by Duke University researcher Redford Williams, M.D., and his colleagues, reported that people who suffer a heart attack, but who have no spouse or intimate partner, are three times more likely to die within five years of the event than those who have an equally severe coronary event but have a loving partner.

"What we found was that those patients with neither a spouse nor a friend were three times more likely to die than those involved in a caring relationship," said Dr. Williams.

Well-known immunologists Janice Kiecolt-Glaser and Ronald Glaser have conducted numerous studies on how the quality of a relationship affects the immune system. In one study, the researchers compared the immune systems of married women, each of whom was given a questionnaire to determine the quality of her marriage. Those women who said that they had loving and supportive husbands also had far better immune functions than those who said their marriages were difficult and unsupportive. In general, the immune systems of married women were stronger than those who were unmarried. But it was the quality of the relationship that had the greatest impact on health.

The Glasers found similar results in men. Unhappily married men had weaker immune systems than happily married men. Moreover, the men who were separated had the lowest immune response of all.

Separation and fear can grow, like a deepening night, until they engulf us in the darkness of isolation, self-doubt, and even self-hatred. Love, like the dawn, can send the shadows fleeing.

Into Another Realm

It is a mysterious and wondrous experience to have your special powers recognized by someone else. Love illuminates and magnifies the best in you. It alters your perception of what's possible for you to achieve in this life. Indeed, it gives you a glimpse of your heroic nature, your ideal self. Once you have entered that realm, you are suddenly more creative, more powerful, and less afraid. You can see new possibilities and perform feats that your lesser self could not imagine, much less believe possible. The heroic nature is the part of you that gives your life meaning. And, needless to say, it is also the part of you that can heal you of any illness.

Love lets us glimpse the lofty worlds that live inside of us, but we cannot fully occupy those worlds until we learn to love others. Until we can love consistently, we are trapped in a childlike relationship with those around us, secretly waiting for others to give us the love we need so that we can feel strong and secure enough to be our best selves. If those we care about do not give us that love, we shrink a little and settle into our lesser selves, which is to say, the part of us that is fearful and angry for not getting the love we need.

Only when we love can we come fully into our power to transform ourselves and others. Your love must manifest, first, as love for yourself; that self-love must manifest as acts of self-love. It guides you in all your health habits, such as your dietary choices, your exercise regimen, your need for rest, your need for gentle touch, your need to be heard and understood, and your need to be alone. Your love of yourself allows you to recognize toxic relationships and to gently eliminate such people from your life, while spending time with people who love you and support your healing.

The love you have for others makes you supportive, understanding, and compassionate. In this way, your love inspires those around you and, in the process, makes you the creative force in your relationships. The more you love, the more you set the tone for your relationships. Your ability to love transforms you from victim to creative catalyst. As you support others and make them aware of their own best selves, you naturally shift into your own heroic nature, or higher self, which is the realm from which miracles can flow.

The heroic nature's primary relationship is with its own perception of truth and love. The higher self is willing to sacrifice the comforts of old and familiar behaviors in order to heal. For example, the person who is functioning from the higher self and wants to heal is willing to give up favorite foods or drinks because he knows intuitively, if not from direct experience, that they are harming his body. In the same way, he is willing to break up old behavior patterns, forgive old hurts, and rekindle love so that he might experience life's greater possibilities. The higher self keeps us from denying truths that we already know. And then it demands that we align our actions with those truths.

Mohandas Gandhi (known throughout the world as Mahatma, or "great soul") was speaking from this higher self when he wrote in his auto-biography, *Gandhi* (Beacon Press, 1957), "I worship God as Truth only. [Caps his.] I have not yet found Him, but I am seeking after Him. I am pre-pared to sacrifice the things dearest to me in pursuit of this quest. Even if the sacrifice demanded be my very life, I hope I may be prepared to give it."

Your higher self forces you to recognize your body's most elemental truth, which is that it will age and die. Life is short. That wisdom awak-ens the heart's greatest truth, which is that the only thing that will make this life worth living is love.

All of which makes the fourth step essential to our physical, emo-tional, and spiritual healing. The question everyone who arrives at this place must answer is: How do I create a loving and healing community?

Begin by Finding Healers for Your Body

Your body, now suffering and struggling to live, is desperately in need of love. That love must come in different forms, including the healing foods you eat. But in the context of the fourth step, that love must come from others, and specifically from healers, including those who can touch your body with love and healing energy.

Most Americans are touch-deprived. Other warmer cultures, such as many Southern European, or Hispanic, or South American peoples, recognize that touch is an essential form of love and therefore must be communicated and experienced many times each day. A curious and charming little study revealed our varying attitudes toward touch. Re-searchers observed four couples sitting over coffee for one hour. Each of the couples was of a different nationality. One couple was American, an-other English, a third French, and the fourth Puerto Rican. The ob-servers found that the American couple touched each other twice during the entire hour. The English couple did not touch each other at all. The

French touched 110 times, and the Puerto Rican couple touched 180 times—in a single hour!

This is more serious than we might think. Touch is an essential way to communicate love. We all need to be touched in order to sustain physical and mental health. Infants and young children who are deprived of touch have weaker immune, endocrine, and digestive systems, studies have shown. Researchers reported in the scientific journal *Adolescence* that children who are not touched in positive ways experience heightened emotional and mental stress, adverse hormonal conditions, antisocial behavior, and a greater tendency to violence. When a group of these children underwent regular therapeutic massage, they experienced increased brain levels of serotonin (the neurotransmitter that creates feelings of relaxation, confidence, and well-being), decreased brain levels of dopamine (the neurotransmitter that promotes aggressive behavior), and a significant decrease in aggression and violence. By touching the body with love and care, we soothe the mind and relieve it of so much distress.

Our memories, stress, and so much painful emotional trauma are held within the tissues of the body. Think back when you were a child and were scolded by an adult. Your first reaction was physically to recoil. With repeated attacks, that recoil becomes a habitual response. Eventually, the physical and emotional tension that was caused by such events is held within our shocked muscles and organs. If there was physical abuse, the shock and tension are even more acute.

Tension in the body causes tissues to contract in one place and expand in another. Some sets of muscles go into spasm, like a tightened fist. Those tightened muscles will prevent optimal blood circulation to flow to organs and cells, causing these organs to function at less-than-optimal levels. Waste, in the form of carbon dioxide, dietary and environmental toxins, will build within tissues, and the organs will struggle for life. This polluted environment forms the basis for disease.

Expansion and contraction occur even on the cellular level. In the coronary arteries, inflammation causes artery tissue to swell, the artery pathway to narrow, and the heart to become swollen and desperate for oxygen. These events form the basis for heart disease and heart attack.

Picture yourself, full of stress, lying on a healer's table. Someone with a gentle healing touch applies his or her hands to your tightened shoulders, painful back, swollen rib cage, cramped legs, tortured feet. Slowly, these parts of your body start to relax and come out of spasm. Gradually, your body learns to trust the compassionate love that flows through the therapist's hands. Your breathing gets slower, deeper, and more rhythmic; your muscles surrender their tension and release more energy into your body; and your long-standing misalignments start to come back into balance. The biological impact of such changes is enormous.

Studies have shown touching premature babies increases their chances of survival, encourages more rapid physical growth, and promotes immune, nervous, digestive, and reproductive system development. A study published in the *Journal of Alternative and Complementary Medicine* (February 2002) showed improved immune function among patients receiving therapeutic touch.

There are many forms of therapeutic massage and healing touch. Among the oldest and most widely practiced are acupressure, shiatsu (the Japanese version of acupressure), chiropractic, cranial sacral therapy, deep tissue massage, therapeutic massage, Bioenergetics (created by pioneering physician Dr. Alexander Lowen), Network Chiropractic, Reiki, and Swedish massage. Choose a practitioner who has been trained by a reputable massage or chiropractic school. In the Resource Guide at the end of this book, I have described the most common massage practices and provided a resource guide for contacting qualified massage and chiropractic practitioners.

Healing massage and therapeutic touch can directly relieve many of the physical and psychological conditions that support your illness. At the same time, it will promote the forces of healing now rising within you.

Forgive and Seek Forgiveness to Restore Love to Your Most Important Relationships

Certain relationships are essential to our psychological health and well-being. Only you can determine which of your relationships fall into that category. It may be your wife or husband, a life partner or longtime friend; it could be your children, or your mother or father. Whatever the relationship, one thing is certain: Forgiveness has been essential to maintain the free flow of love between the two of you. In fact, you've probably had to forgive each other not once but many times. Forgiveness is love's best friend, because without forgiveness, love cannot endure.

We have all witnessed countless examples of the living hell that is created when two people in an essential relationship don't forgive. In many cases, they are relegated to what seems like lifeless conversation (which is often hurtful by virtue of its neutrality), or surreptitious sniping, or outright war, even as they remain inextricably linked or committed to staying together. Yet their words and actions make the very nature of their relationship destructive. Sadly, many such couples secretly hope that the other will soften and express remorse for what has happened between them. Each mistakenly believes that something said in anger will somehow soften the other's heart. Of course, such hopes are illusions. Pain only causes more pain.

If you find yourself in such a situation, your heroic nature may be whispering a single question to you over and over again: How can I forgive and get back to love? Below are four steps that can help you forgive and restore love in an essential relationship. While these steps can be used to promote forgiveness in any relationship, I am only suggesting that they be used in essential relationships, or a relationship you are committed to maintaining. Sometimes we complicate the subject of forgiveness by including nonessential relationships in our discussion. Do I have to forgive the person who stole my wallet? people ask, or the person who took away my job? Only you can say whether you need to forgive that person. If it is eating away at you, and thereby serves as an impediment to your health, the answer is yes. But more fundamentally, we must acknowledge that forgiveness is essential in all relationships that involve love—especially if we want that love to continue, or to be restored. Here are four steps to help you forgive someone you truly care about.

1. Give Up the Need to Be Right

All ongoing conflicts are sustained when each partner insists that he or she is right and the other is wrong. Being right is a powerful and seductive illusion. Within it lies a relentless yearning for victory, a yearning that will not let you rest until you are vindicated. Unfortunately, many people take that yearning to their graves, still unsatisfied. Meanwhile, the campaign to prove that you are right has the effect of molding you into a frustrated, hardened, and embittered person who secretly longs to be loved, but is deprived of love, in part by your own stubborn defense of your position.

If there is a single lesson to be learned in all essential relationships, it is that there are always two truths present in every disagreement. Each person has his or her own personal needs and experience of life. Each sees the world from his or her own unique perspective. One or both may be unable to express fully his or her truth, but those truths are both equally real. Until each truth is understood and expressed, we cannot know what is motivating our actions, or our partner's.

In a relationship that is driven by the need to be right, real listening is impossible. Instead, each partner is furiously thinking about what he or she will say next as soon as the other takes a breath. Every fiber of one's being is dedicated to proving the other wrong, and in the process annihilating his or her truth.

Only when you recognize that you both have an incomplete understanding of each other's truth, and allow the other's truth to be expressed, can a state of understanding, compassion, and love arise. The best approach, therefore, is to give up being right. Instead, try to understand your own and your partner's needs and motivations. Know that, at bottom, both of you yearn to be understood, validated, and loved.

2. Accept Responsibility for Your Own Mistakes and Ask Forgiveness

In all essential relationships, neither party is free of error. Find your own mistakes, however buried inside you they may be, and admit them to yourself. Once you have reflected upon them, confess them to the person with whom you are in conflict. Acknowledge that your error hurt the person you love. Promise him or her that you will do everything in your power to avoid making that mistake again. Apologize and ask for forgiveness.

Your honesty, courage, and vulnerability will change your relationship with the person you love. More important, it will also change your relationship with yourself. We often insist on being right to avoid facing the underlying awareness of our own mistakes. When we confess our mistakes, something inside of us relaxes and celebrates our reconnection with truth and the divine.

In the mid-1990s, I wrote a long piece about a medical doctor who volunteered much of his time on a hospice ward at his local hospital. One day, I followed him on his rounds and spoke to the people whom he treated. Every person I interviewed expressed the same message. Love, forgiveness, and honesty were the most important lessons of life, they told me. Those who expressed their love honestly and directly, who forgave others and were forgiven, were also at peace at the end of their lives.

After the doctor and I spent time with his patients, the doctor told me of a former patient who had a wife and four children, all of whom he abused with his violent and angry temper. By the time he arrived at the hospice ward, he was ninety-three years old and had only weeks to live. The proximity of death made him realize how sorry he was for the way he treated them, the doctor said. Deeply humbled, he begged his wife and children to forgive him for his abusive behavior. He told each of them how much he loved them. He later told the doctor what he had said. "I was so hard on my children that I ruined my family," the doctor recalled the man saying. "I said to each of them, 'I am sorry. My anger came from my fear. I always believed that if I didn't do things just right, my life would be ruined. What could happen, I didn't know. I had too much pride. I was arrogant. I wanted everyone to reflect well on me. If they didn't behave just as I wanted . . . '" With that, he made a gesture with his hand, indicating that he hit them.

Miraculously, the man's full confession and his humble plea satisfied a deep need in his wife and children and elicited their love. "I remember how that family huddled around him at the end," the doctor recalled. "His approaching death drew them closer to each other, and the love they all felt for each other was a beautiful thing. Were all their wounds healed? No, of course not. But when someone important to you has hurt you, and then acknowledges that he hurt you and begs for your forgiveness, you are changed in a positive way. Your wounds begin to heal. You experience some form of justice and a kind of closure. You can love yourself more, and you can even start the process that leads to forgiveness of the one who hurt you. That is very healing."

Remember Gandhi's statement: God is truth. When we admit our own mistakes, we experience greater wholeness and reconnection with our hearts and all that is right in the universe. We embrace with love that part of us that made the mistakes and desperately wants to be accepted and returned to love. And in the process, we are redeemed.

A short word of warning. Most of us have been so well trained in self-defense that we can easily use confession as a subtle, manipulative tool whose real purpose is to elicit the confession of our loved one. We may start out confessing our own mistakes and end up accusing our loved one of failing to reciprocate. That's not the point of this step. On the contrary, we should be interested in one thing only: to honestly state how we have contributed to the conflict with the person we love. Only by making such a confession can we enjoy its rewards. In any case, your partner will know whether or not you are sincere. And anything less than sincerity will backfire and reinforce your conflict.

3. Share Your Gratitude for Your Loved One, with Your Loved One

All your essential relationships have great meaning, if only because these people have filled such important roles in your life. Conflict with these people—your spouse, children, a dear friend, your mother or father—tears at the soul and changes the quality of your life. Consider how much of a contribution your loved one has made to your life. Experience your gratitude for that contribution and express how important it is to you.

Not long ago, a couple came to see me for health advice and support for their marriage. I asked each to consider why he or she needed the other, and what each did to enrich the other's life. The man spoke first and listed the many reasons he needed his wife, and what she gave to him. When he finished, she was in tears. "It's so good to hear that," she said. "I didn't know you felt all of that. I didn't even know that you no-ticed." He was equally moved when she expressed all the reasons she needed him. Each was fulfilling a role in the other's life that was unique and irreplaceable. There is only so much time in life, the body tells us, which is why the heart says that love is sacred.

4. Find a Healthy Outlet for Your Emotions, Especially Your Anger

Forgiveness is not abandonment of self and one's own feelings and truth. You may have many feelings, such as anger, fear, and disappointment, that you need to honor and explore. Seek out the help of a compassionate therapist who can you lead you deeper into your memories and feelings with the intention of helping you understand and love yourself. Your doctor, a friend, or clergy member may be able to recommend such a person.

Many massage therapists, especially those who do therapeutic massage, Reiki, and healing touch, encourage their clients to express the deeply held emotions that often arise during their healing sessions. We hold our emotions—especially anger, fear, and sadness—in the body as physical tension. The emotions held within your tissues can be released by someone with a gentle, healing touch.

Finally, pour out all your negative emotions, especially your anger, disappointments, and fears in a diary or journal. Write in it as frequently as you can—every day, if possible.

Community Can Be Found in a Support Group and Counselors

Much is being said today about the global village that we're supposed to be living within, but the fact is that more people are isolated than at any other time in human history. On any given day, we are likely to have as many interactions with machines—voice mail, ATMs, online stores, and computers—as we do with people. Amtrak and Federal Express are just two of hundreds of businesses today that require patrons to interact, at least initially, with a computer-generated personality. (Amtrak calls the mechanized voice "Julie.") In our increasingly dehumanized world, we must consciously seek out community in order to meet our fundamental need for social contact and belonging.

One of the best ways to do that is with a support group, especially one that is designed to help people cope with serious illness. Support groups are often facilitated by well-trained, compassionate, and highly effective group leaders who can create safety, trust, and honesty among the group's members. In such environments, people can share their feelings—including their fear and anger—and get the love and understanding they need. The effects of such groups on your healing powers can be truly miraculous.

Studies have repeatedly shown that support groups strengthen immune systems and increase survival among people with serious illness, including various types of cancer, such as breast cancer and malignant melonoma. In one such study, Stanford psychiatrist Dr. David Spiegel and his colleague James L. Spira, Ph.D., found that women with advanced breast cancer who participated in a support group lived twice as long as those who did not participate in such a group.

One of the ways that support groups appear to help people is by alleviating depression and its related side effects by providing a sense of camaraderie and belonging. Researchers at the University of Michigan found that when people lose a sense of belonging, depression rises dramatically. "The need to get connected with others is paramount in recovery from depression," said Dr. Reg Williams, who led the study. Williams, whose research was published in the July–August 2003, issue of the *Journal of Nursing Research* was quoted as saying, "A sense of belonging is the best predictor of what an individual might experience in terms of depressive symptoms." A superficial sense of having friends is not enough, Williams said. "An individual may have friends," but he may still experience depression if he "doesn't feel they belong to him," Williams said.

Depression is important, of course, because many people who are diagnosed with a serious illness become depressed. Moreover, depression is often associated with surrender, which, for those with a serious illness, is tantamount to death.

If Your Heart Leads You Back, Go . . . The vast majority of us yearn for spiritual support and a sense of connection with the divine. That yearning is especially strong after a diagnosis of a serious illness. (See Chapter 6 on Faith.) If your higher nature is encouraging you to join a religious community, go back. Those who do are strengthened in both body and soul. In a follow-up to the Alameda County study, researchers found that frequent church attendance was associated with lower rates of death from cancer, and circulatory, digestive, and respiratory disorders.

Turn to Qualified Healers and Teachers of All Types A sense of connection and belonging can be created and experienced by turning to healers and teachers of all types. Most ministers and priests will set aside time to counsel you on an ongoing basis for free. There are many hands-on healers in churches throughout the country who will give you body-work for no charge. There are also many forms of healing services provided by all types of religious communities.

Virtually every community offers several types of twelve-step pro-grams, all of which are free. Many communities offer low-cost, individ-ual psychological counseling programs, as well. Believe it or not, many state departments of mental health offer free psychological counseling to anyone who cannot afford such counseling. All such services can be found in the yellow pages of your phone book under "Social and Human Services."

In addition, there are excellent schools for bodywork throughout the country, where volunteers are needed so that students can practice and develop their skills. In many cases, these sessions are provided free of charge or for minimal fees.

In virtually every town and city, there are low-cost programs for yoga, gentle stretching exercises, meditation, and writing workshops. Any combination of these types of programs can give you a sense of community and belonging. At the same time, they provide extremely beneficial services and an opportunity to express your innermost feelings and thoughts.

Participate in a Healing Community Communities all over the country have sprung up around specific healing modalities, such as the macrobiotic diet and lifestyle, or the Pritikin program, or the McDougall diet. In many cases, community newsletters offer services, potlucks, and gatherings throughout the country. Such communities provide enormous support and practical information about healing. In many such gather-ings, people can be found who have faced and overcome the very condi-tions with which you may be struggling.

Finding the Right Support Is Easier Than You Think

As I said, the yellow pages of every telephone book contains a section under "Social and Human Services" that offers a wide variety of social support groups and services for every demographic group. Among them are programs for children, the elderly, twelve-step programs, drug abuse counseling, AIDS counseling services, low-cost medical assistance programs, support groups for people with various types of cancer, men's groups, women's groups, home care assistance, and various types of charities, such as the United Way, which can either help you directly, or refer you to other helpful organizations and groups. Your telephone book also includes a "Self-Help Guide" to support services offered in your community. (The Resource Guide in the back of this book can guide you to health-related programs, communities, and support groups in towns and cities across the country.)

In general, support groups allow people who face a common challenge to help each other cope, to share information, and to provide comfort and compassion. In short, they do the very things that traditional communities provided but, for so many of us, no longer exist.

Conquering the Unconquerable

The fourth step is itself an integration of many of the steps on the healing journey. Many people who work with healers or join support groups are already actively involved in strengthening their healing forces. They have begun to care for themselves in nurturing, loving ways; they have taken personal responsibility for their recovery; they've changed their diets; and they are seeking out healing connections with others.

That was certainly the case for Norman Arnold, who was forced to combine these and other important healing steps all at once if he had any chance of surviving pancreatic cancer. But above all else, Norman's experience illustrates the need, and the potential rewards, that can flow to the person who seeks connection with others, and the love and knowledge such connections can bring.

In 1982, Norman Arnold, then fifty-two years of age, was one of the most successful men in all of South Carolina. Married and the father of three sons, Norman had only recently sold his wine and spirits distribution company after making it the largest such retail company in the state and among the top ten in the country. Having achieved all the financial success he could have dreamed of, he was now looking around for something to do with the rest of life, something that gave his life purpose, meaning, and even rebirth. So far, nothing was showing up.

There was one small physical problem, however: He had a nagging pain in his back that had persisted for nearly a year. His doctors weren't sure what was wrong, but most agreed that it must be his gallbladder. On July 27, 1982, he entered Providence Hospital in Columbia and was operated on the following day. The surgery was expected to be routine. It was anything but.

The surgeon who performed the operation was a longtime friend of Norman's, Dan Davis, M.D. Dr. Davis opened Norman's abdomen and was about to turn his attention to Norman's gallbladder when he decided to examine the other organs that were available for inspection. He scrutinized Norman's pancreas and discovered a tumor the size of an egg. Davis biopsied the growth, sent it to pathology for analysis, and was soon informed that it was malignant. At that point, Davis might have sewn Norman up and braced himself to tell his patient the bad news, but the surgeon decided to look elsewhere and discovered three lesions on Norman's liver. Pathology confirmed that they were also cancerous.

Pancreatic cancer is incurable, with an average life expectancy of 5.1 months after diagnosis. Norman's gallbladder seemed irrelevant at that point, but Davis nonetheless turned his attention to it and found, as expected, that it was filled with gallstones. He removed the organ and closed the abdominal incision. Norman was sent to intensive care.

Meanwhile, Dan Davis went to the waiting room and found Norman's wife, Gerry Sue. He escorted her to the lounge and proceeded to tell her, as gently as he could, how perilous Norman's condition was.

"It took time for his words to register," Gerry Sue recalled. "I kept asking him what we would do next, and he gently explained that there really wasn't anything left to do." Two terrifying questions kept pressing themselves into her mind, but Gerry Sue dared not ask them: Is Norman going to die? And if so, how much time does he have to live? But she had to know.

"We have reservations for a skiing trip at Christmas, Dan," Gerry Sue said, obliquely. "Can Norman go on that trip?"

"I think you should go," Davis said.

Gerry Sue's mind raced. "We've got a bar mitzvah in April. What about that?"

Davis paused, calculating the months. "Can you move it up?" he asked.

Gerry Sue had her answer.

When Norman awoke, Dan Davis sat down on the end of his bed and gave his friend the terrible news: Norman had adenocarcionoma of the pancreas with metastatic lesions to the liver. The situation was hopeless. Norman could expect to live perhaps five to nine months, tops.

Once he told Norman the news, Davis left Norman's side, and Gerry Sue rushed into the intensive care unit. The two embraced and, as he would say much later, Norman felt the world come down on him. "We're all sitting ducks," he muttered.

Norman was soon moved to a private room, where an oncologist, Dr. Bill Babcock, explained that Norman should undergo chemotherapy. Norman questioned the effectiveness of such a procedure on his illness. The chemotherapy would have only a palliative effect, Babcock admitted.

"As I listened to his words, I disengaged from reality," Norman recalled. "I sank into my pillow and entered a fog."

When Babcock left, Gerry Sue tried to assure Norman that the two of them would fight this disease. "Our first few conversations were us grasping at empty hope," Norman recalled. "We were just fighting the darkness."

Later, Norman forced himself to think about his situation and what he could do. "I still had my three sons to raise," he told himself. "My wife was still young. Since I was an only child, my mother would be left without her son to care for her. But there was also an emptiness in my soul. I had been given a great deal by life, but I had the sense that I had not given back all that I should have. And now everything was about to be washed away."

At this point, Norman was in despair. He realized that he had reached the end of what conventional medicine could give him. Yes, there were possible experimental treatments out there, but they were long shots, at best. He knew that if he became a compliant patient, and surrendered to his doctors, he would soon be dead. He had to regain his composure and somehow take control of his situation. The first thing he decided was to get out of the hospital. Nothing positive could be done from his bed, and lying there only made him feel like a victim.

On the afternoon of August 5, 1982, Gerry Sue arrived at Providence Hospital and proceeded to make her way to Norman's room. She had regained her characteristic composure and, like Norman, was ready to find something, anything, that might help her husband. When she entered Norman's room, she was shocked to find him dressed and ready to bolt. Even before she had a chance to say hello, Norman announced, "I'm getting out of here. Either you're going to drive me, or I'm calling a cab." With that, he marched down the hallway of the hospital and headed for the door. A nurse ran after him like a chicken announcing the presence of a cat.

"Mr. Arnold, Mr. Arnold, you can't leave, you can't leave, sir," she said.

"My dear, I am doing just that," Norman replied, and didn't lose a step.

"You can't do that, Mr. Arnold. You'll have to sign some papers before we can let you go," she said. "The hospital can't take responsibility for you if you leave now, sir."

"That's fine," said Norman. "Where do I sign?"

It took a few minutes to gather the paperwork and without even reading it, Norman signed his name and headed for the parking lot, Gerry Sue hurrying at his elbow.

He was only a few feet inside his front door when the phone rang. Dan Davis was on the other end.

"Norman, you left before I had a chance to take out your stitches," he said. Norman had been in such a hurry to leave that he didn't consider the sutures, nor the small tube in his side that was meant to allow fluid and air to drain from his abdomen. That, too, would have to be removed.

"That's right, Dan," said Norman. "When do you want to take them out?"

"I'm leaving for the beach tonight. I'll be over this evening." That night, Dan Davis arrived at Norman's house. He had Norman lie on his kitchen table, where he plucked the stitches from his body and closed off the drain.

"I felt like a big bird being prepared for the oven," said Norman. "But at least I felt some control over my life again."

With the help of his cousin, Charles Banov, M.D., Norman immediately began considering the possible treatment options that were available to him. Standard chemotherapy was out of the question, since the evidence clearly showed that it was useless against his illness. All the other treatment options were experimental. One of them was malaria therapy, which involved injecting the cancer-afflicted organ with malaria in the hope that the resulting fever might kill the cancer. Another, hyperthermia treatment, treated the cancerous organ by heating the organ in the hope that the heat would also kill the cancer. Neither of these seemed to offer much hope. Two experimental treatments seemed vaguely plausible. One was an experimental chemotherapy, which might extend Norman's life a year. The drugs had severe side effects, however, which did not buoy Norman's spirits. The other was monoclonal antibodies, which were antibodies produced by mice that were exposed to human blood that contained cancer. It was theorized that the mouse would produce antibodies against the cancer. These antibodies would be removed from the mouse and injected into the patient where, it was hoped, they would be effective in combating the patient's disease. It was further hoped that the antibodies would stimulate the patient's immune system to produce similar antibodies that would be effective in killing the cancer. There was no proof that the monoclonal antibodies might be effective against pancreatic cancer, or any other type, but the idea appealed to Norman.

But then the unexpected happened. Without being asked, another of Norman's cousins, Sandy Gottlieb, arrived one day with the current issue of *Life* magazine. It featured an article about a Dr. Anthony Sattilaro who had used a macrobiotic diet to recover from his own terminal cancer.

Sattilaro had been diagnosed with prostate cancer that had spread throughout his body. After much unsuccessful surgery and hormone therapy, Sattilaro was given between eighteen months and three years to live. A short time later, he chanced upon the macrobiotic diet, which, the *Life* article said, consisted mostly of whole grains and vegetables. Within eighteen months, bone tests, x-rays, and blood analyses revealed no sign of his cancer. The piece published photographs of Sattilaro's before-and-after bone scans, which revealed the presence of cancer before the diet and the absence of malignancy a year and a half later.

"Had I not been ill, the macrobiotic diet would not have appealed to me in the slightest," Norman recalled, "but given the desperation of my circumstances, I now thought seriously of looking into it. I placed macrobiotics at the very top of my list."

Norman shifted into his business mentality and did his due diligence on the macrobiotic diet, instructing his lawyer to find out all he could about macrobiotics. Soon the lawyer found a medical doctor, Keith Block, in Evanston, Illinois, who uses conventional and complementary medical practices to help people with cancer and other illnesses. Dr. Block had successfully treated people with a wide array of illnesses, including cancer, using the macrobiotic diet. Norman sent his lawyer to meet Dr. Block and to get as many case histories from the doctor as he could. He then instructed his lawyer to follow up on those case histories to determine if they were valid. As it turned out, they were. Many of Dr. Block's patients had used the macrobiotic diet, under his care, to reverse serious illnesses, including cancer.

Norman needed to meet people in South Carolina who practiced macrobiotics. He called the Kushi Institute in Boston, the macrobiotic teaching center mentioned in *Life* magazine. A person there gave him the name of Becky Kabuto, a macrobiotic cook who lived in Asheville, North Carolina. Norman called Becky and asked if she could teach him and Gerry Sue the diet. Becky and her Japanese husband arrived at Norman's house the following day.

Becky was in her mid-twenties. She was shy and sweet and six months pregnant. Becky and her husband, who spoke little English, brought a variety of macrobiotic staples, including several kinds of seaweeds, brown rice, vegetables, and a salad press. They established themselves in Gerry Sue's kitchen and proceeded to cook a meal. As they did, Becky instructed Gerry Sue and Norman on macrobiotic cooking and philosophy.

The basic idea was that Norman's previous diet and lifestyle helped cause his cancer. His former diet, rich in fat, sugar, and chemical additives, had caused the accumulation of toxins within his system. These toxins coalesced into a mass that affected the DNA of his cells and caused the onset of cancer in his body. The macrobiotic diet would help rid his body of the illness by eliminating the toxins that were supporting the life of the cancer. The whole philosophy of macrobiotics revolved around the idea of balance. If Norman stopped eating the poisons that were causing his cancer, he would "discharge," or eliminate them, as well as the cancer, from his body, Becky told him.

Becky was no scientist or doctor, but she was so sincere and so obviously altruistic in her motivation that Norman could not help but be moved. Her simple and unpretentious explanation of how diet worked had a sort of poetic persuasiveness to it, Norman thought. In addition, she gave him a gem of an image that would prove reassuring and extremely helpful later on. Becky said that once Norman's blood became healthy, it would erode the tumors in his body. The cancer would melt away, she said. Norman liked that image a lot.

After preparing the meal, Becky and her husband left the Arnold house, and Gerry Sue, Norman, and their three sons ate their first macrobiotic meal. Their dinner that night consisted of brown rice, a variety of green vegetables, a seaweed called hiziki, and navy beans. "The meal wasn't bad," Norman decided. Moreover, the philosophy behind the diet fascinated him. He had always been vaguely interested in nutrition, although his past orientation was toward vitamins and vitamin therapy. Still, the idea that diet was the foundation of health sounded right to him. Still, he needed more.

On August 9, 1982, he went to Baptist Hospital in Columbia for another CT scan and a further attempt to confirm or deny the earlier diagnosis. The CT scan revealed the clear presence of tumors on his pancreas and liver.

Norman had to start on a treatment as soon as possible. On August 11, Gerry Sue, Charles Banov, and Norman went to Georgetown University to meet Dr. Phillip Schein, one of the world's preeminent specialists on pancreatic cancer. Dr. Schein was an impressive man who radiated competence and professionalism. Yet he gave Norman little hope. Schein knew better than anyone in the world that Norman faced a death sentence. Instead of offering a cure, Schein offered the possibility of time.

"How long will the chemotherapy give me?" Norman asked.

"Some patients survive eighteen months on this protocol," Dr. Schein said. He pointed out that new therapies were being discovered and that within eighteen months a new method of treatment might be available.

Dr. Schein's approach was to prescribe a chemotherapy protocol of five-flurourcil (5-FU) plus adraimycin and mitomycin-C, with the addition of another drug, hexamethylmelamine. These drugs would be administered together initially. One week later, the 5-FU would be injected by itself. Three weeks after that, the mitomycin would be administered, which would complete the cycle. The whole process would begin again in three weeks.

Gerry Sue and Norman were buoyed by the possibility that he might survive a year and a half. They were grateful for that small hope. Norman agreed to undergo the treatment, but only if he had Dr. Schein's assurance that Norman would be Dr. Schein's patient first, and a member of his study second. "Dr. Schein, I need you to assure me that as your patient I will take precedence over your study," Norman said. Norman asked that if at any point the chemotherapy appeared to be doing him more harm than good, he wanted Schein to tell him the truth. Dr. Schein assured him that he would. Norman agreed that he would return to Georgetown on August 17, for his first round of chemotherapy. The remainder of the first series would be administered at Baptist Hospital by his oncologist, Dr. Bill Babcock.

As Norman pursued a medical approach to his disease, his mind kept going back to macrobiotics. He went to a local bookstore and asked for anything the clerk had on macrobiotics. There were a couple of books, including one by Jean Kohler, who, remarkably, had used macrobiotics to help him recover from pancreatic cancer. The book was entitled *Macrobiotic Miracles*. Norman bought the book, and he and Gerry Sue read it cover to cover that night.

Another round of telephone calls yielded the telephone number of Michio Kushi, the leading teacher of macrobiotics. When he called Kushi's home in Brookline, Massachusetts, a secretary answered. Norman explained the reason for his call. It would be impossible for him to see Michio Kushi, the secretary told Norman, because Kushi was leaving for Europe that evening. He'd be gone for about a month.

"Does he have any time to see me this afternoon?" Norman asked.

"Yes," she said. "He could see you at 5 P.M. for about an hour."

"Well, I'll be there at 5 P.M. today. I'll be traveling from Columbia, South Carolina, so you won't be able to get back in touch with me to cancel," Norman said.

She asked Norman his name and told him that Mr. Kushi would see him at 5 P.M. As soon as Norman hung up the phone, he called the Columbia airport and chartered the next available plane for Boston. A few hours later, Norman and Gerry Sue landed at Logan Airport in Boston and took a cab to the Kushi house in Brookline.

The house was an enormous stone mansion with a large portico before the front door. "It reminded me of the television show, *The Munsters,*" Norman recalled. "I didn't know what to make of the place."

Norman rang the doorbell and the two were allowed to enter a small foyer, where perhaps a dozen pairs of shoes were lined up. He and Gerry Sue took off their shoes, looked at each other with skepticism and a touch of humor, and followed a young woman into a larger anteroom where other people waited, presumably to see Michio Kushi.

Soon, they were ushered into a large library that was solid with books. Michio Kushi got up from a chair and hurried over to them with his secretary a step behind. The minute Norman saw Michio, he had a good feeling. He was smiling and greeting them in an unpretentious, warm-spirited way. The three shook hands, and Michio directed Gerry Sue and Norman to a small alcove off the library that had large windows through which the late-afternoon light entered.

Once the three were seated, Norman told Michio the full extent of his illness and the options he faced. Kushi listened carefully, then proceeded to give Norman a very strange examination, looking closely at his face, eyes, arms, and feet. Occasionally, he would ask a question, such as, "Do you have pain here?" He put his hand precisely on the spot where Norman did indeed suffer a mysterious pain, which no one could yet explain. Norman had not mentioned the pain, and he was surprised to have Michio bring it up.

While Michio conducted his examination, Norman examined Michio. He had a large head, straight black hair, a high forehead, and round, soft eyes. He had a wide nose and a tightly closed mouth. There was nothing about him that was affected or contrived, Norman later recalled. He was as natural and unself-conscious as any person Norman had ever met.

"I have prided myself on my judgment of character," Norman recalled years later. "The Ben Arnold Company [Norman's business] employs more than two hundred people, and over the years I have dealt with a small army of employees. In addition, my experience in business has brought me into contact with all types, including strong men such as the one who now examined me. I sensed a gravity about Michio Kushi. Without making the slightest contrivance, he nevertheless radiated an air of substance and knowledge."

When Michio concluded his examination, he resumed his seat.

"You are nice people," he began, "but your diet and way of life has caused your disease," Kushi said. "You have eaten too much fat, from steaks and other red meat, cheeses, and eggs. This, with smoking and drinking, staying up too late, working too hard, has caused your cancer."

"I've been told by my doctors that my cancer is incurable," Norman said.

Michio smiled. "What is medically impossible is macrobiotically possible. Your constitution is very strong. You can recover," he said.

Norman was inspired, to say the least. It wasn't just his words, he later realized, but the fact that Michio was someone he trusted and respected. That's what gave credence and power to those words. Michio proceeded to outline the diet Norman should follow. It was composed chiefly of whole grains, such as brown rice, millet, barley, whole oats, corn, and buckwheat; fresh vegetables, especially the leafy greens, such as collard greens, kale, and mustard greens, and the yellow vegetables, such as squash and carrots; sea vegetables, with names like hiziki, arame, nori, wakame, and kombu; beans, including adzuki, navy, pinto, black, soy, and lentils; small amounts of the white meat of fish; and small amounts of fruit.

Michio encouraged Norman to avoid all oil, fatty foods, refined flour products, sugar, and refined salt. Norman was to use sea salt and high-quality fermented soybean products, such as shoyu, miso, and tamari. He was to drink a small bowl of miso soup daily. Michio then encouraged him to wear only natural fabrics and to take short, brisk walks daily. He suggested that Norman pray before every meal, and use a towel to scrub his body while he was in the shower. Michio said that this would improve circulation and help the skin eliminate toxins. He told Norman to swim in the ocean, not the pool. Chlorine would sap minerals and strength that his body needed to overcome his illness, he said. He told him to listen to peaceful, inspiring music every day, and to fill his house with plants, which pumped oxygen into the air.

He then gave him one last bit of advice that I thought was both funny and wise. "Every day, sing a happy song," he said. Norman and Gerry Sue laughed, but they knew what he meant. As Norman would say later, Michio had given him more hope and inspiration in the space of sixty minutes than all the doctors he had seen in his lifetime. Norman was elated.

"Michio," Norman began, "I've been very successful in business and I can be a generous fellow. I would like to be helpful to you by making a substantial contribution to your work."

Michio looked at him warmly, and said, "When you get well, you'll help me help others." For Norman, that was the clincher. From that day on, Norman, Gerry Sue, and their three sons ate a macrobiotic diet.

Norman Arnold is a pillar within the Columbia community, with many social contacts, his synagogue being among the most important. That September also saw the arrival of the Jewish new year, or Rosh Hashanah. Norman and Gerry Sue went to their synagogue, where Norman read from the Torah, which he did every new year. Word of Norman's condition had spread quickly through Columbia, and that Rosh Hashanah service was filled with the weight of Arnold's approaching death. After Norman finished his reading, people from the congregation came up and embraced him, many with tears in their eyes. They were saying good-bye. Norman was moved. He, too, felt the tears begin to flow. Norman didn't know how to tell them that he wasn't out yet, and that he was going to fight this disease. As he returned to his pew, Gerry Sue leaned over to him, and said, "What are they going to do next year when you're back?" Norman smiled and hugged his wife.

In 1982, Gerry Sue and Norman had been married twenty years and had been through many emotionally rocky times together. Norman's illness brought a whole new set of problems to their marriage. But rather than drive them apart, the illness brought them closer together. "You realize how important someone is when you are about to lose them,"

Gerry Sue said years later. "The love you have rises to the surface, and you hold on to one another for dear life. At that point, you make the most of whatever time you have left together. If the time is spent searching for a cure, than that's what you do, but you're really loving each other as you do that." Gerry Sue poured her love into everything she did for Norman, including her cooking. In some mysterious and alchemical way, macrobiotics became traditional chicken soup, the healing balm for all that ails a loved one.

That same September, Norman was given an injection of the monoclonal antibodies. There would be only one injection. He would simply have to wait to see what effect the antibodies had, if any.

That same month, Norman began taking the experimental chemotherapy protocol under Dr. Schein's direction. Arnold underwent five treatments of chemotherapy. The effects of the drugs were devastating: weight loss, chronic fatigue, muscle wasting, nausea, and total loss of body hair. His weight dropped from 160 to 112 pounds. He looked like a refugee from Auschwitz. At times, he became despondent. By the time fall arrived, he wondered what good the chemotherapy might be doing for him and why he was even subjecting himself to such treatment.

By Thanksgiving, Norman realized that he could not go on taking the chemotherapy. Dr. Schein had made it clear to him that the chemotherapy was not a cure; it wasn't even a guarantee of a few more months. But he wanted Norman to continue the chemotherapy on the chance that it might extend his life. Now Norman asked himself: What kind of life did chemotherapy offer? He was wasting away.

"I'd rather die in some more dignified way than have my sons remember me like this," Arnold said.

Norman sought out many social and spiritual therapies that might be helpful. He and Gerry Sue attended the Carl Simonton Clinic in Dallas, Texas, where the two learned positive-imaging techniques to treat the disease. Norman practiced the mind-body imaging techniques diligently. He also remained active in his synagogue and derived support from his spiritual community. And then there was the social aspect of the macrobiotics community. After finding other people in the area who practiced macrobiotics, Norman and Gerry Sue attended classes on cooking and macrobiotic philosophy; they also participated in potluck dinners where other people shared their own healing stories. They visited large and vibrant macrobiotic communities in Florida and other Southern states, where they received support. Both Norman and Gerry Sue remained in close contact with many of the people they met on these trips.

It wasn't long before the entire regimen was showing some results, not all of which were entirely reassuring. True to Becky Kabuto's prediction, Norman soon began to experience physical changes. Initially, he lost more weight, which frightened both him and Gerry Sue. Michio told him that the weight loss was expected and that he would gradually return to his optimal weight. Second, he got a cold, which was more of a nuisance than anything else. This, too, was one of the ways the body was cleansing itself of toxins, Michio told them. But then Norman's tongue turned black, which shocked him and Gerry Sue. In a panic, they called Michio, who gave them the same response: This was a discharge of poisons from his liver and pancreas and that it was, in fact, a good sign. His body was ridding itself of the cancer, Kushi said. Norman was baffled and incredulous, but what could he do but wait and hope that Kushi was right? Sure enough, within a few weeks, his tongue returned to a pink, healthy hue. These symptoms were followed by some clear signs of improvement, however. For one, he started to regain some weight, which pleased him immensely. His face lost its formerly ghostly pallor and became clear and vibrant. And then his energy and overall strength increased dramatically. None of these were signs of advancing disease. On the contrary, Norman and Gerry Sue believed that Norman was turning things around.

On June 24, 1983, just nine months after he was diagnosed, Norman had another CT scan, this one showing only the faint presence of tumors in his pancreas and liver. Clearly, the cancer was in retreat. For the next six months, all of Norman's outward physical signs continued to improve. His doctors were amazed. None could explain what was happening to him, because none of them had seen such a reversal before. And then, on December 22, 1983, Norman underwent another CT scan. This one was unequivocal. All clear! The test showed no signs of cancer anywhere in his body. Numerous other tests, including liver, blood, and ultrasound, confirmed the CT scan: There was no indication of cancer.

At the time of this writing, twenty-one years later, Norman Arnold, at the age of seventy-three, remains a vigorously healthy and active man. He is heavily involved in philanthropic endeavors, continues to follow a macrobiotic diet, and has endowed the University of South Carolina Medical School's Department of Alternative and Complementary Medicine. Like Marlene McKenna's story, described in Chapter 1, Norman Arnold's recovery has been meticulously documented and was part of the documentation that persuaded scientists at the National Cancer Institute's Cancer Advisory Panel for Complementary and Alternative Medicine (CAPCAM) to formally study macrobiotics as a possible therapy for cancer.

※

Make a Commitment to Healing and to Life

It doesn't just happen. We have to make it happen. We restore health by acting wisely and consistently, day in and day out, until our actions make small changes in our biochemistry, changes that, with time, gain momentum and grow more powerful. Soon, the toxins in the blood and tissue that support the illness fall significantly, stress hormones decline, excess weight falls off, circulation improves, blood levels of phytochemicals increase, and the immune system gets stronger. These changes wear away the supports of the illness, causing it to weaken at its roots. Eventually, the effects of our actions become so pervasive and powerful that they are the equal of the disease. And then, after months of consistent behavior, the balance tips, and the garrisons of health run roughshod over the illness and trample it into oblivion.

Commitment, the fifth step on the healing journey, is the underlying force that makes this chain of events possible. To commit means to give all you have, without reservation, to a specific goal or person. The realization of your goal may lie in the future, but the nature of commitment is to keep you focused on the present. Commitment guides your choices in the here and now, by forcing you to decide if your present actions get you closer to achieving your goal or further away from it.

A Buddhist teacher once told me that we can learn the meaning of commitment by considering how a lion attacks its prey. A lion falls upon a small animal with the same ferocity with which it attacks a water buffalo. There is an absolute commitment of all its powers, both physical and spiritual, to the attack. And because the lion brings its entire being to the act, it succeeds even before it lays its claws into its target.

True commitment has the effect of imbuing your actions with the power of your entire being. In ancient China, the sages said that all living things are imbued with a life force, which the Chinese called *Qi* or *chi*. This life force flows through the human body and gives power to every one of our actions. A person can act, the Chinese said, and still withhold his life force from his action. Such an act has little power, because it lacks *Qi*. Therefore, it is doomed to failure. Commitment is the act of giving your life force, your spirit, unfettered, to your goal. In the end, the presence of your spirit is what gives your actions healing power.

Commitment is the warrior's path. Two characteristics make deep and lasting commitment possible—the first is our ability to know our own heart, which is to say, to know what is true for each of us; the second is the courage to follow the dictates of the heart, no matter what the outcome. Because the warrior is able to do precisely this, he or she acts patiently and consistently.

Consistent behavior causes your actions to accumulate momentum and power. Like the relentlessness of the wind that can reshape a rocky cliff, or the constancy of water that can wear away an entire coastline, consistency can make soft things more powerful than the hardest of substances. This is especially important when using alternative or complementary medicine, whose practices are clearly softer and less invasive than conventional medicine.

In 1996, I wrote a book with Alice Burmeister entitled *The Touch of Healing* (Bantam Books, 1997) that described the gentle but powerful art of Jin Shin Jyutsu, or the placing of one's hands at precise locations on the body. (See the Resource Guide for more on Jin Shin Jyutsu.) In *The Touch of Healing,* we report many remarkable case histories of people who used Jin Shin to recover from serious illnesses. One of those people was Amy Tandy, of Dallas, Texas. In 1994, Tandy was suffering from severe kidney disease and had lost all but 21 percent of her kidney function. Her doctors insisted that if it fell to 20 percent, she would require immediate kidney dialysis and, when a donor was found, a kidney transplant. She was forty-nine years old. Amy had been suffering from failing kidneys since 1983, and the long road had just about reached its inevitable conclusion. One day, after seeing her physician, she sat in her car in a state of shock. What could she do? she asked herself. Suddenly, some inner strength welled up inside of her. She was not going to have kidney dialysis or a kidney transplant, she decided. She was going to find her own answers.

Amy had recently begun seeing a bodywork therapist who practiced Jin Shin Jyutsu. The Jin Shin Jyutsu session left Amy feeling noticeably better—more relaxed, energetic, and optimistic. For the next year, Amy underwent Jin Shin treatments three times per week; she also did a Jin Shin self-help routine every day. She did this practice with complete commitment and soon discovered that her kidneys were becoming stronger. When her kidney function crept up to 30 percent, her doctor was amazed. "If you get up to 40 percent," he told her, "I'll learn this Jin Shin Jyutsu." In August 1995, her kidney function reached 43 percent. Her physician told her that there no longer was any need to discuss kidney dialysis or transplant. According to all of his tests, she was healthy.

Amy Tandy's commitment to Jin Shin Jyutsu—which included her work with a practitioner and her daily use of self-help practices—turned this gentle practice into a powerful tool for healing.

Our commitment can make both alternative or conventional treatments more powerful, and in the end sufficient to overcome even the most terrible of conditions. Ralph Donsky is living proof of that.

"Resolve to Survive": Ralph Donsky's Remarkable Healing Odyssey

In the summer of 2003, Ralph Donsky, then fifty-three years of age, stood five feet four inches tall and weighed about 130 pounds. He was tanned and fit, the picture of good health. He played tennis twice a week, basketball once a week, and did at least twenty minutes a day of aerobic cross training. Ralph, an electrical engineer who recently moved to St. Petersburg, Florida, spent most of his life in Connecticut. In addition to his day job, Ralph continues to volunteer in hospitals, where he performs magic and recounts his remarkable story to patients, a story that he believes can inspire even the most hopeless of people. Ralph remembers when he was one of them.

On June 22, 1993, Ralph, then forty-two, was about to go on vacation with his wife and two daughters to Ocean City, New Jersey. He had loaded their bags and placed the family's bicycles on the rack on the back of the car. As he lifted the last bike, Ralph felt a stabbing pain shoot through his back. The pain was of such intensity, Ralph recalled, that it "knocked the air out of me and caused me to bend over and put my head between my legs to catch my breath."

Ralph collected himself, got up off the ground, and was relieved when he realized that the pain was gone. Undaunted, he and the family went to Ocean City for a pleasant and uneventful vacation.

Three weeks after he got home, the pain returned with all of its original intensity. This time, it was no longer confined to his back, but radiated throughout his rib cage. Over the next few days, the pain got worse. Soon, he couldn't sit for more than fifteen minutes without intense and terrible pain that spread throughout his ribs and down his spine.

Alarmed, he went to his family doctor, who could not find anything physically wrong with him. The physician referred Ralph to an endocrinologist, a specialist in conditions related to hormones and bones. Ralph underwent an exhaustive series of tests. When the test results came back, there was only one conclusion: Ralph had Cushing's disease, a rare disorder that, among other things, causes bones to disintegrate. Ralph's ribs and vertebrae were crumbling under the weight of his body.

Cushing's disease arises when a tumor appears in the brain, usually in the pituitary gland. The tumor causes the brain to produce exceedingly high levels of the hormone ACTH, which in turn triggers the adrenal glands to produce excessive amounts of the stress hormone, cortisol. At such high levels, cortisol prevents the bones from absorbing calcium, which was why Ralph's bones were decomposing. The weight of his body was too much for his bones to carry.

It wasn't long before Ralph couldn't stand, or lift even a light object without breaking a bone. He was forced to lie in bed in a slightly elevated position in order to prevent the weight of his body from placing too much pressure on his spine.

The tumor would have to be removed from his brain, his doctors said. That procedure, they hoped, would stop the excessive production of ACTH and the hormonal cascade that led to bone loss. Unfortunately, numerous MRIs (magnetic resonance imaging) could not find the tumor in Ralph's brain. For weeks he was brought by ambulance to the hospital to undergo yet another MRI, but each one proved fruitless. To this day, Ralph's tumor has never been found.

His doctors said that the only course of action was to remove the pituitary gland in the hope that the tumor was there but too small to detect. The pituitary was removed on November 5, 1993, but after thorough analysis, no tumor was found. Meanwhile, the tumor— wherever it might be—continued to stimulate Ralph's body to produce high levels of ACTH and cortisol. And his bones continued to crumble.

A few days after his surgery that November, Ralph was transported home by ambulance. Every little bump in the road caused a tiny fracture in his back and rib cage and triggered an unbearable shock of pain. "The second the ambulance left the emergency exit of the hospital, I knew that the ride home would be difficult," Ralph recalled. "As the ambulance went over tiny potholes in the road or took sharp turns, pain began shooting through my ribs and back. The half hour ride seemed like six hours. The paramedic saw that I was in pain and tried to distract me by asking about my family. I prayed for God to give me the strength to hold on until I got home to my wife and children and perhaps some miracle to cure me."

Ralph was placed on high doses of morphine, which dulled his mind as well as his pain. The drug drained him of his energy and distorted his perceptions. Every one of his movements seemed to occur in slow motion. It took him two hours to eat a meal. At times, he felt as if he were floating inside a giant pool.

A month later, on December 6, 1993, Ralph suffered a massive heart attack. He was rushed to the University of Connecticut Health Center, where he fell into a coma for five days and was listed in critical condition.

When Ralph emerged from the coma, he found himself in the critical care unit of the University of Connecticut Health Center. Ralph's cardiologist came to his bedside, and said, "Don't be afraid, but you have just awakened from a coma. You had a serious heart attack." Ralph gazed furtively around his bed and found himself attached to a multitude of wires and tubes. Suddenly, the memory of months of pain, broken bones, and crumbling vertebrae came rushing back. He sank into his pillow and felt despair engulf him. How was he going to face the future? he wondered.

A few days later, Ralph's doctor explained that Ralph's adrenal glands would have to be removed. The Cushing's tumor, wherever it might be, was still producing extraordinary amounts of ACTH, which meant that his bones were still crumbling. The only thing doctors could do for Ralph was to remove his adrenal glands, which would eliminate the cortisol and allow the bones to start absorbing calcium. Without the surgery, Ralph's bones would continue to crumble, his doctor said. By then, Ralph had already lost six inches of height and was standing five feet four. If that process didn't stop, he would soon be dead.

The surgery could not be done immediately—his heart had not recovered sufficiently to withstand the stresses associated with the operation. Thus, Ralph was released from the hospital, crumbling bones and all, and told to come back regularly so that doctors could check on his heart.

When Ralph emerged from the hospital, he was shocked by the severe curvature of his spine. "I looked like the hunchback of Notre Dame," he said. "I worried about how I was going to face the world in this disfigured state."

What was far worse, however, was the intense back pain that he suffered. "I was in continuous pain for eighteen months," Ralph said. "I couldn't ride in a car for more than five minutes, because the position it put my back in was too much for me to bear." He was given daily doses of morphine, which left him feeling as if he were living inside a dream— a dream that was rife with pain and fear. The fear and the pain opened up a dark portal inside of him and allowed all his demons to emerge.

"I was afraid of going to sleep at night," Ralph recalled, "thinking that I would not wake up in the morning. I was also afraid of the dark. I correlated darkness with my life coming to an end. The pain, the drugs, the surgery on my pituitary gland, and my heart attack had all combined to wreak havoc on my mental state." All of this terrified and exhausted his wife and children. "Sometimes my family couldn't bear it anymore," Ralph recalled. "I was depressed and obsessing. It was too much for my family to deal with."

In April 1994, four months after Ralph awakened from his coma, surgeons removed both of his adrenal glands, which allowed his bones to start to heal. That job was facilitated by daily injections of Calcitonin, a drug that promotes the uptake of calcium by the bones. Ralph's wife, Wendy, administered the injections each day for six months. So began his long and arduous journey back to health.

Ralph's heart attack was due to his Cushing's disease, his cardiologist told him. The illness caused a blood clot to form in his coronary artery and blocked blood flow to the left side of his heart, causing that part of the heart to die.

"How can I prevent that from happening again?" Ralph asked.

The only way to prevent any further danger, his cardiologist said, was to keep his arteries free of cholesterol plaques. The arteries must be clean. The only way to do that was with a very strict diet and exercise.

Already familiar with the Pritikin Program—his father-in-law had adopted it to treat his own health problems—Ralph began eating a diet composed strictly of whole grains, lots of vegetables, beans, and fruit. He emphasized the green vegetables, such as broccoli and collard greens, because of their calcium content. He also took a calcium supplement. In no time, Ralph became an adept cook, learning how to prepare his food so that it was delicious, satisfying, and medicinal, all at once.

As for exercise, he knew he had to start out slow. His father-in-law had given him a stationary bicycle, which he started riding for five minutes a day, at five miles an hour. That small amount of exertion exhausted him. "Don't give up," he kept telling himself. "It's not going to get better overnight. You've got to commit to the long haul if you are going to make it all the way back," he said. Soon Ralph hit upon a single phrase that would become his mantra. "Resolve to survive!" he kept telling himself. That phrase embodied his complete commitment to his healing approach and to life itself.

After his stationary bicycle ride, Ralph would walk the length of his driveway to the sidewalk, then back. As with the bicycle riding, any little bit of exertion terrified him. He was afraid of breaking a bone or having a sudden heart attack. Ralph told his cardiologist that he wanted to get to the point where he could ride an hour before breakfast every morning.

"You can do it," his doctor told him. "But you have to go very slowly and carefully." The doctor told him to extend the duration of his workout by five minutes every two weeks. The important thing, said his doctor, was consistency. "If you maintain consistency," the cardiologist said, "you'll be able to reach your goal." Ralph rode the stationary bicycle seven days a week, often in severe pain. "Resolve to survive!" he kept telling himself.

Slowly, his strength improved. Ralph looked around for another form of exercise and found an aquatic workout class in a local health club. The pool was kept at ninety-two degrees, which made his body feel relaxed and capable of exercising when he entered the water. The exercises, done with barbells, consisted of rowing motions and swirling patterns beneath the surface of the water. The resistance was ten times that of the air. The bike strengthened his legs; the water aerobics his arms and upper body. It wasn't long before Ralph could feel himself getting stronger.

"The aquatic workout was an incredible confidence builder," Ralph recalled. "I went twice a week, every week, for three years. When I started, I could barely move the plastic barbells through the water. With time, I became one of the strongest members of the class, almost stronger than the instructor. I remember my incredible determination and resolve. Once I started gaining some muscle back, there was no stopping me."

Meanwhile, Ralph continued to adhere strictly to his plant-based diet. He permitted himself a single serving of chicken and fish once a month. "I made up this diet, based on the Pritikin Program," Ralph said. "Pritikin allows a small amount of fat in the form of low-fat animal products, but I wanted to eat a stricter diet that was even lower in fat," said Ralph. "I would not back down on this."

As a way of maintaining his spirits, Ralph kept careful track of the things that made him feel good, versus those that brought him down. He recorded these things in a journal that he kept faithfully. "I became really good at listening to my body," Ralph said. "When my body told me 'no more,' I stopped. When I felt strong again, I resumed. I learned to pace myself."

Having established a morning workout routine, Ralph added tennis twice a week, and basketball once a week. The results were nothing short of astounding. Six months after he started this routine of bicycle riding and aerobic workouts, he was riding his bicycle for a full hour, at a minimum of twenty miles per hour. Sometimes he would increase his speed and get up to thirty-five miles per hour. He was six months ahead of his schedule. In the process, he had undergone a metamorphosis. Though still small of frame, Ralph had created extensive muscle development in his arms, shoulders, back, abdomen, and legs. In some respects, he was in the best physical condition of his life.

In September 1994, at the age of forty-three, Ralph finally returned to work—fifteen months after his Cushing's disease was diagnosed. He was still in a back brace. He still suffered some pain, though it was significantly diminished, but he was still struggling with his fears. Even as he found himself recovering physically, he inexplicably fell into a deep depression.

"There is no isolating your mental health from your physical health," Ralph would write years later. "Your brain, which drives all of your bodily functions, also is the recipient of your pain and anxiety. After fighting a severe physical illness, my mental health had suffered as a victim." Ralph knew that it was time for him to heal his mind, as well. He plunged himself into therapy. He also saw a variety of healers. Just as he had done with his physical illness, Ralph addressed his mental and emotional issues with the same commitment and resolve.

A year later, he had made a full recovery—physically, mentally, and emotionally. He no longer experienced any pain; he was free of the brace, and all his tests—including those for his heart—showed that he was in excellent health. Remarkably, his body was no longer producing abnormally high levels of ACTH. On the contrary, his hormone levels were normal, his doctors discovered. Somehow, Ralph's medical and personal self-help methods had combined to destroy the Cushing's tumor and shut off ACTH production. "I'm back to being a normal guy," he said then. "No, I'm even better. I'm stronger than I ever was."

His doctors continue to shake their heads in amazement. Ralph's cardiologist put it this way: "Ralph, if you had not taken care of yourself the way you have, you would not be standing here in front of me . . ." Another doctor told him, "Ralph, you are alive today because of who you are as a person. You are responsible for where you are today." His psychological health was just as good. All symptoms of anxiety and depression were gone.

Nevertheless, Ralph's illness and recovery cost him more than he would ever have dreamed. He and his wife divorced in the winter of 2001. That was another dark time for him, he said, but in the spring of 2002, he met Barbara and was married in May of 2002.

"Life is full of surprises," Ralph said in 2002. "Sometimes the greatest adversity can bring out the best in a person, and the worst. But if you resolve to survive, good things can happen, even when it seems like everything is falling apart. Today I'm happier than I've ever been, but if someone had told me in 1994 that I would be this happy in 2003, I probably wouldn't have believed him."

Your First Commitment: To Life

As Ralph Donsky's story shows, a sincere commitment to healing can awaken the spiritual forces that lie deep within us. Those spiritual forces are perhaps the real sources of recovery—even those recoveries that are attributed to a particular medicine, surgery, or alternative approach. Scientists know very well that without a commitment to health, or life itself, the immune system mysteriously weakens, and for some even shuts down.

Researchers have known for decades that bereavement—an entirely emotional reaction—can, in some people, weaken the immune system and even result in death. Scientists have repeatedly shown that people who suffer prolonged bereavement experience far higher rates of mortality in their respective age groups than those who have not experienced such a loss. Dr. Steven Schleifer, at Mount Sinai Hospital, wanted to know what, if any, physiological changes took place in those who were suffering from what society typically refers to as a "broken heart."

Schleifer and his colleagues studied men who had recently lost a loved one and discovered that bereavement caused a deadening effect on the immune system. For those who were suffering from the stress of emotional loss, a certain type of white blood cell, called a lymphocyte (or CD4 cell), failed to react in the presence of a pathogen or an aberrant cell.

Schleifer concluded that in the face of such a loss, these men gave up the desire to live. Once the will to live was shut off, the body's defense mechanisms no longer functioned. Thus, an emotional state known as bereavement was having a very physical reaction.

Interestingly, as people overcame their bereavement, their immune systems righted themselves. Research has shown that there is a six-month-to-one-year window when people are at their most vulnerable. After they emerge from that weakened period and sufficient emotional healing has occurred, their chances of living on are greatly enhanced.

Other studies at Mount Sinai suggest that the hypothalamus gland, found in the brain, has an enormous influence on the endocrine and immune systems. The hypothalamus is highly sensitive to emotional and psychological conditions. Such research has shown that when a person's will to live is shattered, he or she suffers a far greater chance of premature death than those who struggle to survive.

Surrender often leads to depression, which in turn weakens the immune system profoundly. Michael Irwin, a psychiatrist at the San Diego Veteran's Center, studied women whose husbands were terminally ill with lung cancer or had recently died. He found that the women who were most depressed had the lowest natural killer cell activity.

Depression is associated with higher-than-normal levels of cortisol, an immune-suppressing hormone. There is some evidence that high cortisol levels may weaken the immune response to disease-causing agents, perhaps by reining in natural killer cell activity.

Here's How You Can Strengthen Your Commitment to Healing

There is one healing method, above all others, that can strengthen your ability to commit to, and sustain, a healing program. That approach is physical exercise. No other healing activity so thoroughly empowers the will and focuses the mind like regular, moderate exercise. Just take a walk or do some other form of gentle exercise—such as yoga, Tai Chi Chuan, or Qigong—every day for a week, and you will experience first-hand a significant improvement in your willpower and discipline. You will also notice a shift into your more heroic nature. You will feel more in control of your life and more positive about your future.

You should not overexert yourself, as Ralph Donsky's experience illustrates. On the contrary, you should start out slowly and increase the distance you walk, or the length of time you exercise, very slowly and deliberately. It's essential that you consult your physician before you start exercising, and undergo regular examinations throughout the time that you exercise.

With continued and consistent exercise, your stress levels will fall significantly. At the same time, your feelings of optimism will rise. You will start to believe in possibilities that you could not even see before you began exercising. Remarkably, all your other health-promoting activities will also get stronger, especially your ability to adhere to a healing diet. In fact, scientists have found that exercise is the single greatest factor when it comes to predicting whether or not a person will remain on a healing diet.

Peter Wood and his coworkers at Stanford University followed a group of middle-aged men who ran or jogged every day for two years. The researchers gave the runners no nutritional advice, but nonetheless closely monitored their dietary choices through the two-year period. Among the findings was the fact that the men who exercised experienced an increase in their appetites. That was to be expected, since they had increased their calorie burning. But what was surprising to the scientists was that the diets of the men changed to include more plant foods and complex carbohydrates. Carbohydrates are the body's primary source of energy. Whenever we exercise, we burn off our carbohydrate reserves, which in turn creates cravings for carbohydrates. As long as people choose complex carbohydrates, from plant foods—as opposed to simple sugars—they will be consuming all those additional nutrients and phytochemicals so essential to the immune system. Exercise causes the body to crave the very foods that are the source of these substances.

Exercise has the odd but remarkable effect of putting you in touch with your best self and giving you the confidence that you can become that best version of yourself. No other health-promoting activity has this same effect. The bottom line is that if you want to commit truly to a healing program, make daily exercise a fundamental part of it.

Cleansing Your System of Toxins and Fighting Disease

All forms of regular, moderate exercise, including walking, yoga, riding a stationary bicycle, dancing, or doing some form of martial art promote the cleansing of your internal system. Exercise moves lymph, which collects waste from your cells and tissue fluids, and helps to eliminate them from your body. It also eliminates toxins from cells and tissues through sweating and deep breathing, as well. In the process, exercise reduces and in some cases eliminates many of the poisons that your illness needs to survive.

Exercise improves the efficiency of your heart, meaning it makes the heart pump more blood per beat. As you exercise regularly, your heartbeat slows down, causing the resting period between beats to become longer. Rather than 90 beats per minute, your heart soon beats only 70 or 65 times. A heart that beats only 60 times per minute is resting twice as long as the heart that beats 90 times per minute.

Exercise elevates HDL (the good cholesterol) levels, which significantly reduces your risk of heart disease and stroke. It also your lowers blood pressure. Exercise reduces the stickiness between blood platelets; sticky platelets cause your blood to sludge and form clots, which are the basis for most heart attacks and strokes. In fact, regular exercise dissolves clots and improves circulation to your heart and brain.

In the late 1970s, when the Pritikin Longevity Center first opened, Nathan Pritikin used to ask people to do a simple math test upon entering the Center in Santa Monica, California. All the questions were easy ones—2 × 5; 5 × 7; and 2 + 8, for example. He would time people while they did the test. One month later, after they had been on the Pritikin Program for Diet and Exercise for four weeks, Nathan would ask his participants to do a test with similarly simple math problems. This time, they raced through the test. Many took half the time to do it as they did the first time out. Nathan conducted this little experiment to show people how dramatic was the improvement in their mental function when they ate a low-fat, grain-and-vegetable-based diet that provided optimal amounts of oxygen to their brains.

In addition to all of this, moderate exercise significantly strengthens your immune system and helps fight cancer. With regular, moderate exercise, all major classes of immune cells increase in both number and aggressiveness in the face of a disease-causing agent, including cancer cells and tumors.

Finally, exercise strengthens bones, increases muscle mass, and elevates mood significantly by increasing brain levels of endorphins, the body's natural opium-like compounds. Some studies have shown that regular, moderate exercise can be as effective as medication in the treatment of mild to moderate depression.

Commitment to Practical Change

Those who get well not only make a commitment to living, but are able to translate the will to live into practical, everyday healing activities. In the process, they find and commit to a healing approach, one that they maintain as an outward expression of their commitment to life.

Your commitment must be eminently practical, meaning that it must change many of your most fundamental behaviors if it is to be real and have any effect on your illness. Among the changes that your commitment to your healing must create are the following.

1. Dietary change. Breakfast, lunch, and dinner must all be fundamentally different. Ideally, your commitment will lead you to adopt a plant-based diet, low in fat and processed foods, and rich in nutrition, immune-boosting antioxidants, and cancer-fighting phytochemicals. In order to sustain that diet, your commitment will lead you to learn how to prepare the foods so that they are delicious and satisfying. Attending cooking classes, reading cookbooks, and experimenting with these foods are all a direct outgrowth of your commitment to your healing.

2. A daily exercise program. Your exercise program can be as simple as a daily walk. At the outset, the distance doesn't matter. Rather, you should do as much as you can without exhausting or harming yourself. As you get stronger, you can add distance to your walking, as well as other types of exercise routines. Gentle

yoga, stretching, light resistance or weight training, a martial art (such as Tai Chi Chuan), Chinese exercise (Qigong), or some form of dance—any one of these practices can be incorporated into your life as you experience a return of your strength and overall vitality. Do not push yourself beyond your limits. Go slowly and do only what is safe and comfortable. Consult your doctor before starting an exercise program; tell him or her what you are planning to do and allow him or her to guide you in your choices.

3. Gentle body care from a competent massage practitioner. Therapeutic massage, acupressure, Jin Shin Jyutsu, and other types of bodywork are forms of healing love. Give your body the physical touch and attention it needs to promote healing. Try to get a gentle, noninvasive massage once a week, or twice a month.

4. Take time for yourself every day to become aware of, and to understand, your own personal needs. Being able to satisfy your needs begins with making them conscious. Once you are aware of your needs, you will find it much easier to make wise choices that elevate the quality of your life. This is a fundamental part of acting compassionately toward yourself and others. It is part of developing the healer within you. Working with a therapist or healer can help you better understand yourself, your needs, and help promote a more compassionate relationship with yourself.

5. Stay connected. Attend your support groups and get the love and care you need to promote your healing. Your commitment to healing will naturally lead you to develop a supportive community of loved ones, friends, teachers, healers, and spiritual guides. Fill your healing community with a diverse group of people who can bring a wide variety of life-promoting qualities and characteristics to your life. When you find yourself in despair from loneliness, pick up the phone, call a friend or someone who supports you. Look forward to your next appointment with your healer, therapist, priest, minister, rabbi.

6. Study. Your commitment to healing will make you thirsty for information and knowledge that will promote your recovery. Read books and articles written by people who have spent their lives investigating the healing arts. Change your behavioral patterns as

you encounter information that resonates as true and essential for your life.

7. Engage in some form of prayer, meditation, or spiritual practice on a daily basis. Develop a strong belief in your recovery and deep faith in the love that underlies life. (More about all of this in the next chapter.)

Overcoming the Despair of the Dark Night of the Soul

Commitment to the healing path inevitably leads us to a confrontation with ourselves and the dark impulses that helped to create the illness in the first place. The fact is that it's easy for us to say that we should exercise, or eat a healing diet, or join a support group, or meditate and pray. If doing these things were as easy as listing them, we all would be a lot healthier. But something inside stops us from engaging in such healing activities. Indeed, something compels us to engage in behaviors that are self-destructive and even promote self-loathing.

For many of us, the moment we commit to a healing path is the moment when we begin to face our resistance to healing. That resistance, like a great stone in a river, can block us from making progress and plunge us into despair or depression. We feel alone in our struggles. And in our weakness, we cannot bring ourselves to do a single positive thing for ourselves.

This is an archetypal confrontation, the dark night of the soul, when we are forced to ask ourselves, What blocks me from doing what I know to be right? In the depths of his own despair, St. Paul himself confessed, "For the good that I would, I do not, but the evil which I would not, that I do." Most of us find ourselves nodding in agreement with St. Paul, because, as much as we would love to think of ourselves as good and perfect, we know better.

In the midst of our own pain, we are forced to ask: What can I do to escape this despair? The first thing we must do is understand its source, then act in gentle ways to relieve it.

The troubling reality for all of us is that we are driven by opposite forces, light and darkness, altruism and selfishness, of good and evil. As the great Swiss psychiatrist and philosopher Carl Jung wrote in his autobiography, *Memories, Dreams, and Reflections* (Random House, 1965), "The psyche . . . rests on a foundation of antithesis, on a flow of energy between two poles." We are founded upon opposites, said Jung, and those opposites are inescapable. And the more we deny our darker impulses, the stronger they become, it seems.

Jung maintained that all our urges, drives, and behaviors that do not conform with our idealized image of ourselves are pushed back into the unconscious, where they coalesce into a kind of secondary personality that Jung called the *shadow*. In *Memories, Dreams, and Reflections,* Jung defined the shadow as the part of ourselves that we decide is "[t]he inferior part of the personality; [the] sum of all personal and collective psychic elements which, because of their incompatibility with the chosen conscious attitude, are denied expression in life and therefore coalesce into a relatively unconscious 'splinter personality' with contrary tendencies to the conscious . . . The shadow personifies everything that the subject refuses to acknowledge about himself and yet is always thrusting itself upon him directly or indirectly." In other words, those urges that we would like to keep hidden, somehow compel us to express them, oftentimes in secret ways.

Whenever we commit to a healing path, we must inevitably face the shadow within us. In fact, this is a fundamental part of the healing process—to bring those aspects of ourselves that we have repressed or denied into the light of love and acceptance. This confrontation with the darkness within each of us can seem like an eclipse of the sun. But like all eclipses, the light is restored by movement. The light is still within you. The power and desire to heal is there. But in order to rally those healing forces, we must express some of the darkness—and in the process release some of its related tension—so that the impasse can be resolved. It is important to realize that even this painful moment is part of the healing process. Indeed, many great and inspiring insights can be experienced by understanding the conflict and pain that wants to be brought into the light of your awareness.

Sometime ago, I interviewed a woman who had a long-standing problem with overeating and overweight. For years, she saw these problems simply as the consequence of her lack of discipline, for which she berated herself regularly. When she reached her mid-thirties, she felt compelled to deal with early experiences of sexual abuse. She entered therapy and joined a support group. Eventually, she discovered that she feared relationships with men so intensely that she was using overweight as a way of keeping men at a distance. On the other hand, she also yearned for a healthy, loving relationship with a man. That yearning led to intense internal conflict, anxiety, sadness, and physical tension, all of which she relieved with food. That, of course, kept her overweight. As her therapy progressed, she made her fears and her desires for a relationship conscious. She began to develop compassion for herself and her own needs. She learned that, as an adult, she had the power to determine how a relationship developed, and how close or intimate anyone could be with her. This was a power that she did not have as a child; but in order to find satisfaction and balance in her life, she would have to learn to use her adult authority.

That awakening gave her the confidence to start dating and searching for a fulfilling relationship, which she eventually found. As she became more fulfilled, she did not have to turn to food to satisfy needs for love and tenderness, which meant that she naturally lost virtually all of her excess weight.

In the interview, she told me, "You know, I didn't realize it, but I wasn't just keeping men out of my life—I was keeping a lot of good things away. I was spending my life protecting myself from the very things I needed, and using food to compensate for my empty life. I was starving, and I didn't know it."

Serious illness is often the consequence of a lifetime of imbalances that arise when we repress needs and impulses that have long been buried in the shadow. These buried elements of our nature attempt to reintegrate and reunite into our awareness and our love. They start to push against our conscious minds, like water against the wall of a dam. The more they push, the more tension we begin to experience. That tension can manifest as anxiety, fear, anger, a hunger to be seen, a desperate need to speak our truths and to be loved.

It's common for us to turn to food, cigarettes, alcohol, television, video games, and drugs (both pharmaceutical and recreational) to reduce the tension that arises when repressed needs, long buried in the shadow, start to surface. All of us know that food is used at least as much to love ourselves, and for the purpose of self-medication, as it is for nutrition. Ice cream, chocolate, cookies, pastries, potato chips, soda pop, greasy hamburgers, and oily french fries are not known as comfort foods for nothing. The fact that these foods dominate our food supply says much about how much suffering is occurring in our society today. There can be no doubt, however, that these foods, when eaten in excess, lead to life-threatening disease. We can only postpone the pain for so long before it rears up and takes control of our lives, oftentimes in the form of an illness.

The emergence of an illness can become the moment when we open up to our pain and attempt to restore some degree of balance in our lives. To do that, we must examine the deeper urges that long to be expressed, and to allow them to emerge from the shadow and into the light of consciousness, acceptance, and love. This process, which is essentially making the shadow conscious, can be accomplished through a very simple process, a process that at least one expert refers to as confession.

How You Can Escape the Shadow and Restore Your Hope

Psychologist James W. Pennebaker, Ph.D., a professor of psychology at Southern Methodist University (SMU) in Dallas, Texas, studied the effects of confession on the immune systems and psychological health of college students. Pennebaker devised a study in which students wrote about their most traumatic experiences for twenty minutes a day, for four consecutive days. After they performed the four-day writing exercise, Pennebaker and other scientists measured the students' immune responses and compared them against a control group, or students of similar health who did not do the writing exercise. Pennebaker found that the people who wrote about their traumatic experiences had dramatically stronger immune responses, and made fewer visits to the health clinic, than their matched controls.

Pennebaker found that the most profound improvements in immune power occurred in the people who made the fullest confessions, meaning they confessed feelings and events that they had never before expressed, even to themselves. Many of these people, whom he called "high disclosers," thanked him profusely for giving them the opportunity finally to tell their stories.

After the study, Pennebaker theorized that the transforming power was catharsis. He pointed out that inhibition, the mechanism by which we keep the contents of the shadow hidden, even from ourselves, requires a certain amount of psychic and physical energy. As he puts it, inhibition is a demanding form of work, especially when very painful events or memories must be kept secret. Inhibition, Pennebaker found, is frequently associated with an array of physical symptoms, including a weakening of the immune defenses and elevations in blood pressure, heart rate, breathing, skin temperature, and perspiration levels. These and other symptoms are released when we no longer struggle to keep the contents of the shadow hidden but instead allow it to emerge and become conscious.

Pennebaker studied the effects of confession on crime suspects who underwent polygraph or lie detector testing. Working with the Federal Bureau of Investigation, Pennebaker found that when suspects confess their crimes during polygraph testing, they experience a dramatic shift in physical health. They become deeply relaxed, and the physical symptoms associated with inhibition disappear.

The effects go well beyond the physical, however. Pennebaker found that criminals who confess during polygraph tests emotionally bond to their confessors. Years after making their confessions, many former criminals send well wishes in the form of letters, birthday, and Christmas cards to their FBI inquisitors. The reason for the profound effect on health, Pennebaker theorized, was that confession allowed certain repressed parts of one's being—parts that were submerged in the shadow—to surface and be reunited with consciousness and acceptance. The energy that was maintaining the inhibition, or repression, has been released, and psychic equilibrium has been restored. With balance come feelings of peace, tranquillity, and resolution, as well as better physical health.

You can use what has become known as the "Pennebaker method" to release parts of your shadow into the light of awareness and compassion. The exercise is simple and cost-free. You simply take at least twenty minutes per day, for four days, and write about the most traumatic experience of your life. You should write about the same experience during

the four-day period. Once you have spent four days on the same experience, you can do the exercise again by writing about another painful experience that you have had.

Pennebaker found that during the first two days of writing, people
experience and write about negative emotions, such as anger, sadness,
anxiety, and grief. On the third or fourth day, however, they experience
relief, insight, and resolution of those feelings. This suggested to Pennebaker that, by the third day, the study participants were releasing the
inhibiting energy and integrating the traumatic events into their consciousness. The energy that was released could then be integrated back
into the body and utilized for improvements in physical and immunological health.

Pennebaker suggests that you adhere to four rules while doing the
exercise.

1. Write continuously about the single, most upsetting experience,
   trauma, or shame-filled event of your life.
2. Write about this event or experience for at least twenty minutes,
   for four consecutive days.
3. Don't worry about grammar, spelling, or structure of the piece.
4. Write your deepest thoughts and emotions regarding the experience. Include all the details you remember and insights into the
   events. The more you confess in your diary, the greater the impact on your psychological and immunological health.

Once you have done the writing, share it with someone you love, or
with a therapist, healer, or religious or spiritual figure. Let this confession be the basis for an enriching therapy.

Pennebaker found that people who do this exercise, then share their
feelings with a close intimate, never see themselves, or the experience
they write about, in quite the same way. Indeed, many discover that their
former guilt is replaced by compassion for themselves, a newfound self-
respect, and far greater self-love.

Seeing Destructive Behaviors in a New Light

All too often, we criticize ourselves for behaviors that we deem to be inappropriate, or undisciplined, or somehow a consequence of poor character. These are all the wrong words, the wrong labels, which may have no other purpose but to keep us from knowing what truly is driving us to engage in self-destructive behaviors. In most cases, our destructive patterns are some form of comforting behavior that we use to take us out of emotional pain or physical and psychological tension.

When looked at in this light, we can see that changing these behaviors depends on dealing with the underlying energies that exist in the shadow, forces that want to be reintegrated into consciousness. In effect, the psyche is attempting to restore wholeness and health. We can facilitate the healing process by addressing our imbalances, and trying, as best we can, to make conscious the contents of the shadow that want to be reintegrated into our lives. We can do that by writing about our imbalances, by changing our behavior, and doing the Pennebaker method.

The Pennebaker method is only one way of doing this. In fact, when confronted with the dark night of the soul, we often need help in resolving our despair. Many hands-on healers, such as Reiki masters or massage therapists, encourage their clients to become intimately aware of the places in their bodies where symptoms arise. These are places where we may be holding injuries that originated during moments of trauma and shock. When someone with a healing touch places his or her hands on these wounded places, and encourages us to express what we feel, we can often remember painful events and release traumas that the body has been holding for decades. As physical tension is reduced, cravings and other compensatory behaviors lessen. We become more relaxed in the body. Guilt dissipates and disappears. Energy increases significantly. Immune function is boosted. We are more at peace with ourselves and the world around us. We understand and feel compassion for ourselves and others. We experience, at a much deeper level, what it means to be human.

What has happened to us? We committed to a process by which we come to know ourselves and, in the process, become whole.

To What Are You Really Committing?

As you practice your healing program, and begin to change, new questions start to emerge from within you. To what am I really committing? And what am I becoming? Yes, you are committing to your survival and to a healing program that you believe can help you survive. But as you sincerely practice that program, and struggle to survive, you cannot help but wonder how this experience and your healing program are changing you. You are taking good care of yourself. You are forgiving those closest to you and seeking forgiveness; you are practicing greater love for yourself and others. You are evolving as a human being. A new version of yourself is emerging. Slowly, you come to realize that your commitment is no longer fueled by fear alone. Rather, you are seeing yourself in a new light, a light that reveals the best version of yourself. At that point, you realize that becoming this wiser, more spiritually alive version of yourself is now part of your commitment, and may even have been the most important reason to do your program in the first place. To be sure, the need to survive is driving you, but the critical knowledge that you now possess is that your way of survival is causing something altogether good and spiritually awakened to emerge from within you. Which means that your commitment leads you inevitably to the larger issue of faith.

STEP 6

✳

Believe in Your Ability to Heal—Have Faith

Believe in yourself! Have faith in your abilities! Without a humble but reasonable confidence in your own powers you cannot be successful or happy."

So begins Norman Vincent Peale's classic, *The Power of Positive Thinking* (Prentice Hall, 1952). Those words, written more than fifty years ago, are as alive and true today as they were when Peale first wrote them. They are not only relevant to success and happiness, however, but to the restoration of health. In his book, *Anatomy of an Illness,* writer and medical investigator Norman Cousins, yet another person who cured himself of a so-called terminal illness, put the matter succinctly when he wrote, "Drugs are not always necessary. Belief in recovery always is."

Words like belief and faith are doorways that lead us into the mystery that lives behind the curtain we call reality. What we find, when we explore the meaning of these words, is that they have the power to alter reality. Your beliefs, subjective as they are, can infuse tremendous power into your healing program. Native American medicine man, Rolling Thunder, used to say that even a glass of water can be powerful medicine if the person believes sufficiently in the water. The miracles at Lourdes are certainly proof of that.

At the sixth step in the healing journey, the path leads, as it were, to a mirror. It's time to look at yourself and ask: Do I believe in my healing program and my ability to recover? Am I optimistic about my chances? Many of the tools you need to restore your health are already in place and are being practiced every day. Your commitment to these healing tools, by itself, strengthens your belief in them. But at this step on the path, you must move ever more deeply into the mysterious world of belief and faith if you are to proceed on your journey.

It's important to know what you believe, because negative feelings, once they are recognized, can be the basis for intelligent decisions and positive changes in your approach. Some aspects of your program may need adjusting, or discarding altogether. Other aspects may be sound. Subtle doubts may be your inner voice telling you to make changes now, or to seek additional counsel. Your doubts may also be encouraging you to become more conscientious in your habits. Making the appropriate changes is an essential part of the healing journey.

It's important, as well, to distinguish between your subtle awareness for the need to change and a generalized pessimism or doubt in yourself. Belief translates into optimism. And believe it or not, optimism can be learned and implemented consistently. Researchers from the University of Pittsburgh Medical School, Yale University, and the Pittsburgh Cancer Institute successfully trained people with cancer to be more optimistic and to overcome self-defeating beliefs. Not only did they succeed in causing the study participants to have a positive outlook, but that outlook dramatically improved their immune systems, the researchers found.

The scientists examined the effects of optimism training on thirty patients, all of whom suffered from cancers that had an extremely high probability of recurrence. "The course was designed to make them more optimistic about events in their lives," said Martin Seligman, a psychologist at the University of Pennsylvania, who also participated in the study. "It didn't focus on cancer."

The scientists found that as optimism within the patients grew, their natural killer cells became more numerous and aggressive than those of the control group who were equally ill but got no such training.

As long as your immune system has not been irrevocably weakened, your body still possesses awesome healing powers that are capable of overcoming disease. For your healing program and your body to be sufficiently powerful to restore health, you must believe in them. It's that simple. Your belief gives your program and your body the power they need to restore health.

At this stage of your journey, you are asking yourself to believe in three things. First, the power of your healing program to create the conditions your body needs to heal. Second, your body's ability to overcome its illness and restore health. Third, a higher power, which most people refer to as God. All three are the basis for optimism, faith, and healing. These three were the basis for one of the most famous of all recovery stories, that of Anthony Sattilaro, M.D.

Where Medicine and Spirituality Become One

On June 1, 1978, doctors at Methodist Hospital in Philadelphia, Pennsylvania, informed Anthony Sattilaro, M.D., that he had prostate cancer that had spread throughout his body. Specifically, x-rays and bone scans had revealed that the tumors appeared in his skull, spine, sternum, left sixth rib, right shoulder, and prostate. A biopsy of his prostate revealed that it was filled with cancer.

Sattilaro, who was then president of Methodist Hospital, was told that he had between one year and eighteen months to live. Sattilaro was forty-eight years old. Prostate cancer in men younger than fifty is a highly virulent and lethal disease. He did an exhaustive investigation of his illness and sought the counsel from medical experts across the country, all of whom agreed that he had little chance of recovery.

In order to give him as much time as possible, doctors surgically removed Sattilaro's left sixth rib—which was filled with cancer—and both of his testicles. This was done to reduce his testosterone levels. Testosterone can fuel the cancer and makes it spread more rapidly. Sattilaro was also given therapeutic estrogens in the hope that the drugs would also slow the cancer. It was soon discovered that neither of these approaches had any real effect on his disease, but did cause significant side effects, including profuse itching of Sattilaro's skin and intense nausea and vomiting. His body also became bloated and overweight. The five-foot-six-inch Sattilaro soon weighed 170 pounds, 25 pounds above his normal, healthy weight.

The tumors in Sattilaro's spine caused him tremendous pain, for which he was taking an array of powerful analgesics, including Percodan and a concoction known as Brompton's mixture, which is composed of morphine for pain relief, cocaine for euphoria, and compazine to control nausea. Unfortunately, the drugs tended to wear off long before he could safely take another dosage, which meant that he was forced to endure many hours of agonizing pain each day.

While all of this was going on, Tony's father was dying of lung cancer. Tony watched his father wither away and realized that he himself would soon follow in his father's footsteps. On August 7, 1978, Sattilaro's father died and, on August 9, the family buried him in their hometown of Highland Park, New Jersey.

It was a beautiful summer day when the family laid its patriarch to rest. After the funeral, Sattilaro got into his car and drove back to Philadelphia. On the highway going home, Sattilaro, depressed and weary with pain, spotted two hitchhikers by the side of the road and decided to pick them up. It was an uncharacteristic thing for him to do, especially since he had prejudices against young people with long hair and scruffy clothing. What made him do it is anyone's guess. In any case, he stopped and Sean McLean and Bill Bochbracher got into his car, McLean in front, Bochbracher in the backseat.

The two travelers were on their way to North Carolina to study cooking. They were affable young men, both in their mid-twenties. Soon Bachbracher went to sleep and eventually Sattilaro told McLean that he had just buried his father, who had died of cancer, and that he himself was dying from the same disease. The next words that came from McLean's mouth have come to be famous in certain circles of natural healing. Certainly, they are responsible for altering not only Sattilaro's life, but many lives since.

"You don't have to die, Doc. Cancer isn't all that hard to cure," the young cook said.

Sattilaro was utterly offended. "I looked at him and thought, 'This is just a silly kid,'" Sattilaro recalled years later. "Here I was a doctor for twenty years. I knew that cancer was very difficult to cure, and we didn't have the answers."

McLean, a student of macrobiotics, insisted that such a diet and way of life could restore Sattilaro's health. He then pressed Sattilaro to drive to Essene Natural Foods Store, then located on South Street in Philadelphia, where he might meet the local macrobiotic teacher, a man named Denny Waxman. Sattilaro took McLean and Bochbracher to Essene, but Waxman was out. Reluctantly, Mclean and Bochbracher left the doctor and resumed their travels, but not before they got Sattilaro's address. Two weeks later, a large manila envelope arrived at Sattilaro's door with sixty-seven cents postage due. The envelope, sent from McLean, contained a booklet entitled, *A Macrobiotic Approach to Cancer*. Sattilaro gave the thing a perfunctory perusal and was about to toss it in the wastebasket when his eye caught the name of a Philadelphia physician whose written testimonial described her use of the macrobiotic diet in her treatment of cancer. Sattilaro looked up the physician's name in a medical directory and telephoned her home. A man answered. Sattilaro explained the reason he was calling and asked for the woman.

"I'm sorry," the man said. "My wife isn't here. She's in the hospital dying of cancer."

"Oh, I see," Sattilaro replied. "Well, you've answered my question. Macrobiotics doesn't cure cancer." With that, Sattilaro was about to hang up when the man answered Sattilaro with enthusiasm. "Listen, it really works," the man said. "While she was sticking to the diet, it really did help her. She showed real signs of getting well. But she couldn't stick to it. She hated the food."

"Do you think it's worth looking into?" Sattilaro asked. "I'm dying of cancer."

"Yes, definitely," the man replied.

The next call Sattilaro made was to Denny Waxman. The two met on August 27 at Denny's home in Bala Cynwyd, a suburb of Philadelphia. Denny Waxman, then thirty years of age, was lean, healthy-looking, and serious. He gave Sattilaro a very strange examination in which looked carefully at his face, arms, feet, and the sclera of his eyes. Sattilaro was wearing a battery-driven acupuncture device on his back in an attempt to stem the pain, but Waxman paid it little attention. Once he completed his examination, Waxman outlined the diet he wanted

Sattilaro to eat. It was composed of cooked whole grains, such as brown rice, fresh vegetables, beans, sea vegetables, and soup that contained miso, a base made from fermented soybeans. The diet also included a variety of condiments and some seeds and nuts. Waxman said that when Sattilaro became stronger, he could include fish and some fruit, but until he showed real signs of improvement, he should abstain from these foods. After he finished describing the diet, Waxman encouraged Sattilaro, saying that he had a strong constitution and a good chance of recovery.

"What the hell," Sattilaro told himself as he left Denny Waxman's house that day. "I'm going to die anyway, so I might as well give this diet a try."

Sattilaro did not cook—he ate all of his meals in restaurants—and after a few failed attempts in his kitchen, he soon accepted Denny's invitation to eat his meals at the Waxman table. There Sattilaro learned about macrobiotics. It was not a subject that gave him much peace.

Sattilaro soon found that the world of macrobiotics was more than simply a diet or a nutritional approach to illness and health. Rather, it is a philosphical approach to living. Unlike modern science, traditional medical systems, such as those of the Chinese, Hindu, Native American, and Greek combine practical healing arts with a philosophy about the underlying forces that shape reality and drive our lives. In these systems, the philosophical principles guide the practitioner in the use of the healing tools, which means it's impossible to separate the philosophy from the actual practice.

At the core of the macrobiotic philosophy is the theory that two prevailing forces, known in China as yin and yang, are present in all phenomena and are constantly seeking to establish balance or harmony. The yin force creates rest, passivity, cool temperatures, and expansion, while the yang force creates movement, action, aggression, heat, and contraction. Everything we do, from sleeping, to work, to the foods we eat, has some yin or yang effect on our bodies and minds. When one or the other dominates our lives, we experience some degree of imbalance. As our imbalances become more exaggerated, the risk of illness increases. Extreme imbalances give rise to extreme diseases, such as heart disease and cancer. Food is among the most concentrated manifestations of yin and yang and therefore can be used to manipulate these forces to create balance, harmony, and health. Hence, the macrobiotic emphasis on diet. On the other hand, all behaviors have yin and yang effects. Everything from sleep (yin) to exercise (yang) to lovemaking (initially yang but turning into balance and rest, more yin) can be used to restore balance and harmony within the body and mind. Though the macrobiotic diet is made up of a core group of foods, practitioners emphasize certain foods in order to create balance. For those whose conditions are dominated by yin influences (caused by excess consumption of sugar, processed foods, and soft dairy products), practitioners recommend the core diet, with slightly more yang influences, such as more whole grains, root vegetables, and limited fruit intake. For those whose illnesses are caused by yang influences (such as from meat, salt, chicken, and hard cheeses), practitioners recommend the core diet, plus more yin influences, such as softer grains, more vegetables, beans, and some cooked fruit. Lifestyle factors are also employed. More vigorous exercise (a yang influence) is recommended for those who are too yin; more gentle exercise (relaxing or yin), such as yoga or Tai Chi Chuan, is recommended for those who are too yang.

All of this was a huge stretch for Sattilaro to accept, but there were other ideas, even more spiritual in nature, that ran counter to what Sattilaro had come to believe about life. The most important of these was the theory that all living things are imbued with, and animated by, an immanent life force. Virtually all traditional healing systems are founded on such a philosophy, including the Greek (where the life force is *pneuma,* or breath), Hindu (where it is called it *prana*), and Chinese (where it is called *chi* or *Qi*). The belief in a life force is also present in Judaism and early Christianity. In these traditions, the life force is linked to spirit— that is to say, one's own individual spirit, and also the larger life that permeates the universe.

Sattilaro's medical training gave him a scientific and materialistic orientation in life. He had come to believe that if you couldn't see the object in question, or measure it with a machine, it didn't exist. Hence, he thought the macrobiotic ideas were ludicrous.

"When I came to Denny's house," Sattilaro recalled years later, "I thought that this was the biggest bunch of weirdos I'd ever seen. They were all sitting [Japanese-style] on the floor, ready to eat with chopsticks. Then they started to pray, and I just thought that this was a bunch of crap."

The only potentially valuable idea in macrobiotics that Sattilaro could discern was the relationship between food and health. The belief that too much consumption of meat, eggs, chicken, dairy products, sugar, and processed foods caused disease made sense to him. At least that was something he could hold on to. On the other hand, he strongly doubted that the macrobiotic diet could reverse his illness. Still, he was dying, and anything that gave him even the smallest hope was worth looking into. Moreover, he had to eat, and the macrobiotic diet seemed sufficiently nutritious that it probably wouldn't hurt him, so there was little to lose.

There was something else that kept him coming back to macrobiotics, however. On an intuitive level, he felt that what he was doing was right. He couldn't articulate the source of his feeling. Yet, his gut urged him on. So every evening he returned to the Waxman table and ate this very strange food with his chopsticks. After dinner, Denny's wife, Judy, sent Tony off with additional food for breakfast and lunch the following day.

Despite his skepticism, Sattilaro made a complete commitment and followed the diet with absolute strictness. Anything that Denny recommended, Tony did. The diet was the only thing that gave him hope, he said, and he would not weaken his chances of recovery by being self-indulgent. It wasn't long before his diligence was rewarded.

On the morning of September 26, just one month after he met Denny Waxman, Sattilaro got out of bed, reached for his Percodan and, still half-asleep, suddenly realized that the pain in his back was gone. He jumped out of bed and searched his back with his mind. Nothing. He walked around his bedroom and did some gentle stretching. Gone. Not a trace of pain could be found in his back, or anywhere else in his body. He had been suffering with this agonizing pain for the previous two years. Only the most powerful narcotics could put it down. And now, for reasons he could not understand, the pain had disappeared.

That milestone convinced Sattilaro that the diet was deeply affecting his health, and perhaps his cancer. From there, Sattilaro began to make steady and, at times, seemingly miraculous progress. His energy levels dramatically improved. His appearance changed. He lost the excess weight, regained a youthful glow in his features, and looked years younger. Soon, it became clear to those around him that Sattilaro was not following the standard path of a man dying of cancer.

One of Tony's friends and colleagues, John Giacobbo, M.D., then vice president of Methodist Hospital, recalled Sattilaro's progress. "When Tony first started the macrobiotic diet, people thought it was some kind of far-out idea," Dr. Giacobbo said. "Some people at the hospital thought he was a kook. I told him he was crazy. Pretty soon, though, you could see he was improving mentally and physically."

Sattilaro's health continued to improve through the fall and as it did, his confidence grew. That was a dangerous moment for him. With his energy levels and his optimism at an all-time high, he decided in December to travel by train with his mother to Florida. On the train, he widened his diet to include foods that he did not normally eat. He did not believe that these foods would affect him, but he soon became nauseated, threw up the meal, and the following day, suffered the recurrence of his back pain. Terrified, he returned to Philadelphia and resumed his strict macrobiotic diet. Within a couple of weeks, the pain was gone again. The experience taught him a valuable lesson, he said. His condition was delicate, he realized, and he would have to eat absolutely perfectly if he had any chance of recovery.

During the winter and spring of 1979, his health improved once again, and he felt certain that he was on track to be healed entirely of his disease. In June 1979, he stopped taking the therapeutic estrogens, despite his doctor's strong opposition. Rather than suffering any decline in his health, as his doctor predicted, he only got stronger.

As his health improved, Sattilaro underwent a spiritual transformation. He went back to his Roman Catholic roots and became deeply involved in the Church. He regularly traveled to monasteries and took part in meditative retreats. He prayed throughout the day, formally in the morning and evening, and in small ways throughout the course of his day. He read spiritual literature voraciously and sought the guidance of clergy. In fact, the macrobiotic experience reinforced many of his own fundamental spiritual beliefs. And in the process, he came to see his life's most profound imbalances.

Sattilaro realized that he had been dominated by the rational intellect and its tendencies to see people and events as separate and distinct from each other. He realized, as well, that such a point of view, though important in certain contexts, was only a partial understanding of reality. There was another way of seeing things—a more unified approach to life in which all events, all people, all phenomena are united by the web of life, a web that itself might be understood as a living, spiritual entity. These two points of view give rise to very distinct ways of thinking and behaving, and indeed very different qualities of life. The intellectual view, which insists that all beings and phenomena are separate, promotes criticism, fear, and selfishness. This understanding sees people as striving after limited resources. It's a dog-eat-dog world, says the intellect. Get what you can and survive. In fact, this was Sattilaro's way of life, prior to getting cancer. He was profoundly ambitious and determined to get all that he could for himself. Now he saw clearly how he had to change. As it happened, that change was staring him in the face. It was there in his healing path all the while.

The belief in a universe infused with a life energy that is constantly seeking harmony suggested that life itself is a perfectly coordinated entity in which all people and events are joined in a harmony that only God could comprehend or orchestrate. The unified worldview recognizes the commonalty among us all and our inherent unity with the universe itself. From this monistic worldview comes not separation and fear, but unity, compassion, love, and healing. In order to heal himself, Sattilaro knew he had to change his thinking and his way of living to conform with this unified view of life. The new way of thinking was essentially positive and optimistic. He had to start believing in the possibility of a miracle.

On September 25, 1979, Sattilaro underwent a bone scan and x-rays, all of which showed no sign of cancer in his body. He had been completely healed of his disease. Those who watched him go through his healing odyssey were convinced that his macrobiotic approach restored his health. Said Giacobbo: "Most people at Methodist were convinced that Dr. Sattialro was going to die. The five-year survival rate for this type of illness is zero. Now, he is completely cured, and I'm amazed. I think the diet did it."

Many people argued that Sattilaro's recovery was some kind of miracle. "Of course it was a miracle," he would reply. "God directed me to pick up Sean McLean and Bill Bochbracher. There's no doubt in my mind that God has been with me every step of the way."

Tony Sattilaro lived another ten years. In 1990, his cancer returned, and he died in Fort Lauderdale, Florida. Just before his death, he told me that he had been asked to leave Methodist Hospital in the late 1980s. He was essentially removed from the job and the profession he loved. With the loss of his job, his life purpose had been lost, he told me. "I became a walking reminder of a healing approach that medicine didn't want any part of," Sattilaro told me. "People didn't want me around." In fact, shortly after Sattilaro had cured himself and become famous, he regularly heard that highly placed physicians predicted he would be dead inside of two years. That didn't happen. But it did reveal how much of an embarrassment he was to those who insisted that diet had no place in the treatment of cancer.

When we spoke again after his cancer had returned, Tony could not help but draw the obvious parallel to that other famous figure who had been raised from the dead. "I was just like Lazarus," he said. "After Lazarus was restored to life, people wanted him dead again, because he was a reminder of Jesus. Many people in my profession wanted me dead, too, because I was a reminder of the role diet could play in healing."

He moved to Florida, fell into depression, and soon gave up his macrobiotic diet. "It took two years of eating fatty foods and sugar for my cancer to return," he said. When it was clear that his cancer was back, he telephoned Michio Kushi, who began counseling Sattilaro again. That summer, Sattilaro attended the Kushi Institute Summer Conference at Simon's Rock College in Great Barrington, Massachusetts. Before the few hundred people gathered at the conference, Sattilaro announced that he had twice proved that macrobiotics cured his cancer.

"The first time was when I got cancer and adopted macrobiotics and cured myself," he said. "The second time was when I went off the diet and got the disease back." Later that summer, Sattilaro died of cancer.

Belief As the Healer

Tony Sattilaro's story is a journey in faith. Like all recovery stories, it began with a small belief in the possibility of recovery, which, like a seed, sprouted and grew. Belief in recovery is, by itself, a powerful healing force. It often serves to balance the fears and limitations placed upon us

by the rational intellect, which states that that reality is fixed and im-
mutable. Believe what you want, the intellect says, but getting well depends on having an effective drug or surgery. That was Tony Sattilaro's
most fundamental belief at the outset of his healing journey. Sattilaro was
a man dominated by a materialistic worldview. He was also a symbol of
materialistic medicine. Neither that worldview, nor the medicine that
comes out of it, could save his life. But mysterious forces led him to another way, one that might be called a spiritual approach to healing. Macrobiotics opened him up to a larger view and a greater set of
possibilities, which is the source of miracles. In fact, Sattilaro's spiritual-
ity was always waiting to emerge. The confrontation with death and the
sudden presentation, as it were, of a philosophy that was both practical
and spiritual gave him a new way of looking at life. The transformation
that followed freed him from much narrow and negative thinking. Suddenly, he had a new set of beliefs that gave him hope and brought about a
kind rebirth and enthusiasm for living. There was nothing else to do, at
that point, but humbly turn to God and pray for help.

This process, which is archetypal in nature—meaning that those who
enter it tend to experience a similar transformation—begins with a small
belief that something unexpected, perhaps even miraculous, could happen. Belief, by itself, is a powerful healing force, as the research on
placebo has confirmed again and again.

The placebo effect is a very real and measurable improvement in
health that cannot be attributed to any form of medical treatment. It is
most often observed when scientists want to test a particular medication. In such cases, researchers divide a population of people into two
groups, one that gets an active drug—this group is called the experimental group—and another that gets a nontherapeutic pill or potion, usually
containing sugar or starch. The latter group is referred to as the control
group. Inevitably, large portions of the control group report an allevia-
tion of symptoms and a restoration of health, even though they received
nothing that would actually treat the illness. The same effect turns up in
people who undergo what they believe will be an operation. Men who
suffered from arthritis in the knee report a complete relief of symptoms
after being wheeled into an operating room, anesthetized, and having
two small incisions made in the backs of their knees to make it seem like
they were operated on. No such operation occurred, but months and

even years later, they continue to report a complete restoration of their knees and no recurrence of arthritis pain. The same has been shown in both men and women with angina who underwent a sham operation that involved nothing more than a couple of superficial incisions made in the chest.

"The truth is that the placebo effect is huge," wrote Margaret Talbot in the *New York Times Magazine* ("The Placebo Prescription": January 9, 2000). "Anywhere between 35 and 75 percent of patients benefit from taking a dummy pill in studies of new drugs—so huge, in fact, that it should probably be put to conscious use in clinical practice, even if we do not entirely understand how it works."

Placebos are constantly disrupting scientific studies because they oftentimes prove just as effective—and sometimes more effective—than the active drugs that they are supposed to be compared against. In fact, 30 to 40 percent of any test group will respond to placebo, said Harvard scientist Henry Beecher. Other studies have shown that, in certain conditions, the numbers are even higher. In patients treated with placebo for pain, depression, heart disease, gastric ulcers, and asthma, as many as 50 to 60 percent of patients respond positively to placebo.

Irving Kirsch, Ph.D., a psychologist and researcher at the University of Connecticut, believes that up to 75 percent of the effectiveness of Prozac and similar antidepression drugs can be attributed to placebo.

"The critical factor is our belief about what's going to happen to us," Kirsch told the *New York Times*. "You don't have to rely on drugs to see profound transformation."

Three elements must be present to invoke your belief fully. First, we must have an intellectual basis for believing in the efficacy of our program. In other words, there must be some explanation for efficacy that the rational mind can comprehend and entertain, if not fully accept. Second, we must see positive results within a reasonable amount of time. In short, the program must make us feel better. Again, such feelings of improvement may have less to do with the therapeutic approach than with the healing effects of belief. Third, we must come to believe that a power greater than ourselves is at work in the healing process. These three elements tend to arise in succession, meaning the first factor eventually leads to the second, which in turn leads to the third.

Anthony Sattilaro had grave doubts when he adopted an alternative treatment for his metastatic prostate cancer. He took up the program because he had run out of choices and because another doctor had said it might work. However, part of the explanation for macrobiotics—that diet could both cause illness and help to heal it—made some initial sense to him. He followed the diet strictly and soon experienced a cessation of pain. That moment turned the tide for him. Now his belief in the program was engaged, which only made it stronger for him.

Perhaps the placebo effect is nothing more than the use of an external agent to stimulate the body's own healing forces. That certainly is one of the underlying beliefs in all of alternative or traditional medicine—that given the right conditions, the body can heal itself. And, as Norman Cousins and other observers have noted, those healing forces are invoked and strengthened when we have a strong belief in recovery.

Belief has a very specific growth pattern. It may start out as belief in a therapeutic tool, but, if maintained long enough and allowed to grow, often leads us toward the spiritual part of our nature. As Tony Sattilaro experienced, belief in macrobiotics soon led to a deeper experience of his own spiritual life and a regular practice of prayer and meditation.

In Prayer and Meditation Lies a Power to Heal

From a purely pragmatic and rational standpoint, prayer and meditation make good sense because both have been shown to have a profound effect on health. Scientists from UCLA and other university research centers have found that the daily practice of transcendental meditation (TM)—in which one silently repeats a single word, or mantra, over and over again—reduces blood pressure, atherosclerosis, and the incidence of heart attacks and strokes in humans.

Daily meditation has been shown to boost significantly the immune system. A study done on men with HIV showed that those who meditated daily experienced an increase in the number and aggressiveness of CD4 cells—the immune system's commanding general that directs the system's attack against disease. Under normal circumstances, men with HIV experience a steady decline in this important class of immune cells, but, at least in this study, the men who meditated daily were less likely to see their HIV infection escalate to full-blown AIDS.

Similarly, a study done on medical school students showed that daily meditation or relaxation exercises increased the number and aggressiveness of both natural killer cells and CD4 cells. Natural killer cells play a pivotal role in the treatment of cancer.

Other research has shown that daily meditation or relaxation techniques can reduce anxiety and alleviate mild depression.

Harvard Medical School professor Herbert Benson, M.D., famed for his study of the effects of prayer and meditation, says that all of these effects stem from what he calls the "relaxation response." Ten to twenty minutes of meditation each day can lower blood pressure, slow heart rate, balance hormones, relax muscles, and boost immune function, Benson says.

"Any practice that can evoke the relaxation response is of benefit, be it meditation, yoga, breathing, or repetitive prayer," said Benson. "There is no reason to believe that one [method] is better than the other. The key is the repetition, but the repetition can be a word, sound, mantra, prayer, breathing or movement." Benson went on to say that, "Just about any condition that is either caused or made worse by stress can be helped with meditation."

Praying or meditating daily can dramatically affect your health. It appears that scientists can even explain why it works, at least in part. But our understanding of material reality begins to break down when we consider what happens when sick people are prayed for by others at a distance.

Distant Prayer: Changing Our View of Reality

"Who has not, during a time of illness or pain, cried out to a higher being for help and healing?" Randolph Byrd, M.D., asked in the introduction to his study, "Positive Therapeutic Effects of Intercessory Prayer in a Coronary Care Unit Population," published in the *Southern Medical Journal* (vol. 81, no. 7, July 1988). "Praying for help and healing is a fundamental concept in practically all societies, though the object to which these prayers are directed varies among the religions of the world."

Dr. Byrd, a professor of medicine at the University of California, San Francisco, was among the first scientifically to document the power of prayer to promote healing. He and his colleagues divided a group of

393 patients who had recently undergone heart surgery into two groups. The first group, composed of 192 patients, were prayed for by members of several local churches of Protestant and Roman Catholic denominations. Each person who prayed was given the patient's first name, the patient's diagnosis, condition, and regular updates on the patient's health. At the same time, 201 patients, who had also undergone coronary procedures in the same hospital, were not prayed for and were used as controls. There were no statistical differences in health between those who were prayed for and those who were not. None of the patients knew that they were being prayed for; nor did the scientists know who was being prayed for and who wasn't.

After nine months, the researchers found that the prayed-for group experienced much more rapid healing and far less need for medical intervention than the controls. Those who were prayed for had fewer incidents of congestive heart failure, cardiopulmonary arrest, pneumonia, and required less medication and high-tech support than controls. On the other hand, "The control group required more ventilatory assistance, antibiotics, and diuretics than the IP (intercessory prayer) group," Byrd and his colleagues reported. "These data suggest that intercessory prayer to the Judeo-Christian God has a beneficial therapeutic effect in patients admitted to a CCU."

Other studies found similar effects from distant prayer. Perhaps the most impressive of these was done in 1998 by Duke University researchers who studied the effects of distant prayer on 150 people who had invasive cardiac operations. The Duke researchers compared those who were prayed for against a control group composed of people who had undergone the same kinds of procedures but were not the focus of a specific prayer group.

The Duke researchers asked seven religious groups to pray for the 150 participants in the experimental protocol. Those seven groups included Carmelite nuns from Baltimore, a Buddhist group in Nepal, and Virtual Jerusalem, an organization that prays for people upon request and inserts written prayers into the Wailing Wall. As with Randolph Byrd's study, none of the study participants knew that they were being prayed for; nor did the scientists themselves know who was being prayed for and who wasn't. The Duke researchers found that those who underwent surgical procedures and were prayed for experienced nearly a third fewer adverse outcomes, such as heart failure, postprocedural is-chemia, repeat angioplasty, or heart attack, as compared to the control group.

How is it possible that people can pray for others and affect their health? Such phenomena cannot be explained according to the laws of Newtonian physics, which posits that objects do not influence each other unless they interact in a physical or otherwise known way. Since prayers did not interact with those they prayed for in any way that is understand-able according to Newton, prayer should not have any effect on people, especially over a distance spanning from, say, the U.S. to South Korea. Yet, in study after study, those who are prayed for experienced better health or more positive outcomes.

Research on prayer paints a very different picture of reality than the one most of us have been taught and come to accept. Rather than being separated by space, the studies on distant prayer reveal a more unified world where all of us are much more united than we are used to think-ing. (More about prayer groups below and in the Resource Guide in the back of this book.)

A Two-Sided Reality Where the Ordinary and the Miraculous Live Side by Side

Here's an odd contradiction in which virtually all of us indulge. We all realize that people are separate from each other. Yet we think nothing of praying for our loved ones. If we are separate from our loved ones, how can our prayers help them? We answer that question by saying that God intervenes on behalf of those we love. In other words, all of us are sepa-rated by space, until God overcomes the separation. But if God is pre-sent everywhere and all the time, how can there be any separation?

Paradoxes make our heads spin because they cannot be reconciled in ordinary ways. We think of our lives as separate from others, yet some of our behaviors are based on the belief that all of us are united in some mys-terious way. Our most advanced science, quantum physics, tells us that both beliefs are true. We are separated by space and time and yet we are all united. Which reality you experience depends on what you believe.

At the root of this contradiction is another paradox. Everything, including each of us, is composed of both matter and energy—that is to say, we are solid objects, and at the same time luminous balls of energy that have no solidity at all.

Quantum physicist and author of the book, *Taking the Quantum Leap,* Fred Alan Wolf, explains it this way. We are taught to believe that matter is composed of atoms, which are like "itsy-bitsy baseballs," says Wolf. Yet, when the physicist looks closer at these tiny particles, "the little baseballs do not behave like little baseballs—they refract or bend and spread out like waves, producing wave patterns . . ." When the atom is examined closely, it stops being solid, but instead turns into waves of energy. And in the process, the material world disappears.

"At the quantum level, nothing of the material world is left intact," writes Deepak Chopra in his remarkable best seller, *How to Know God* (Random House, 2000). "It is strange enough to hold up your hand and realize that it is actually, at a deeper level, invisible vibrations taking place in a void . . . At the quantum level the whole cosmos is like a blinking light. There are no stars or galaxies, only vibrating energy fields that our senses are too dull and slow to pick up given the incredible speed at which light and electricity move."

Both realities are true—we are solid and we are energetic beings. And each one of these conditions offers us very different sets of possibilities. In the material mode of reality, we bump our toes and try to avoid large moving objects in order stay alive. In this mode, prayer makes no sense at all, because everything is separate. But on the energetic mode of reality, prayer makes complete sense because everything is united by energy, even our thoughts.

"The universe can appear to be fundamentally paradoxical," writes Wolf. "The more we determine one side of reality, the less the other side is shown to us."

That's where belief and faith come into the picture. People can insist that reality is based on rational, material laws, and they have good reasons to think they're right. But as Wolf points out, if you insist on seeing only one side of reality, that's the reality you get and the one you must live with.

In *How to Know God*, Deepak Chopra offers a simple metaphor to show how these apparent opposites can be reconciled to better understand our relationship with God. Chopra states that reality is like a three-layer sandwich. The first layer is the material world, bound by all the laws of physics. At this level, there appear to be no phenomena that cannot be explained through rational science. Indeed, all rational arguments against the existence of God seem entirely persuasive. The top layer of the sandwich is what we refer to as God. And in between, there is a transitional zone where "God and humans meet on common ground," writes Chopra. "Somewhere miracles take place, along with holy visions, angels, enlightenment, and hearing the voice of God. All of these extraordinary phenomena bridge two worlds: They are real and yet they are not part of a predictable cause-and-effect."

Chopra refers to this transitional zone as the quantum reality, where events occur that transcend the laws of Newton and our picture of ordinary reality. The quantum dimension is the transitional zone where energy becomes matter. Or to put it another way, the quantum reality is that dimension of existence where prayers (energy) change our health (matter)—and even the health of people at great distances. As inhabitants of the quantum reality, we can call upon that power, God, to turn energy into matter, or make our hopes and our prayers a reality.

"Each of us can live in the victory of spirit, claiming for ourselves the miraculous power that has been given to us as children of God," writes Marianne Williamson in *Everyday Grace: Having Hope, Finding Forgiveness, and Making Miracles* (Riverhead Books, 2002). "It is our *faith* that miracles are possible—that the very fabric of the universe is miraculous—which opens the mind, and thus the future, to unimaginable possibilities. 'Dear God, please send a miracle' is a powerful prayer for cosmic support. To pray is to take spiritual action."

In September 1982, Gerry Sue Arnold, wife of Norman Arnold, whom I wrote about in Chapter 4, drove across her hometown of Columbia, South Carolina, to purchase a pressure cooker so that she could prepare rice for Norman and her family. Her drive was fretful, as she considered her husband's fate, as well as her own. What lay ahead for them? she wondered. How bad would it get for Norman, for her children, and for her? She pulled over to the side of the road and sat for a moment in an effort to clear her head. In the midst of her acute distress, she asked God to give her strength to see Norman through this crisis. Suddenly, she was engulfed by an overpowering sense of peace. A chronic pain in her stomach suddenly disappeared. And then she heard a voice come ringing into her ears. "Norman's going to be all right," were the words she heard. An irresistible calm passed over her. In a single moment, she was changed. Despite all the grim pronouncements from Norman's doctors, Gerry Sue knew that Norman would live.

In 1981, I interviewed Mona Schwartz, who at the time was forty-six and the mother of two children. Mona had beautiful red hair, large, dark blue eyes, and a strong, wide mouth that revealed a radiant, energetic smile. She stood five feet three inches tall and had a slim figure. At the time of the interview, Mona was showing me photographs of her children. Finally, she removed a picture of herself from an album and handed it to me. It is of Mona, standing on a boat deck, wearing a raincoat that was bursting from her girth. She weighed 170 pounds, and her stomach was so distended that it looked like she was carrying a beach ball under her raincoat. Mona, a native of Philadelphia, Pennsylvania, had suffered from a litany of severe illnesses, including acute thyroid, kidney, gallbladder, and liver disorders. She suffered from toxemia, idiopathic edema, severe back and neck pain, and chronic diarrhea. She also suffered from borderline leukemia. She had undergone more surgeries than she could remember and was taking numerous medications every day for her many disorders.

Doctors had already informed Mona that there was little they could do for her, but in 1974, they suspected that she suffered from liver cancer and scheduled a biopsy of her liver at Graduate Hospital in Philadelphia. On the night before the surgery, Mona walked the halls of the hospital, despondent. She decided that she didn't care if she lived or died—life had become too much for her to bear. Soon, Mona found herself in a poorly lit, silent, empty corridor. Tall windows were on both sides of the hall, but outside the world was dark. Suddenly, a strange light appeared directly in front of her. The apparition asked Mona if she wanted to live. Deeply stirred, Mona fell to her knees, and said, "I want to live, God. I want to live." Her words were met by empty silence.

The following morning Mona underwent biopsy surgery. After the operation, she was returned to her room. As she gradually regained consciousness, Mona heard the words, "Then you shall live." A week later, she encountered a diet and lifestyle that led to the full recovery of her health.

"No problem is too hard for God to solve," writes Marianne Williamson in her book, *Everyday Grace*. "This is very important to remember, as it's hard to have deep faith in a kinda-sorta-powerful God."

Surrender to Love

Belief is not faith. There is an intellectual insistence in belief, because belief is the human struggle to overcome doubt. With belief comes hope, but in hope lies the shadow of uncertainty. As we have seen, belief is essential to the healing process, but it does not have the power of faith. Faith is beyond belief. It arises from having experienced what some call the realm of spirit, or what Chopra refers to as the quantum level of existence, where events occur that cannot be understood or explained in ordinary terms. Those who have ventured into this realm know it as a world of love, peace, and miraculous occurences.

It is said that mystics and saints live at this dimension; they never leave the realm of love, and therefore have a power to perform miracles that the rest of us cannot comprehend. As French philosopher Teilhard de Chardin said, "One day, after we have mastered the winds and the waves, gravity and the tides, we will harness for God the energies of love. And then, for the second time in human history, mankind will have discovered fire."

Perhaps this is what Jesus meant, when he says, in Matthew's gospel, "If you have the faith of a mustard seed, you shall say to the mountain, move from here to there and it shall move." There is a power in faith to alter reality as we know it, to change events, and to experience the miraculous.

How can we develop faith? By practicing belief, and daily prayer, and being open to experiencing spirit in our daily lives.

In *The Power of Positive Thinking*, Norman Vincent Peale tells the story of a former major league baseball pitcher, Frank Hiller, who pitched a complete nine-inning game in temperatures that were well in excess of a hundred degrees. In the process, he lost several pounds and at one point his energy began to flag badly. In a very short period, however, his strength returned, and he appeared to grow stronger as the game progressed. Asked after the game how he pulled off such a feat, he told a reporter that he repeated a phrase from the Old Testament over and over again. "But they that wait upon the Lord shall renew their strength; they shall mount up with wings as eagles, they shall run, and not be weary; and they shall walk and not faint." (Isaiah 40:31). Every time he said these words, he felt himself get stronger. "I passed a powerful energy-producing thought through my mind," he said.

As Peale says, "Contact with God establishes within us a flow of the same type of energy that re-creates the world and that renews springtime every year. When in spiritual contact with God through our thought processes, the Divine energy flows through the personality, automatically renewing the original creative act. When contact with the Divine energy is broken, the personality gradually becomes depleted in body, mind, and spirit. An electric clock connected with an outlet does not run down and will continue indefinitely to keep accurate time. Unplug it, and the clock stops. It has lost contact with the power flowing through the universe."

Prayers, Meditations, and Chants

Prayers can be as simple as clearly stating your request, or as elaborate as repeating favorite passages from sacred literature, or reciting the prayers you were taught as a child. Many people feel more comfort during prayer when they create an altar in their home. An altar can be a low table upon which you can place spiritual articles that inspire your reverence for the sacred. Of course, the altar should be set up in a very private place in your home—a quiet corner of your bedroom, for example, or a room that does not get much traffic. This altar becomes the outward symbol and a reminder of the sacred in your life. Whether you create an altar or not, it's important to pray in a quiet setting that allows you to go deeply inside yourself and allow your feelings to emerge.

Two ideas are of paramount importance regarding prayer. First, we are instructed by many religious traditions to pray continuously throughout the day. A wonderful short volume entitled, *The Practice of the Presence of God* (Paraclete Press), written by Brother Lawrence, a French monk who lived in the seventeenth century, instructs us merely to talk to

God on an ongoing basis through the day. Treat God as if he were at your side as you walk through your life. As you walk with God, share all your thoughts, emotions, fears, and desires. Turn all that you are burdened by over to Him. This, says Brother Lawrence, is the practice of the presence of God. As he wrote to a fellow member of the clergy in 1682, "There is no manner of life in the world more sweet or more delicious than continual conversation with God. They alone can understand it who practice it and savor it . . . Believe me; make a holy and firm resolve never voluntarily to withdraw yourself from God's grace from this time on. Live the rest of your days in God's holy presence . . ."

The second step that is important, especially as it relates to health, is to pray until you feel relief from your fears and anxiety. As you begin, you may be overwhelmed with both of these feelings. Keep praying until they pass and you experience a degree of serenity and protection.

As you pray, concentrate on your image of the Deity, a holy figure, patron saint, or an ancestor who loved you and watched over you while he or she was alive. You may instead want to concentrate on the image of a sacred light, which many believe is the closest image we have of God. Whatever the symbol, try to communicate all that you feel. Relax into its embrace and feel yourself coming into communion with it. As you pray, your emotions will begin to change. You may simply experience relief from your fear. You may experience anger or even sadness. Keep praying. As the meditation I described in Chapter 1 showed, anger eventually leads to sadness, which can release so much emotion. Let it come out. Sadness is a gateway to compassion for yourself and others. Once you feel compassion for yourself, you may want to stop praying and simply feel the emotions rise through your body and heart. Feel the love you have for yourself and others. Sit with those feelings and allow them to comfort you.

It can be helpful to recite the prayers you learned in childhood. As Herbert Benson says, it doesn't matter whether you pray or meditate; what matters is that you say the words over and over again until you achieve what he calls the "relaxation response."

Here are some suggestions for prayers, meditations, and chants that can inspire strength and hope. I have also provided a list of organizations that, upon request, will pray for you. The addresses and other contact information for these organizations is provided in the Resource Guide in the back of this book.

- Pray directly to the archetypal Holy Mother, however you conceive of her. The mother is seen by many as the source of unconditional love. Pray to her in the morning, during the day, and at night. Praying to the Holy Mother is especially powerful whenever we feel anxious or afraid.
- A very simple, yet powerful spiritual practice is to read a chapter a day from either the Old or New Testament. If you do practice this consistently, you very likely will experience a profound transformation in your feelings about yourself, your life, and your relationship with God. Consistent reading of the Bible promotes strong belief and deep faith in the God's love.
- Read passages or chapters from other sacred literature, such as the Koran, the Bhagavad Gita, the Sutras of Shakyamuni Buddha, the Vedas, and the Upanishads.

Chanting

You can purchase CDs and tapes for all types of chanting, including Sufi, Hindu, Buddhist, Jewish, and Gregorian chanting. Among the most commonly chanted words is *om,* which, in the Hindu tradition, is the sacred sound of the universe. It is widely believed that when you chant the sound of *om* again and again, you align yourself with the rhythm and the energy of the Self, Atman, or God. Chanting *om* creates for many a deep state of reverence, relaxation, and meditation. For those who have trouble emptying their minds during meditation, chanting *om* before meditation can free you of much distress, anxiety, and excessive thinking. Therefore, it is an ideal chant to use before you meditate.

Nam Myo Ho Renge Kyo is a Buddhist chant that means devotion to the mystic law of cause and effect through sound. Nam My Ho Renge Kyo is believed, by some Buddhist sects, to be the highest sound or vibration people can utter. It opens the spiritual channel, or tube of energy that runs down the center of the body, boosting the life force to every cell and fiber of the body and spirit. Nam Myo Ho Renge Kyo is one of the most physically and spiritually empowering chants ever created. Try chanting it slowly or rapidly and rhythmically and see what effects it has on your physical and emotional well-being.

An ancient Japanese chant is Su, a sound that is designed to open the heart. Another ancient chant is a derivation of *om,* A-U-M, which is designed to open three centers of the body-mind. The sound "A" is intended direct energy to the bladder, reproductive, and pelvic region; "U" directs energy to the center of the chest and opens the heart; "M" directs energy to the throat and head. This chant grounds you deeply in your body and autonomic nervous system, the branch of the nervous system that runs to your organs and muscle tissue. It will reduce excessive thinking and allow you to feel centered and balanced in your body.

Chanting is incredibly energizing and strengthening. Choose any sound that you have a heartfelt connection to and chant it throughout the day. You can chant a sacred sound quietly to yourself and out loud in the privacy of your home or in a peaceful natural environment, such as a forest or by a lake or the sea.

Meditations

Watch Your Breath

Among the oldest, simplest, and most powerful meditation techniques is the act of sitting peacefully and concentrating on your breath. This meditative tool can be used in a quiet setting, such as your home, but also at any time in the day, even in the most crowded or stressful situations. It will immediately bring about feelings of greater calm and self-control.

Wherever you are, begin this meditation by placing both feet on the floor; place your hands comfortably in your lap; and drop your shoulders. Release a long exhalation. Feel the tension drain from your body. Envision the muscles in your low back and pelvis releasing and opening. Feel yourself sinking ever more deeply into your body.

Now, observe your breath with your mind. As you breathe, concentrate on the out breath. With each exhalation, feel the tension leaving your body. Your exhalation is actually allowing you to settle ever more deeply into your body. Your exhalation becomes a tool for releasing deeper and deeper layers of tension.

When thoughts arise, observe them as if you were merely witnessing them. You are an observer, a witness to your mind, but not a participant. As much as possible, do not engage your thoughts, anxiety, or fears. They are merely clouds passing gently before you. Let the wind take them where it will.

Memories and emotions may rise as you do this exercise. Observe these with the same dispassion. Your body is an enormous vase that contains many thoughts, emotions, and memories. As you relax and watch your breath, your body will try to release these mental images. They create tremendous tension and fear in your body and contribute to your illness. Let them go. Let your body cleanse itself. Come back to your breath. When a thought or memory or emotion rises, it will try to pull you into its drama. Observe it as it rises and fades away. Do not judge anything that comes up. Don't get hooked by it. Don't fight it. Don't repress it. Allow it to rise, appear before your mind's eye, then fade away. If you find yourself engaging in any thought, memory, or emotion, come back to your breath. Don't engage in any recrimination of yourself. This is a practice that you will get better at. Exhale. Let the tension be released from your body. Watch your breath.

Eventually, you will come into a state of deep relaxation and calm. With practice, you will get so good at this that you will want to stay for as long as possible.

The Light Meditation

(Before doing this meditation, you may want to tape record the instructions in advance and then play the tape as a guide to your meditation. When you record the meditation, speak slowly in a calm, supportive, and loving voice.)

Begin this meditation by sitting peacefully in a quiet place in your home, or in nature. Choose a place where you will not be disturbed or interrupted. Get comfortable. Place your hands in your lap and release a long exhalation. Drop your shoulders. Observe your breath with your mind and concentrate on releasing the tension from your body with every exhalation. Feel yourself sinking ever more deeply into your body. Let your mind relax and try to empty it of any thoughts. Observe your breath.

When you feel sufficiently relaxed, imagine a small diamond of light suddenly appearing in the area of your heart. Observe this light and notice that it is extremely powerful and determined. You realize that this is a living entity that is connected to an infinite source of energy. It has the purest, most loving of intentions. It has come to help you.

As you observe this light, you see it slowly grow larger. The center of the light is expanding, as are its radiant beams. It fills your heart with a warm sensation of love, joy, and peace. It continues to grow. Now it is filling your entire chest with these same healing sensations.

A thick beam of light grows from the bottom of this starlike energy and moves into your stomach, intestinal area, and pelvis. It permeates every cell in your digestive tract, abdomen, reproductive organs, and your entire pelvis. You feel its healing energy invading every square inch of your lower body. No cell is left in the dark. All are alive and strengthened with this healing energy of light. All the tension in your lower body is giving way to this light. Any obstruction must break up and dissolve before its overwhelming power. You can see the darkness and blockages break up and fade into the atmosphere outside your body. Every cell that is diseased is either restored to the light or dies instantly.

From the star at the center of your chest, another beam grows upward and spreads this same healing energy into your shoulders, armpits, neck, and head. It infuses your entire upper body with a powerful light that overcomes all darkness, all tension, all resistance. You feel it permeating your entire nervous system, every cell and fiber of your upper body. The light fills your head with love and compassion.

From your armpits, the light is moving down into your arms and hands, again filling every cell with healing energy. It bursts forth from your fingertips.

From your pelvis and reproductive organs, the light moves down into your thighs, knees, calves, ankles, and feet. The light fills every cell, then bursts out from your toes.

Your entire body is now infused with light, love, and healing energy. The light grows beyond the boundaries of your body so that you find yourself sitting in a ball of light and love.

Notice that the light that engulfs your body is now radiating outward and joining an enormous source of energy just above your head. You are now aware that the energy that imbues your body is joined with an infinite source of unconditional love and healing energy that is being channeled into you. It pours into your body and soul so that your radiance is suddenly a hundredfold brighter. Your heart welcomes this abundant energy and distributes it throughout your body, especially to those places that need it most.

Bathe in this energy and the love, warmth, and compassion in which it holds you. Use your breath to direct the energy to anyplace that it is needed. Relax and sit in this energy until you are ready to emerge from the meditation.

Ask Others to Pray for You

Every church, synagogue, and temple offers community prayers for those who are suffering with illness or some other difficult circumstance. Ask your local religious community to include you in their prayers. If you have a close-knit group of friends who are spiritually oriented, ask your friends to form a prayer support group.

There are many religious-based groups that will pray for you, however. Among them are the Carmelite Nuns, which have monasteries throughout the world. The Carmelite Nuns, an order of cloistered Catholic nuns, spend their entire lives praying for those in need of help. They will pray for anyone in need of help. Virtual Jerusalem, an organization of Jewish people found on the Internet, accepts prayer requests from anyone. There are also many Protestant sects that also accept requests for prayers on an ongoing basis. Addresses for these and other organizations can be found in the Resource Guide in the back of the book.

All spiritual practices, no matter what their religious source, should bring us back into an intimate and loving relationship with ourselves and with our perception of God. Spiritual practice is the act of attuning your awareness to your soul. So many people who became ill later told me that somewhere along the way, they lost track of themselves. The demands of their lives overtook them. Life sped up and got out of control. In the course of things, they found themselves relating more to the demands of the world than to the subtle urges of their inner lives. This, they say, is how they lost connection with themselves.

Prayer and meditation allow us to detach from the intensity and the demands of the world, so that we can come back into integrity with ourselves and the peace that lies within. Inside of each of us is a harmony that is not unlike healing waters. We slow down in meditation and drink from that harmony. Soon, we feel restored to our own center, and to a peace with the Presence that we refer to as God. In that peace, we can come to know ourselves at much deeper levels. We can open up to the guidance of our hearts and souls. With continual practice, we make decisions and act from a deeper knowing of who we are, what we need, and what we want to do with our lives. Ultimately, such practices can help us answer the question all of us are asking ourselves: What is my purpose for living?

STEP 7

Establish Goals and Find
a Purpose for Living

In 1993, Ann Moss, then fifty-eight years of age, suffered from severe heart disease and a form of cancer known as Hodgkin's disease. All of her coronary arteries were blocked, including the left main artery—one of three primary arteries that bring blood to the heart—which was 95 percent closed. Her blood cholesterol level was 300 mg./dl. "I had chest pain all the time," Ann recalled. "I couldn't brush my teeth or take a shower without having terrible chest pain. Every step I took caused more pain and fatigue. Most of the time, I had pain even at rest. I was taking nitroglycerin constantly. I had zero energy. I couldn't live a normal life anymore."

Ann, a resident of a Pittsburgh suburb, was already taking all the drugs that her doctors could prescribe. Her only hope lay with a coronary bypass operation, which bypasses one or more arteries to the heart with unobstructed vessels taken from the leg or chest. Without bypass surgery, she would be dead in three months, her doctors told her.

There was a problem, however. Radiation treatment, which Ann had been receiving for her Hodgkin's disease, had depleted her rib cage of calcium, leaving her bones thin and brittle. Her doctors feared that if they opened her chest, her rib cage would shatter to pieces, making it impossible for her bones to heal. As if this were not concern enough, Ann had already suffered a stroke and was twenty pounds overweight. Clearly, she might not survive the surgery. Yet, she needed the surgery to survive. Her doctor told her that, despite the risks, there was no alternative but to go ahead with the operation. But then something unexpected happened.

That summer, Ann's daughter saw a television show that featured John McDougall, M.D., who told his audience that virtually all major illnesses are caused by a diet rich in fat, protein, and processed foods. He also said that these illnesses could be prevented and many of them reversed by eating a diet such as the one he recommended. McDougall had a clinic in the Santa Rosa, California, area, where he treated people with a wide range of illnesses with his diet and gentle exercise program. Ann's daughter told her mother of McDougall's statements and urged her to go to McDougall's clinic. Immediately upon hearing about Dr. McDougall, Ann realized that she had to go to Santa Rosa and soon told her doctor that she would not undergo the surgery.

"What are you going to do?" her doctor asked her. "Wait to die?"

"I'm going to California to be treated at Dr. McDougall's clinic," Ann replied. "Dr. McDougall has a diet, and it may be able to help me."

"How are you going to get there?" her doctor asked her.

"Fly, of course," Ann said, surprised by the question.

"The trip alone could kill you," her doctor warned. As for the idea that a diet could cure her of her multiple conditions, Ann's doctor thought the notion was ridiculous.

That September, Ann flew to San Francisco and was driven to McDougall's center, just outside of Santa Rosa. She arrived in a wheelchair, frail and obviously near death.

At first, all Ann could do was rest and eat McDougall's vegetarian diet. After a few days, however, Ann realized that her chest pain was subsiding. Encouraged by the small but significant progress, she got on the stationary bicycle and pedaled slowly for a grand total of three minutes. That's when exhaustion and pain hit her again. "That was all I could do," Ann said. "But it was a sign that I was getting better."

Ann spent twelve days at McDougall's center, and when she got home, she threw out all of the foods in her cupboard and refrigerator and restocked her kitchen entirely with whole grains, fresh vegetables, beans, and fruit. "When I got home, I followed the diet strictly. It was my only hope," Ann recalled. "I also started to walk. At first, I walked just to the end of my block, which has a slight elevation. I would go that far, and then turn around and come home. But I set these little goals for myself. Gradually, I started to increase the distance I walked. And then I bought a stationary bike and started doing two minutes, and later three minutes on the bike. I increased my time on the bike the same way I walked. I would say, 'Okay, today I'm going to four minutes on the bike,' and after a couple of weeks, I'd do five. I know that sounds like such small potatoes, but I was frightened all the time that I might kill myself."

Many of the routine activities that most of us take for granted were beyond Ann's capabilities. Which meant that she could mark her progress by her ability to do things that she couldn't do before.

"Things people take for granted, I was thrilled to do," said Ann. "As the months passed, I gradually realized that I could do more and more. By Christmas, I was also doing things I hadn't been able to do in years. I took showers without pain and walked every day. I was even able to go to the stores and shop again. One day I said to myself, 'Gosh, I'm doing all these things that I have not been able to do in years.'"

Her doctors were "amazed," Ann said. "They couldn't believe my tests. My heart was strong, I had lost weight, and my cholesterol level had fallen to 181. I have had no recurrence of my Hodgkin's disease. I weigh 114 pounds and I wear a size 6 petite dress. I have incredible energy and no health problems at all. I'm off all medication. My doctors just marveled, but they couldn't believe that through diet and exercise I could do all of this."

Ann said that changing her diet was not nearly as hard as she thought it might be. "I love to eat. I love food. But I was willing to switch over and for me it was easy because I love beans, rice, and vegetables, too. Then I saw the results, how much I was benefiting, and at that point the other lifestyle meant nothing to me."

As Ann became well, she underwent a remarkable metamorphosis. "I became an advocate for Dr. McDougall. I tell people everywhere about the power of diet to heal. And I am living proof of that power." At a certain point in her healing process, Ann realized that it was not enough for her simply to enjoy her newfound good health. She wanted to help others get well, too. Ann found ways of helping others by telling her story to people who were ill and by allowing reporters to write about her recovery. "I really want people to know that even when the doctors tell you you're finished, there's still hope."

The transformation that Ann underwent—from being overwhelmed by her disabilities to being an enthusiastic advocate for good health—is among the most common experiences on the healing path. Healing leads us inevitably to our desire to be of service to others.

At the seventh step on the healing path, we start to feel the positive effects of our healing program and begin to see the possibility of recovery. Our life force rises, and we start to believe in our own future. To reinforce that connection with the future, we establish goals. Those goals are both near- and long-term. They are, in effect, points on a map that direct us toward our ultimate goal, which is the full restoration of our health. As our near-term goals are met, we become practiced at creating the future. At first, this is, and must be, a self-oriented process, but as our health improves, the goals we set become bigger and increasingly linked to the health and happiness of others. This growing need to be of service redefines who we are. In the process, we move from a narrow, personal image of ourselves, to a more universal understanding of who we are. That universal perspective offers us the fulfillment of our life's purpose.

The Power of Goals to Promote Healing and Extend Life

There is a mysterious power in having a goal that lies outside of oneself. The goal becomes a bright light hung in a future, a future that would otherwise be in darkness. The yearning to achieve such a goal animates the will to survive and marshals the life-giving powers that still lie within you. Very often, those powers alone are enough to extend your life.

Evidence of this phenomenon came in an odd story published on the front page of the *New York Times*. On January 15, 2000, the *Times* reported an extraordinary rise in the death rate in New York City during the first seven days of the year 2000. That death rate was far above the rates experienced during the first seven days of previous years. The reason for this dramatic increase in mortalities, scientists speculated, was that the year 2000 held very special significance for people. Those who were close to death, and might otherwise have died in December 31, 1999, essentially willed themselves to live long enough to see the sun rise on the new millennium. Once they did that, they departed—in very high numbers, according to New York City statistics.

"The will to live can be pretty powerful," said Robert N. Butler, founder and president of the International Longevity Center, a research center that studies the factors that lead to longer life. Experts interviewed by the newspaper made it clear that "many people who would not have otherwise survived carried themselves into the new year through sheer resolution."

Richard M. Suzman, associate director at the National Institute on Aging in Bethesda, Maryland, told the *Times,* "It's pretty well established that people who are seriously ill will hang on to reach significant events, whether they are birthdays, anniversaries, or religious holidays. In this case, making it into the next century or new millennium certainly counts as that." Suzman said that the mechanisms for prolonging life to meet certain goals are still a mystery, "But the phenomenon is very real."

Pioneering oncologist Carl Simonton, M.D., noticed this same phenomenon in his treatment of people with cancer. Simonton realized that certain patients responded much better to chemotherapy and radiation than others who were equally ill. In his book, *Getting Well Again* (Bantam Books, 1978), written with Stephanie Matthews-Simonton and James L. Creighton, Simonton reported that those who responded well to treatment had strong reasons to go on living. These reasons varied dramatically. Some wanted to resolve issues with their children or spouse. Others wanted to complete an important business transaction. Still others wanted to realize a particular ambition that they had set for themselves. Some of these people made remarkable recoveries. "When asked to account for their good health," Simonton wrote, "they would frequently give such answers as, 'I can't die until my son graduates from college,' or 'They need me too much at work,' or 'I won't die until I've solved the problem with my daughter.'"

Simonton recognized early on that the most health-promoting

goals were those that were both highly personal and extremely important to the person. "Whatever the goals," the authors wrote in *Getting
Well Again,* "they had special meaning to the patient—strong enough,
apparently, to significantly enhance their will to live." Simonton concluded that "those who are 'around longer' are precisely the ones who
make life worth living by investing themselves in something significant
to live for."

How To Set and Achieve Your Personal Goals

The effort to identify and articulate your goals can be a source of inner
comfort and peace. Deciding what you want in life, whether it be an immediate or long-term desire, can be an extremely healing, compassionate, and loving gift that you give to yourself. Sometimes the answers are
less important than the exercise itself. Ask yourself, with real compassion, what you would like for yourself right now. Ask yourself, with true
understanding for how difficult your path has been, what you wanted to
become when you were a child. Is there any part of that dream that has
any relevance to you now? If so, what can you do now to get closer to
that goal? Sometimes this process can get you closer to your true nature
and your long-denied ambitions. In fact, illness itself can be the stimulus
to essential life changes. How many times have we heard of people who,
upon being diagnosed with a serious disease, quit the jobs they hated and
took up an avocation that they always dreamed of pursuing? Such dramatic life changes, though common, are not always necessary. Very often, the new direction that we seek lies buried in the mystery of the
illness itself and the imbalances that gave rise to it.

If you take a little time to reflect, you will discover all kinds of long-
ings within you that have been waiting to be heard and fulfilled. The
kinds of activities people engage in at this stage in their lives are endless.
One man I know took up pool after being diagnosed with prostate cancer in his late fifties. He had always loved watching the game, but only
rarely played—that is, until the diagnosis came. Now, in his late sixties
he's a crack player and has developed a circle of friends with whom he
plays several times a week. A woman I know resumed her piano lessons
after being away from the instrument for more than forty years. "It's the

most calming, soothing thing I do," she told me after performing at a recital. "It puts me in another world, a very beautiful world." Once we start setting and achieving our goals, we become aware of the many things we would like to do with the rest of our lives.

People who haven't set goals before becoming ill often find it difficult to articulate exactly what they would like to accomplish, besides the overriding goal of getting well. Yet, we need short-term, interim goals to help us achieve our larger ambition. Here are five general areas of our lives that we can examine in order to find our own true goals and desires. Keep in mind that these are suggestions to stimulate your own reflections and help you find your own goals.

My goal is to boost my immune system and recover my health by adopting a healing diet. To achieve that goal, I will do the following:

- I will prepare and eat a healing breakfast, lunch, and dinner seven days a week, and enjoy only healing snacks and desserts. (See Chapter 9 for menu plans.)
- I will avoid all foods that injure my health and impede my healing.
- I will attend cooking classes in order to learn how to prepare healing foods and make them delicious and satisfying to my palate.

My goal is to improve my health, fitness, energy levels, and endurance. To achieve that goal, I will do the following:

- I will walk six days a week, for a specific distance, at a specific time of the day (both to be determined by you).
- I will increase that distance and/or the time I walk by this increment (to be determined by you).
- I will adopt one other form of exercise or physical activity that I have always longed to participate in, such as a martial art, or Qigong, or yoga, or ballroom dancing, or tango, or tennis. I will engage in that activity for a specific number of days per week (to be determined by you).

My goal is to heal my heart, to forgive and be forgiven, and to bring more love into my life. To achieve that goal, I will do the following:

- I will start seeing a loving, supportive, and competent healer or counselor for a specific number of meetings each month (to be determined by you).
- I will attend a support group that is specifically designed to help people who are struggling with challenges similar to my own.
- I will write in a journal a specific number of times per week (to be determined by you) in order to confess all my fears, yearnings, anger, and pain; to report my progress on my healing program; to express my gratitude; and to connect to my inner self and personal needs.
- I will change a specific pattern or characteristic in my personality that I have identified as an impediment to my happiness, and the happiness of those around me.
- I will recognize and appreciate a specific talent or ability that I have (such as humor, wit, humility, compassion, nonjudgment) which I love about myself, makes me happy, and makes others happy, and find specific ways to engage in that ability more often.
- I will forgive the person/persons whom I love and who has/have hurt me. (Guidance for forgiveness provided in Chapter 4.)
- I will ask forgiveness from those I love whom I have injured. I will also attempt to establish a new relationship with my loved ones based on forgiveness, compassion, communication, and love.
- I will practice expressing the thoughts and the love that are in my heart, especially to those I love.
- I will do the Pennebaker method (described in Chapter 5) in order to forgive and heal myself from the pain caused by traumatic, shame-filled, and painful experiences I have had.
- My goal is to spend time and strengthen my relationship with a specific person whom I love but haven't been with in some time.

My goal is to improve the quality of my life and to enjoy my life more. To achieve that goal, I will do the following:

- I will listen to my body and rest whenever I feel I need to rest, no matter what demands may be going on around me.
- I will listen to my heart and take a specific amount of time every day to engage in an activity that is meant purely for my own enjoyment and pleasure or to satisfy a specific need that has arisen in me.

- I will take up a hobby or pastime (the activity to be determined by you) that I have always wanted to enjoy. I will do this simply for the fun, the joy, and the satisfaction that this pastime provides me. (Among the activities that people often take up at this time are painting, drawing, singing lessons, building model ships, learning a musical instrument or a second language, or writing their memoirs. Many people research a particular time in history, or study a particular subject, that has always fascinated them.)
- I will carefully plan and visit a particular place that I have always longed to see, or a site that is important to my life.

My goal is to experience reunion with my soul and peace with my Creator. To achieve my spiritual goals, I will do the following:

- I will engage in a specific spiritual or religious practice every day (to be determined by you).
- I will seek out and find an understanding, compassionate, and loving spiritual counselor.
- I will practice nonjudgment of myself and others and refrain from negative thinking about myself and others.
- I will read spiritual or religious literature that uplifts and inspires me. I will do this a specific number of times per week (frequency to be determined by you).
- I will find ways of being of service to others through charitable works and by sharing myself in ways that support and express love to others.
- I will ask a spiritual or religious group to pray for me. (See the Resource Guide for groups who will pray for you upon request.)

Keep in mind that the active pursuit of the goals you identify has an immune-boosting and health-promoting effect. They alone can stimulate your will to live, which in turn can marshal your healing forces.

Finding Purpose in Illness Can Lead to Purpose in Life

The act of establishing and achieving goals is based, itself, on making a deeper connection to your own inner nature. It is as if your happiness depends on your continuing efforts to know yourself. Inevitably, your pursuit of self-knowledge leads you to your greatest need of all—to find meaning and purpose in your life.

Twentieth-century humanistic psychologist Abraham Maslow said that only when our most basic needs are met—our needs for survival and safety—can we even consider our needs for love and belonging. And only when those are met can we consider our greatest need of all, which Maslow called "self-actualization." To be self-actualized, said Maslow, is to be what you were "born to be," or to fulfill your purpose for living. That can only come when you offer up your unique abilities, experience, wisdom, and love to the service of others.

One of the remarkable gifts to be gained from the healing path is that it can show us how illness can offer us the possibility of self-actualization. The knowledge and wisdom gained from your experiences with illness, combined with your unique talents, can become the means for you to serve the greater good.

"We call it, 'getting a second bite of the apple,'" says Robert Pritikin, son of the founder of the Pritikin Longevity Center and its former director. "Many people who come to the Pritikin Longevity Center have been told by their doctors that there's no more hope. They're finished. And then, by some miracle, they recover their health and suddenly they're given a second chance. They get to take a second bite of the apple. Many of them want to do something positive with their lives. They want to fulfill a lot of the dreams that they couldn't even think about when they were sick, dreams that they thought had no chance of ever being fulfilled. Every time we get a second chance, we think those kinds of thoughts."

Perhaps "those kinds of thoughts" come from a part of us that is committed to making the world a kinder, gentler place. In Buddhism, that aspect of our humanity, which all of us possess, is called the bodhisattva nature. It is animated by compassion and a desire to bring all sentient beings to a higher state of happiness and awareness. It's common for people who have had a brush with death to awaken to this aspect of our humanity. Having suffered a serious illness, and having been brought to the edge of the abyss, a change comes over us. We now know firsthand that death is an inevitability, if not now then sometime in the future. This direct knowledge that physical existence has an expiration date awakens us to another dimension of awareness, one that emphasizes spirit over matter, and what we have in common over our differences. In this awareness, compassion, balance, and acceptance of death are guiding principles.

In *The Way of Hope* (Warner Books, 1989), I wrote about long-term survivors of AIDS who adopted a healing diet and way of life that lead to enhanced immune function and, for some, longer life. Virtually everyone who adopted this way of living recognized early on its importance to the survival of their community and society at large. Oscar Molini, a successful New York artist who contracted AIDS in the early eighties, told me that very early in the AIDS crisis, the gay community established an information network to communicate any possible therapies that might be helpful to men suffering from AIDS. Oscar's lifestyle had boosted his CD4 cells count (in those days referred to as T-cells) and extended his life far beyond what his doctors had expected.

"I have survived a lot longer than anyone expected, even me," Oscar told me in 1985. "If I can go on living and sharing my story with people, my life will have made a difference. I think I've already made a difference. That's very important to me."

Ralph Donsky, whom I wrote about in Chapter 5, is another example of how illness can give us purpose. With his ribs and spinal vertebrae crumbling from every sudden movement, Ralph dreamed about the day when he could use his special talents to be of service to others. Since he was a child, Ralph's hobby was practicing magic tricks, and by the time he had reached adulthood, he was a pretty good magician. As he lay in bed, nearly overcome with despair, Ralph fantasized about performing magic for children and telling people about how he recovered from a rare tumor and a heart attack. "I gave myself the goal of performing magic for children who were ill," Ralph told me. "I spent many hours trying to figure out the best way to present my magic tricks and the stories or 'patter' that would accompany it."

Many people fantasize about doing such good works one day, but Ralph made good on his promise to himself. After he recovered, he regularly volunteered at St. Francis Medical Center in Hartford, Connecticut, where he performed his magic for children and adults with cancer.

"I would go to the pediatric and then adult oncology floors every Sunday for two to four hours," Ralph recalled. "I bought myself a Winnie the Pooh bag to transport my magic tricks and made myself a special shirt with the words, 'Magic Ralph' and Disney characters embroidered on it.

"Usually there were family members and friends with the children who were ill, so I tried to get everyone involved in the fun. It's hard on the parents to visit their sick child, so the family needed something to smile about, too. My goal was not only to get the child who was ill to smile, but also to get the child to say a few magic words and laugh. Sometimes I would get the kids to say alakazam or some other magic word so loudly that it would amaze the nurses, who had not been able to get a peep out of the child.

"The feeling of satisfaction I felt in return for getting very ill children to smile or laugh, and to cheer up their families, too, was more rewarding than anything I had ever felt in my life," Ralph recalled.

"When I showed my magic to adults, I would add a short inspirational talk about how I had been a patient lying in the same hospital bed, a short time ago. I would bend over to show them the curvature in my upper back and tell them how I almost died from my heart attack and a rare tumor that made my bones break."

Today, Magic Ralph continues to perform on the second Sunday of each month at the All Children's Hospital in Saint Petersburg, Florida. And he continues to amaze children and adults alike with his magic tricks and remarkable story of recovery.

Having such a purpose is indispensable. Without it, our lives seem pointless and futile. We are reduced to being little more than consumers. With it, we gain clarity and direction. Purpose becomes our organizing principle, our guide for making decisions, our reason for being. Purpose gives us the experience of our own uniqueness, as well as our connection to the greater whole. Thus, it offers us the very balance between the personal and the universal that we all seek. In the end, purpose gives us the experience of being heroic, which, if we direct our thoughts toward the heavens, can give us a sense of connection with God.

Carl Jung expressed it this way. "Nobody could rob me of the conviction that it was enjoined upon me to do what I wanted. That gave me that strength to go my own way. Often I had the feeling that in all decisive matters I was no longer among men, but was alone with God."

In the opening pages of her book, *Everyday Grace,* Marianne Williamson quotes Albert Einstein's famous thoughts on what might be called the delusion of individuality.

"A human being is a part of the whole called the 'universe,' a part limited in time and space. He experiences himself, his thoughts, and feelings, as something separate from the rest, a kind of delusion of . . . consciousness. This delusion is a kind of prison for us, restricting us to our personal desires and to affection for a few persons nearest to us. Our task must be to free ourselves form this prison by widening our circle of compassion to embrace all living creatures and the whole of nature in all its beauty. Nobody is able to achieve this completely, but the striving for such achievement is in itself part of the liberation and a foundation for inner security."

As so many before him, Einstein made clear that the human journey leads inevitably toward what is common among us.

The Mystery Provides the Answers

The inevitable question is: How can I be of service and find my purpose for living?

The answer to that question may be more simple than many of us think. For one thing, service itself is an act of kindness that is possible with virtually every interaction. In addition, every community offers many hundreds of volunteer opportunities, all of them designed to help others. These, of course, are generic answers to a question that all of us want a personal answer to. For that we must pursue what we love. "Follow your bliss," mythologist Joseph Campbell advised, because it is the soul's compass and the surest expression of your heart. The exercises given above that help us establish goals can also help us identify what we love. At that point, it is up to us to follow the path of love. None of us know where that path is leading. But if we pursue it with sincerity and commitment, it can provide answers and open up worlds that we never dreamed possible. Nathan Pritikin is a good example of what is possible when we pursue the healing path to its richest rewards.

Pritikin: The Actualized Man

After he cured himself of heart disease, Nathan Pritikin offered counseling to people with serious illnesses, many of whom were either beyond medical treatment or in need of heroic measures. One of the people he counseled at the time was Eula Weaver, who, at the age of eighty-one, hobbled into Nathan's office suffering from heart disease, severe angina pain, high blood pressure, arthritis, and claudication (obstruction of the circulation of the legs). She had already had a heart attack and couldn't walk more than a hundred steps without severe chest and leg pain. Her circulation was so bad that she had to wear gloves all year round in order to keep her hands warm. Now, after seeing a long list of doctors and taking every conceivable medication, Eula Weaver was diagnosed as beyond hope of recovery. Nathan put her on his diet, taught her to cook whole grains, vegetables, and beans, and asked her not to veer from his recommendations. She didn't. A month later, Pritikin urged Mrs. Weaver to take a short walk each day. Gradually, as her condition improved, Nathan increased the distance Mrs. Weaver walked. A year later, she was off all medication, free of all her previously severe symptoms, and was jogging every day. At the age of eighty-five, Mrs. Weaver entered the Senior Olympics and won two awards for the 800- and 1,500-meter races. She competed in the Senior Olympics for six consecutive years and won twelve awards. She became something of a star at the senior games and was written about in numerous newspapers, including the *National Enquirer*.

That blast of publicity brought Pritikin more patients, many of them suffering from severe and sometimes bizarre conditions. Nathan treated them all, with most experiencing tremendous improvements in health. His love of the subject of diet, health, and science led him to deeper study. Eventually, he wrote a three-volume treatise on the relationship between diet and a wide variety of illnesses, including heart disease, cancer, diabetes, high blood pressure, circulatory diseases, arthritis, hearing loss, and disorders of the eyes.

In 1975, Pritikin set out to prove that his diet could cure coronary heart disease by conducting an experiment in cooperation with the Long Beach, California, Veterans Hospital. Nathan recruited thirty-eight men, all with proven heart disease. Most of them also suffered from other severe illnesses, such as claudication, angina pectoris (chest pain), arthritis, gout, high blood pressure, and high cholesterol. Pritikin also recruited John Kern, M.D., chief of medicine at the Long Beach V.A. Hospital, and his son, Robert Pritikin, who cooked for the men and supervised their practice of the diet and exercise program each day. He then got Loma Linda University to do before-and-after angiograms, a test that could reveal the degree of atherosclerosis in the arteries, on the men's femoral arteries, located in the legs.

Six months later, twelve men remained on the diet and exercise program. Their results were better in many respects than Pritikin had dared dreamed. The twelve experienced a 6,000 percent increase in their walking distance, the greatest improvement in walking distance in people with claudication ever recorded in the scientific literature. Men who couldn't walk a block at the outset of the study were walking five miles, many ten miles by the end of the six-month period. All of Pritikin's patients with angina were relieved of all chest pain and taken off all medication for angina. All of the men with gout, arthritis, and high cholesterol were also relieved of all symptoms and taken off all medication. Of those with high blood pressure, 75 percent were returned to normal blood pressure and taken off drugs. One of the men who was taken off his antihypertension drugs had been on medication for twenty years. Of this group of twelve, two showed reversal of atherosclerosis in the femoral arteries.

Pritikin wrote up his study and presented his results to the American Congress of Rehabilitation Medicine's national meeting, which was held in Atlanta, on November 19, 1975. The next day, the *Atlanta Journal* ran a front-page headline that read: "Heart Disease Breakthrough Offers Hope." "We beat out Franco's death as the lead story," Pritikin later said gleefully. The Associated Press picked up the story, and it was run in newspapers around the country. In a matter of days, Pritikin was swamped with mail asking for more information on his remarkable program.

"And I happened to think," Nathan recalled years later, "this would be an ideal time to put it into practice. If I wait for the medical community, it will be two hundred years. I better do it myself."

Thus was born the Pritikin Longevity Center, which opened initially in Santa Barbara in 1976, and later moved to Santa Monica and Florida. Since that time, the Longevity Center has treated more than eighty thousand people and the results—confirmed repeatedly by independent researchers—have been nothing short of miraculous.

Nathan Pritikin had no college degree and no formal medical education. By conventional standards, he was completely unqualified to have any impact on medicine and health care. Yet he saved the lives of thousands. Today, every medically based diet and exercise program is, one way or another, a copy of his work. Pritikin is proof of what can happen when we commit to a life of service and allow the mystery that we call God to determine how our lives unfold.

In the meantime, we can take comfort in the words of the Jewish sages, who taught the following: "If you save the life of a single person, you save the entire world."

From Me to We

We began the healing journey by embracing the need to practice compassion for ourselves. That is the foundation step, one that never should be let go of. Every step on the healing path transforms us physically, emotionally, and spiritually. As we progress on our path, we set goals for ourselves, goals that serve as points on a map. Our progress mysteriously awakens that part of our humanity that experiences its connection with others and our need to be of service. This aspect of our consciousness embraces what is common, or universal, among us. This larger awareness inside of us is motivated by the knowledge that physical existence is limited.

But that begs the question, If the death is inevitable, what's the point of the healing journey?

What Is the Meaning of Our Search for Health?

Healing, no matter how deeply it occurs, is only temporary. Our struggle for good health ultimately leads to a dead end. How do we reconcile one of life's most vexing paradoxes—that all of us are designed to desire health, yet our struggle to achieve it will end in failure? And that failure will be eminently personal.

When it was reported that the Indian spiritual teacher, Krishnamurti, had pancreatic cancer, one of his students came to him in anguish, and asked the great man, "Why?"

Krishnamurti, who at the time was well into his nineties, looked at his student with compassion, and said, "The body needs an excuse."

Thus, in his profoundly simple way, Krishnamurti had articulated yet another fundamental truth that all of us must finally accept. The body is committed to finding its way to death. It arose from the elements of the earth, and like a river that is bound for the sea, the body is determined to return to its source.

We cannot help but stand back in awe in the face of such a mystery.

It's almost as if that greatest of all mysteries, God, forced us to wrestle with questions whose ultimate purpose was to remind us of our limitations and, indeed, our place in the grand scheme of things.

Many people insist that we are better off ignoring the paradox entirely and instead indulge our desires until the inevitable arrives. But our need to understand health and illness is embedded in our genes. Humans have been designed by nature to adapt in order to survive. Effective adaptation means being able to identify the threat in our environment, then change our behaviors in order to overcome that threat. This characteristic is responsible for all the progress made by the human race—everything from indoor heating and plumbing to the ongoing search for solutions to disease. Whenever we find ourselves beset by illness, we naturally search for answers.

Unfortunately, it is extremely unlikely that we will ever fully understand all the inherited and environmental variables that prevent illness or overcome death. And for all but a small percentage of people, death is preceded by sickness. Being sick and dying is part of what it means to be human. So, too, is our determination to stay alive.

But if we are all doomed to fail in that search, then how could there be meaning in our struggle, except to know that God is bigger than we are? Does our pursuit of health have any greater purpose?

When we look at the behaviors that determine health, we immediately realize that something other than just the body is being affected. As we change our ways of eating and grow more active, as we develop greater compassion for ourselves and others, as we forgive and are forgiven, as we give and receive more love, and as we pray and meditate, we are altering the most fundamental aspect of our nature—the "I" that each of us calls me. That "I," for lack of a better word, might be called consciousness. Consciousness may be nothing more than what we have learned and now know. And at the center of that knowing is that identity each of us experiences as "I", "me," and "self."

Our pursuit of health alters consciousness and the "I" at its center. You are fundamentally changed by each of the seven steps, even when they do not alter your physical health. The healing journey offers transformational experience and knowledge on every level of our existence. On the physical level, we learn that certain types of foods and activities promote our health, vitality, clarity of mind, balance of emotions, and our capacity to understand and to love.

On the psychological and emotional levels, we learn that loving ourselves requires compassion for ourselves, understanding, and a growing acceptance of who we are. We realize that we must be responsible for this marvelous physical gift, the human body, and for its health and healing. Yet, we cannot heal all alone. We need many different types of love—intimate love, friendship, respect, and a sense of belonging in our communities—to experience our wholeness and our health. As we progress on the healing path, we also learn that we can promote our health by remembering our pain, expressing it with compassion, and integrating our past into a state of self-acceptance and self-love. To be fulfilled, we need a sense of purpose that transcends our personal lives and provides love and service to others.

On a spiritual level, we learn that physical and psychological health is enhanced by prayer and meditation. Miraculously, we can be helped by the prayers of others, just as we can help others with our own prayers. We learn that there is a power in prayer, or to put it another way, that a power can flow to us through the act of prayer. Whatever the source of that power is, we realize that it can heal us.

The more we learn about prayer and meditation, the more the nature of the universe is revealed as a unified entity that transcends our rational understanding, or the limits of space and time. In order for each of us to more fully experience health, we must, in our own ways, become more unified, integrated, and whole ourselves. In short, we must strive to become like it.

As we change our behavior to adapt to the underlying laws that support health, we realize that we are being transformed. And perhaps that transformation is less of a physical change than a spiritual one. Perhaps all of these physical trials that we are going through are little more than the lessons our consciousness needs to grow. Or, to become more like the integrated and unified universe from which it springs.

But of what importance is consciousness if it dies with the body? we must ask. As most of us already know, there is a growing body of clues that suggests it doesn't.

A Living Consciousness Rooted in the Body

In the December 2001 issue of the British medical journal, *The Lancet,* Dutch cardiologist Pim van Lommel reported a study in which he and his colleagues interviewed 348 people who had survived cardiac arrest but were considered clinically dead for some extended period of time. These people had lost all signs of life and all brain function. Van Lommel found that 18 percent of these patients—nearly one in five—had had what has come to be known as full-fledged near-death experiences. The characteristics associated with such an experience are now widely known. Upon dying, people report leaving their bodies and examining the events that occur around their bodies from a point above the body itself. Soon they enter a tunnel and move rapidly toward a bright light. When they enter the world of light, they encounter relatives, friends, and a transcendent being who bathes them in unconditional love.

One of the people van Lommel included in his study was a man who suffered cardiac arrest and was pronounced clinically dead upon arriving at the hospital. While doctors attempted to resuscitate him, a nurse removed the man's dentures so that a breathing tube could be inserted into his mouth.

After the doctors saved the man's life, the man was placed in intensive care. Upon waking, he recognized the nurse who had removed his dentures and asked her to return his teeth. This shocked the nurse, because the man had been pronounced dead upon arrival at the hospital and did not regain consciousness while in the operating room. Indeed, he had lost all brain function before the nurse had actually taken out his dentures. Van Lommel later asked the man how he had recognized the woman. He replied that when he arrived in the operating room, he experienced himself leaving his body and witnessing the events from a point above the operating table. Van Lommel realized that since the man had no brain function, he could not have been "observing" the events with his mind, or even hallucinating a fantasy that later proved remarkably accurate. Something else was observing these events and informing this man of what was taking place around him.

Van Lommel speculated that it is possible that consciousness is not necessarily rooted in the brain but is grounded in the body. Van Lommel pointed out that each day 50 billion cells die. Yet the body continues to function as a whole, integrated, and coordinated unit. We do not perceive ourselves as different, even after all the cells of the body have been replaced. Van Lommel states that perhaps there is some form of communication that coordinates cellular function and maintains the body's overall sense of itself. This communication, he said, may very well be consciousness. If that is so, consciousness may not be found in the brain.

In fact, there are clues from other research that corroborate van Lommel's theory. Robert O. Becker, M.D., whom I mentioned in the Introduction, realized that there has to be some coordinating intelligence that maintains the overall function and integrity of the body. Since all the genes needed to grow any part of the body are present in every organ, why doesn't the liver—when it begins replacing cells—grow into a heart? How does a finger know not to grow into a toe or an eye?

These questions stimulated an extraordinary series of experiments by Becker and his colleagues on salamanders, animals that still possess the ability to regrow most of their body parts. If a salamander can regrow a leg or a tail, what stops it from growing a leg in the place where its tail belongs? Becker wanted to know.

In order to answer that question, Becker cut off a salamander's leg and allowed the leg cells to start to regrow. Before the leg had fully been replaced, he cut off the salamander's tail and placed the leg cells on the severed stump of the tail. This should have tricked the animal into growing a leg where its tail belonged, but it didn't. The budding leg cells soon changed and eventually produced a tail.

He then did the experiment in reverse. He cut off the tail and allowed the budding tail cells to grow. Once they started to appear, he cut off a leg and put the regrowing tail cells on the stump of the leg. It didn't take long before those tail buds turned into leg cells to produce a normal salamander leg. Ultimately, the salamander regrew a fully developed leg where the leg belonged, and a tail where the tail belonged.

"There is some mechanism within the living salamander that contains an overall plan for the salamander's body, and provides the information that instructs the blastema [newly formed cells] what tissue it should construct," Becker wrote in his book, *Crosscurrents*. That overall intelligence, Becker showed, was contained in the electrical field that surrounds the body, an energy body he called a "morphogenetic field." This field, he said, acts as a kind of blueprint for the body.

Becker demonstrated that this morphogenetic field permeates and surrounds the living body and directs cells to grow exactly the organs that they are meant to grow. The morphogenetic field holds within it highly complex information that instructs the DNA to produce only those cells and organs that are appropriate to the body's overall design. Becker called this morphogenetic field a second nervous system, with an awareness of a grand design. Another way of describing such an awareness is to refer to it as the human consciousness.

Consciousness Lives On

Traditional healers, religious figures, and shamans have long maintained that the body, mind, and spirit are a single unity, and that spirit is the animating force behind the body. This belief, which is as old as civilization, also asserts that consciousness, or the soul, utilizes the body in order to confront certain lessons that are needed for its own development. Therefore, whatever is happening to the body is also, in some way, happening to the spirit. By attempting to heal the body, the spirit is learning lessons all its own.

Together, Becker and van Lommel provide evidence that some form of energy body exists, and that this energy body contains both consciousness and profound intelligence that not only sustain the human body, but continue to exist after the body no longer survives. Indeed, this energy body, or consciousness, does not need the physical body in order to go on living.

"Consciousness lives on," says Michio Kushi, the world's leading teacher of macrobiotics. "It does not die." Kushi points out that while we are in our mother's womb, which for the fetus is a world of water, the body is nourished and developed within the placenta, or embryonic sac. In effect, the sac grows the body that will live after birth. When we are born, the sac is discarded without a second thought, and the body, which it helped to develop, continues to exist.

"Right now, our physical bodies are serving as an embryonic sac for our consciousness while we live in the world of air," Kushi says. "The consciousness that we are growing now will be our new body when we are born into the world of vibration and energy."

Kushi has long taught that, in the end, healing is a process of spiritual transformation, because as we treat the body in the ways already described, we are transforming the consciousness that lives within it. As he says, "Each of us is developing our new, unique constitution, which is our consciousness. That consciousness will be our new body that will be born into the world of spirit. We are developing that constitution on the basis of what we eat, how we think, and how we act toward each other."

Healing is at once a physical, emotional, and spiritual act. But in the end, it is ultimately spiritual. The healing work we do will help us sustain physical existence and postpone death for a significant amount of time. As we heal ourselves, we begin to experience what Wordsworth called intimations of immortality—the subtle clues that the miracle that we all hope for is true, and that something of us lives on in another form, a form that may be growing inside of us now.

The methods described in this book can help to heal the body, resolve inner conflicts, bring peace to our relationships, and give us an experience of connection with spirit. It can help us develop the consciousness that lives within us. All of which reveals the act of healing as a sacred quest, indeed a sacred path, on which can be found the greatest gifts offered by life.

9

✳

The Recovery Diet Program

The Recovery Diet is perhaps the single most powerful tool available to us in our quest for good health. The program I describe below will provide you with a complete supply of nutrition and an abundance of antioxidants, immune-boosting and cancer-fighting phytochemicals, and fiber. It is low in fat and cholesterol, yet it provides optimal amounts of protein. The carbohydrates on this diet are complex and slowly absorbed. They will provide you with an enduring energy and, very likely, a tremendous boost in your overall vitality. You will likely find yourself thinking more clearly, sleeping more deeply, and waking up with greater energy and inspiration. The diet is low in calories and high in satiety. That means that it will satisfy your hunger, while causing you to lose weight if you are overweight. One of the most common experiences on this diet is the ease with which people achieve their optimal weight, then remain at that weight without having to avoid meals or restrict food intake. You can eat until you are full—if you are overweight now, you'll still lose weight.

As you will see below, there is a great variety of foods to choose from. I have provided a twenty-one-day meal plan and more than fifty recipes to make your meals delicious and satisfying. I've also provided the Resource Guide to help you find dietary counselors, teachers, and other healers who can provide more information and personal assistance. If you are battling a serious illness, I urge you to remain under the guidance of your medical doctor; share the program you are following with him or her; and see a trained professional counselor for any one of the three dietary programs I recommend, namely, the macrobiotic diet and lifestyle, the Pritikin Program, or the McDougall Program. Information about all three programs is provided in the Resource Guide, as well as mail-order suppliers for food and other important supplies. For those with cancer who would like to adopt a dietary program as an adjunct form of treatment, I urge you to investigate and adopt the macrobiotic diet, since this is perhaps the most advanced dietary approach to malignancy.

A Snapshot Picture of the Recovery Diet

The Recovery Diet is composed of the following groups of foods:

Whole grains
Green and leafy vegetables
Round and sweet vegetables
Root vegetables
Beans and bean products
Sea vegetables
Fish
Condiments and oils
Soups
Snacks and desserts

Before I describe the diet in greater detail, I want to give you some tips for enjoying the food and promoting your health.

1. When you are first starting out, you need time. You're probably used to preparing foods that are very different from those on the

Recovery Diet, which means that you'll need time to learn how to cook the foods described here and in the recipe section. You'll also need time to allow your palate to adjust to the new flavors. Most people find that they can prepare and fully enjoy the Recovery Diet within a few weeks. By that time, you're comfortable cooking these foods, and you're already enjoying their flavor. You'll also see their positive effects on your health.

2. Chew your food for maximum flavor, sweetness, and health promotion. Try this experiment. Chew a mouthful of cooked brown rice until it is completely liquefied, which may require you to chew it fifty to sixty times. Notice that when you put the food in your mouth, you get an immediate burst of flavor. As you chew, some of the flavor falls off. However, if you continue to chew the rice, a second, more intense release of flavor and sweetness arises that's even more satisfying than the first hit of taste. Why? After it's been chewed for a short time, the food releases its carbohydrates from their fibrous matrix, thus giving you another round of sweetness and satisfaction. Chewing, of course, makes the food more digestible and the nutrients more easily assimilated into to your bloodstream. That, of course, will strengthen your immune and cancer-fighting forces. If possible, chew every mouthful between thirty-five and fifty times for maximum flavor, digestibility, and nutrient absorption.

3. Eat sweet and pulpy vegetables for fullness and satiety. The sweet vegetables include carrots, corn, beets, parsnips, onions, and squash. These foods are delicious and filling, and they bring flavor and satisfaction to every meal.

4. Use the condiments and sauces described below and in the recipe section to enhance the flavor of your food. Among the most health-promoting condiments are roasted sesame, black sesame, pumpkin seeds, seaweed shakes (tiny flakes of different types of sea vegetables), flakes of nori seaweed, and brown rice vinegar, especially on green vegetables. Vary your condiments. Avoid using fermented soy foods, such as miso, tamari, and shoyu at the table. These foods are delicious but moderately high in sodium. They are best used in cooking.

Let's have a closer look at the Recovery Diet.

Whole Grains

At least 2 servings per day. Whole grains include the following:

Amaranth. A very tiny grain—the size of a poppy seed—but exceptionally rich in nutrition, including protein, calcium, folic acid, magnesium, and iron. Amaranth is quick-cooking—boil for about thirty minutes with a pinch of sea salt—and produces a mild, nutty flavor.

Barley. Rich in soluble fibers that lower blood cholesterol, barley provides folic acid, magnesium, phosphorus, potassium, and zinc. It is immune-boosting and supportive of the heart, kidneys, and bones. In Chinese medicine, barley is used as a medicinal food for the liver, kidneys, bladder, and bones. Barley is typically eaten as "pearled," or slightly refined, but whole barley is available, as well. Cook as a soup with an array of vegetables, such as carrots, onions, leeks, and shiitake mushrooms. Pearled barley is boiled and ready to be eaten in about fifty-five minutes. (See recipes.)

Brown rice. Rich in complex carbohydrates, brown rice is a high-energy food that is also a good source of B vitamins (including thiamine and niacin), iron, phosphorus, and magnesium. It contains lysine, the amino acid often lacking in other grains, which makes it a good source of protein. Brown rice boosts brain levels of serotonin, the neurotransmitter that calms the nervous system and elevates mood and feelings of optimism, well-being, and concentration. Chinese healers use brown rice to strengthen and stabilize all health conditions. It is especially medicinal as an herb for the lungs and large intestine, as well as the nervous system and mood. Brown rice is grown in three sizes: short, medium, and long grain. It also is produced as sweet rice, which is the more glutinous variety. Sweet rice is pounded into patties to make mochi, a highly strengthening food that's delicious when cut into two-inch squares and cooked in soup with vegetables and miso. (See recipes.)

Buckwheat. Often referred to as a grass, rather than a grain, buckwheat comes as "groats" or small, grainlike berries. It provides a delicious, nutty flavor, especially when cooked with vegetables, such as carrots, or with sauerkraut. (See recipes.) Buckwheat is quick-cooking—boiled and ready in fifteen minutes. In Chinese medicine, buckwheat is used to strengthen the kidneys and bladder.

Millet. One of the nutritionally richest grains, millet provides substantial amounts of B vitamins, magnesium, copper, and iron. It is cooked with sea salt and a variety of vegetables, including carrots, onions, cauliflower. Delicious in soups. Millet is quick-cooking. It's boiled and usually ready in twenty-five minutes.

Oats. Oats comes as rolled or steel-cut or whole. Steel-cut are preferred for their nutritional value (they are far less refined than rolled) and quick-cooking—they usually require twenty to thirty minutes of boiling. Oats are especially rich in protein, iron, manganese, copper, folic acid, vitamin E, and zinc.

Quinoa. Considered by some nutritionists as a supergrain, quinoa is especially rich in protein, potassium, riboflavin, magnesium, zinc, copper, manganese, and folic acid. It is also quick-cooking—two cups of grain in four cups of water requires only fifteen minutes of boiling to produce a light, fluffy grain.

Wheat. Wheat comes as whole wheat berries, bulgur, couscous, pasta, and farina, among other forms. Each is progressively more processed than the one before it. Wheat is rich in protein, B vitamins, vitamin E, iron, magnesium, and manganese, just to name a few. Two wheat-derived foods worth mentioning for their flavor and protein content are fu, a chewy addition to soups that provides a mild, delicious flavor; and seitan, also known as "wheat meat." Seitan is meaty, glutinous, hearty, and very rich in protein. Like fu, it's great in soups and stews. Seitan can also be cooked with noodles and added to vegetable medleys.

Grain Products

Whole-grain products, such as wheat bread or pasta, are not whole grains, and are considered secondary sources of carbohydrates. Once a grain is milled, it starts to decay and loses both nutrition and life energy. The carbohydrates in bread and rolls are rapidly absorbed, which means they elevate insulin levels and promote inflammation.

Noodles are more slowly absorbed. That means that high-quality whole grain or lightly milled grains are preferable to bread and rolls.

More Preferred

Whole-grain noodles, made from amaranth, quinoa, brown rice, and whole wheat.

Udon or whole wheat noodles
Soba or buckwheat noodles
(See recipes for delicious noodle dishes.)

Less Preferred

Whole-grain bread and rolls, including breads made from brown rice, whole wheat, rye, and multigrains.

Vegetables

Eat at least nine servings of vegetables per day. Serving size does not matter. A soup with three vegetables constitutes three servings for that day. Eat a wide variety of vegetables from the following categories.

Green and Leafy Vegetables

Preferably steamed or boiled. Choose from any of the following.

Asparagus
Beet greens
Broccoli
Brussels sprouts
Cabbage, including napa cabbage

Carrot tops
Chinese cabbage
Collard greens
Curly dock
Dandelion greens
Endive
Escarole
Kale
Kohlrabi
Green peas
Leeks
Leek greens
Lettuce
Mustard greens
Parsley
Plantain
Scallion
Sorrel
Turnip greens
Watercress

Round and Sweet Vegetables

Beets
Green peas
Shiitake mushrooms
Onions
Squashes
    Acorn squash
    Butternut squash
    Hokkaido pumpkin
    Hubbard squash
    Pumpkin
    Yellow squash
    Zucchini
Snow peas

String beans
Sweet potatoes
Yams

Roots

Burdock
Carrot
Chicory root
Daikon radish
Dandelion root
Icicle radish
Lotus root
Parsnip
Red radish
Rutabaga
Salsify root
Turnip

Beans and Bean Products

Eat one serving of beans or bean products daily.

Beans are the vegetable kingdom's richest source of protein. They are also loaded with immune-boosting phytochemicals, including plant estrogens that protect against cancer. Soybeans and soybean products contain rich amounts of genistein and other isoflavones that protect against and fight cancer. Whole, cooked beans are preferred over tofu. Tempeh, a fermented food made from whole beans, is also preferred over tofu.

Aduki
Black beans
Black-eyed peas
Chickpeas
Lentils

Kidney beans
Lima beans
Navy beans
Pinto beans
Soybeans

Bean Products Include

Miso. A fermented soybean paste used to make soups, stews, and sauces. Miso is rich in friendly bacteria and many phytochemicals, including genistein, a powerful cancer-fighting isoflavone.

Shoyu. A fermented soybean liquid used to make soups, stews, and sauces. Also rich in genistein and other phytochemicals. Shoyu contains wheat.

Tamari. A fermented soybean liquid that does not contain wheat products. Rich in genistein and other phytochemicals.

Tempeh. Tempeh is composed of whole soybeans that have been formed into a patty and fermented. Like other fermented soybean foods, it is rich in friendly bacteria and many important phytochemicals, including genistein. Tempeh is also rich in protein and fiber.

Tofu. Processed to remove much of the fiber, tofu is made from soybeans. It is rich in calcium, protein, and phytoestrogens, including genistein.

Natto. A fermented soybean condiment. Whole soybeans that have been fermented in salt to produce a condiment for whole grains, noodles, and vegetable dishes.

Sea Vegetables

One serving per day. Limit serving size to one-to-two tablespoons.

Sea vegetables are among the most nutrient-rich foods on the planet. They are loaded with antioxidants, vitamins, minerals, and phytochemicals that boost the immune system and fight all diseases, including cancer.

Those who do not already enjoy sea vegetables might consider starting off with sushi nori, or flavored (spicy) nori. No preparation is needed. Simply take the paper-size sheet from the package, wrap some rice, other grains, or vegetables into the nori, and eat as if it were a rice or vegetable roll. Both delicious and highly nutritious.

Use wakame and kombu in soups and stews. Simply break off a few leaf-size pieces of wakame, or place a stalk of kombu in the broth of soups and stews. These sea vegetables provide a very mild flavor—many don't notice the flavor at all—but they enrich your entrée with an abundance of immune boosting nutrients.

(See recipe section for instructions on how to prepare sea vegetables.)

Alaria. Rich in B vitamins, vitamins C and K, many trace elements.

Arame. Rich in vitamins A and B, carbohydrates, calcium, many other minerals, and trace elements.

Dulse. Rich in protein, vitamins A, C, E, and B vitamins, iodine, minerals, and trace elements.

Hijiki. Loaded with nutrition, including protein, vitamins A and B family, calcium, phosphorous, iron, and many trace elements.

Irish moss. Used as a thickening agent for soups and stews, rich in vitamins A and B1, iron, sodium, calcium, and other trace elements.

Kombu. A great source of antioxidants, B vitamins, iron, sodium, calcium, and other trace elements.

Nori (including sushi nori). Perhaps the easiest sea vegetable to use and the one most acceptable to the novice palate, nori is rich in vitamins A, B family, C, and D, calcium, phosphorous, iron, and trace elements.

Wakame. Rich in vitamins A and B1, iron, sodium, calcium, and other trace elements.

Fruit

Preferably in season and capable of growing in your climate.

Fish

Choose white fish, such as cod, scrod, haddock, flounder, halibut, and sole. Avoid farm-raised salmon, which often contain trace amounts of growth hormones and antibiotics.

Condiments

Sesame seeds. Roast for additional flavor.
Black sesame seeds. Roasted
Flax seeds. Roasted
Pumpkin seeds. Roasted
Balsamic vinegar
Mirin
Umeboshi vinegar. A Japanese vinegar made from salted, pickled
    plums. Very tangy and delicious.
Rice vinegar
Wine vinegars
Grated ginger root. Fresh
Horseradish
Lemon and lemon juice
Mustard
Pepper
Pickles
Roasted sesame seeds (see seeds and nuts below)
Roasted sunflower seeds
Sauerkraut
Salsa

Oils

Preferred oils include the following: sesame oil, toasted sesame oil, and olive oil. Oil is liquid fat. Vegetable oils—referred to as polyunsaturated and monounsaturated fats—lower blood cholesterol levels somewhat, but excessive use of vegetable oils can weaken the immune system and may promote cancer. Sunflower oil and corn oil are rich in omega-6 polyunsaturated fats, which depress the immune system and promote cancer. Olive oil, a monounsaturated fat, contains omega-3 fatty acids and many phytochemicals. In small amounts, it can boost immune response, raise HDL cholesterol (the "good" cholesterol), and lower your risk of heart disease.

All oils should be minimized. Sauté twice or three times per week. If you are using diet as an adjunct to medical therapy, minimize oil as much as possible to maximize circulation, reduce weight, and prevent disease.

Snacks

As much as possible, use cooked, natural foods, such as soba noodles in vegetable broth, or cooked vegetables, or soup, as a snack. Avoid oily, sugared, or processed foods. Use whole grains as snacks for their fiber and vitamin and mineral content.

Raw fruit
Cooked fruit
Rice cakes
Puffed grains
Seeds and nuts, including sunflower seeds, pumpkin seeds,
   almonds, and walnuts

Sweeteners

The preferred sweeteners are rice syrup, barley malt, and apple juice. Minimize sweeteners because they contain sugars that are rapidly absorbed.

Beverages for Daily Consumption

- Noncarbonated springwater.
- Black and green tea. Tea contains far less caffeine than coffee—about 20 to 45 mg. of caffeine per cup of tea versus 125 to 200 mg. per cup of coffee, depending on how it is brewed. Tea is loaded with antioxidants and other immune-boosting chemicals. Avoid coffee. It's very toxic to the kidneys, liver, breast tissue, and reproductive organs.

Other Beverages

> Grain coffees, made without coffee beans or caffeine
> Herbal teas
> Kukicha or bancha twig tea

Foods to Avoid

- All red meat, pork, chicken, turkey, eggs, and dairy products.
- Processed foods, including muffins, pastries and rolls, even those made from whole wheat. These foods are rich in calories and are rapidly absorbed into the bloodstream. They often contain trans-fatty acids, as well.
- Cow's milk and cow's milk products, such as milk, yogurt, butter, and cheese.
- All foods that contain refined, white sugar, brown sugar, and sucanat.
- All artificial sweeteners and sugar substitutes.
- Soft drinks, such as colas, 7-Up, diet drinks.
- Hard liquors.
- Coffee.

Below is three weeks of meals on a Recovery Diet. Recipes for each of the foods described below can be found in Chapter 10 of this book. *Bon appetit.*

Menu Plan

WEEK ONE

Monday Day 1

Breakfast	Oatmeal
Lunch	Polenta
	Tofu with tamari and ginger
	Steamed kale with orange miso dressing
Dinner	Simple miso soup
	Pressure-cooked brown rice with gomasio
	Black beans with onion, carrot, and pepper
	Baked winter squash
	Sautéed bok choy with pure lemon dressing

Tuesday Day 2

Breakfast	Simple miso soup
	Leftover brown rice—add water, reheat, and
	sweeten with brown rice syrup
Lunch	Greek spirals
	Steamed watercress and carrots
Dinner	Mushroom barley soup
	Pressure-cooked brown rice with strips of toasted
	Nori seaweed
	Sweet pinto beans
	Marinated vegetables
	Sautéed broccoli rabe
	Kanten

Wednesday Day 3

Breakfast	Bulgur and oatmeal
Lunch	Chinese-style vegetables served over noodles

Dinner	Squash soup
	Millet with cauliflower
	Whitefish salad
	Cucumber, wakame, and watercress salad
	Sautéed kale

Thursday Day 4

Breakfast	Simple miso soup
	Scrambled tofu with whole-grain toast
Lunch	Saucy soba
	Boiled vegetable salad with sesame-lemon dressing
Dinner	Red lentil soup
	Pressure-cooked brown rice with gomasio
	Love those leeks
	Steamed collard greens with vinaigrette
	Blueberry crisp

Friday Day 5

Breakfast	Polenta
Lunch	Root stew
	Pressure-cooked brown rice
	Marinated chickpea salad
	Steamed kale with orange miso dressing
Dinner	Simple miso soup
	Pressure-cooked brown rice with sesame seed and scallion condiment
	Aduki beans with squash and kombu
	Sea vegetable delight
	Rutabaga pickle

Saturday Day 6

Breakfast	Bulgur and oatmeal
Lunch	Split pea soup
	Millet with cauliflower
	Ratatouille
Dinner	Simple miso soup
	Fried rice with shrimp and vegetables
	Daikon radish with tamari
	Steamed collard greens with vinaigrette
	Apple-lemon kanten

Sunday Day 7

Breakfast	Oatmeal
Lunch	Polenta
	Lentils with onions, winter squash, and kombu
Dinner	Fish soup
	Buckwheat and bows
	Steamed watercress with tofu dressing
	Daikon radish salad
	Kanten

WEEK TWO

Monday Day 8

Breakfast	Polenta
Lunch	Simple miso soup
	Macaroni and bean salad
	Boiled vegetable salad with orange miso dressing
Dinner	Baked salmon
	Roasted round potatoes
	Pressed cucumber salad

Sautéed bok choy
Coffee gelatin

Tuesday Day 9

Breakfast	Oatmeal
Lunch	Linguini with white clam sauce Steamed broccoli with sesame-lemon dressing
Dinner	Hardy green lentil soup Pressure-cooked brown rice with gomasio Baked winter squash Marinated vegetables Sautéed brussels sprouts

Wednesday Day 10

Breakfast	Leftover brown rice—add water, reheat, and sweeten with brown rice syrup
Lunch	Saucy soba Ratatouille Cucumber, wakame, and watercress salad
Dinner	Simple miso soup Millet with cauliflower Aduki beans with squash and kombu Love those leeks Steamed kale with tofu dressing Rutabaga pickle Apple-lemon kanten

Thursday Day 11

Breakfast	Bulgur and oatmeal
Lunch	Udon noodles in broth Sautéed broccoli rabe

Dinner   Squash soup
                        Pressure-cooked brown rice with sesame seed and
                            scallion condiment
                        Whitefish salad
                        Boiled vegetable salad with pure lemon dressing
                        Steamed collard greens

Friday Day 12
___

Breakfast   Oatmeal

Lunch   Buckwheat
                        Cabbage with cumin
                        Tofu with tamari and ginger

Dinner   Mushroom barley soup
                        Pressure-cooked brown rice with gomasio
                        Sweet pinto beans
                        Sea vegetable delight
                        Sautéed mustard greens
                        Kanten

Saturday Day 13
___

Breakfast   Scrambled tofu with whole-grain bread

Lunch   Greek spirals
                        Pressed cucumber salad
                        Marinated vegetables

Dinner   Vegetable soup
                        Fried rice with shrimp and vegetables
                        Steamed kale with sesame-lemon dressing
                        Kanten

Sunday Day 14
___

Breakfast   Polenta

Lunch   Millet with cauliflower

Love those leeks
Steamed Chinese cabbage

Dinner   Red lentil soup
              Buckwheat and bows
              Tempeh with sauerkraut
              Daikon radish salad
              Cucumber, wakame, and watercress salad

WEEK THREE

Monday Day 15

Breakfast   Oatmeal

Lunch   Buckwheat and bows
              Root stew
              Steamed Chinese cabbage

Dinner   Split pea soup
              Broiled whitefish
              Roasted round potatoes
              Cucumber, wakame, and watercress salad
              Root stew
              Blueberry crisp

Tuesday Day 16

Breakfast   Oatmeal and bulgur

Lunch   Greek spirals
              Boiled vegetable salad
              Steamed kale

Dinner   Simple miso soup
              Pressure-cooked brown rice with sesame seed and
                  scallion condiment
              Marinated chickpea salad
              Sea vegetable delight

Root stew
Coffee gelatin

Wednesday Day 17

Breakfast	Polenta
Lunch	Hearty green lentil soup
	Pressed cucumber salad
Dinner	Vegetable soup
	Saucy soba
	Tempeh with sauerkraut
	Steamed watercress
	Ratatouille
	Kanten

Thursday Day 18

Breakfast	Oatmeal
Lunch	Whitefish salad
	Sautéed mustard greens
Dinner	Simple miso soup
	Pressure-cooked brown rice
	Sweet pinto beans
	Steamed Chinese-style vegetables
	Root stew

Friday Day 19

Breakfast	Leftover brown rice—add water, reheat, and sweeten with brown rice syrup
Lunch	Linguini with clam sauce
	Cucumber, wakame, and watercress salad
Dinner	Mushroom barley soup
	Polenta
	Aduki beans with squash and kombu

Cabbage with cumin
Sautéed bok choy with tofu dressing
Stewed peaches

Saturday Day 20

Breakfast	Simple miso soup
	Oatmeal and bulgur
Lunch	Pressure-cooked brown rice
	Boiled vegetable salad with orange miso dressing
	Scrambled tofu
Dinner	Baked salmon
	Daikon radish salad
	Roasted round potatoes
	Rutabaga pickle
	Sautéed collard greens

Sunday Day 21

Breakfast	Polenta
Lunch	Macaroni and bean salad
	Steamed Chinese cabbage with miso dressing
Dinner	Squash soup
	Pressure-cooked brown rice
	Sea vegetable delight
	Boiled vegetable salad with dressing of your choice
	Baked winter squash
	Sautéed broccoli
	Apples with apricot sauce

10

$$ \times $$

Recipes

WHOLE GRAINS

PRESSURE-COOKED BROWN RICE

Pressure-cooking will lock in all of the important nutrients in the rice and also make it taste delicious.

> *2 cups brown rice, washed and soaked overnight in 3 cups water*
> *3½ cups water*
> *2 pinches sea salt*

Drain the rice. Place in the pressure cooker with the water and sea salt. Cover with lid and bring to full pressure over high heat. Reduce the heat to low and simmer for 45 minutes. Turn off the heat, let the pressure come down, and remove the rice.

Serves 4.

BULGUR AND OATMEAL

This produces a sweet and tasty morning cereal.

4 cups water
1 cup bulgur
1 cup rolled oats
¼ cup raisins (optional)
1 pinch sea salt
1 pinch cinnamon (optional)

Bring the water to a boil. Add the ingredients. Return to a boil, cover the pot, reduce the heat, and simmer for 30 minutes. Sweeten with brown rice syrup, if desired.

Serves 2–4.

BUCKWHEAT (KASHA)

1 cup white buckwheat groats
2½ cups water
1 pinch sea salt
1 diced onion

Roast the buckwheat groats evenly in a frying pan for 5 minutes. Boil the water and add roasted buckwheat, sea salt, and onions. Cover with a tight-fitting lid, reduce the heat to low, and simmer for 30 minutes or until all the water has been absorbed. Stir and serve.

Serves 2.

BUCKWHEAT AND BOWS

2 cups buckwheat groats
8 cups water
1 pinch sea salt
2 tablespoons olive oil

1 onion, minced
½ pound bowtie noodles, already cooked
1 teaspoon prepared mustard (optional)
1 tablespoon tamari
½ cup parsley, minced

Roast buckwheat groats evenly in a frying pan for 5 minutes. Boil the water and sea salt. Add buckwheat and cook for 30 minutes. Sauté onion in olive oil and add cooked buckwheat, noodles, mustard (if desired), and tamari. Garnish with parsley.

Serves 2–4.

MILLET WITH CAULIFLOWER

1 cup millet
1 onion, diced
½ cauliflower, cut into small pieces
4 cups water
2 pinches sea salt

Wash the millet in a strainer several times. Place the cauliflower and onion on the bottom of a pressure cooker and the millet on top. Gently pour the water into one side of the pot in order to keep the layering intact. Add sea salt and cover. Bring to full pressure over high heat, reduce the heat to low, and simmer for 45 minutes. Bring down the pressure and stir from the bottom to the top of the pot.

Serves 2–3.

OATMEAL

1 cup steel-cut oats, washed
3 cups water
1 tablespoon roasted flax seeds
a handful of raisins
1 pinch of sea salt

Boil oats, sea salt, and raisins for 35 minutes, covered. Garnish with roasted flax seeds. Sweeten with brown rice syrup, if desired.

Serves 4.

POLENTA

> *3 cups water*
> *1 cup cornmeal (may be dry-roasted for a nuttier flavor), diluted in one cup of water*
> *1 pinch sea salt*

Bring water to boil. Whisk in the cornmeal mixture, add sea salt, return to a boil, and stir continually to prevent lumping. Cover, and simmer over medium-low heat for 30–45 minutes. (Cooking time may vary with how coarsely the grain is ground.) For dinner, sprinkle with toasted sunflower seeds or sesame seed condiment. For breakfast, sweeten with a teaspoon of brown rice syrup.

Serves 2.

PASTA

GREEK SPIRALS

> *6 cups whole wheat spiral noodles*
> *1 onion, diced*
> *10 button mushrooms, diced*
> *10 cups spinach, cut small*
> *5 sun-dried tomatoes, soaked for 20 minutes and cut up*
> *3 tablespoons olive oil*
> *1 teaspoon garlic, minced*
> *tamari to taste*
> *handful of pine nuts*

Cook noodles. Drain and rinse thoroughly with cold water. Sauté the garlic and vegetables in oil and add tamari. When vegetables are soft, mix in noodles and pine nuts.

Serves 2–4.

LINGUINI WITH WHITE CLAM SAUCE

1 pound linguini
1 pinch sea salt
1 tablespoon of olive oil
2 cloves garlic
4 scallions
⅔ cup parsley, minced
15 button mushrooms
1 16-ounce can of clams
2 tablespoons tamari

Add linguini and salt to 10 cups boiling water. Cook for 10 minutes or until soft. Drain linguini and rinse with cold water. Mince garlic, scallions, and parsley. Slice mushrooms into small pieces. Sauté vegetables in olive oil and add tamari. Cover and simmer for 5 minutes. Add the canned clams along with the juice. Serve over cooked noodles.

Serves 3.

SAUCY SOBA

½ pound soba noodles, cooked and drained
¼ cup tamari
2 tablespoons unrefined sesame oil
1 tablespoon toasted sesame oil
1 tablespoon brown rice vinegar
2 teaspoons maple syrup
1 teaspoon finely grated ginger
1 teaspoon chopped garlic

1 cup chopped scallions
1 tablespoon toasted sesame seeds

Combine tamari, oils, maple syrup, ginger, and garlic. Mix and pour over the noodles. Add scallions and seeds. Toss together.

Serves 3.

UDON NOODLES IN BROTH

1 8-ounce package of udon noodles
6 cups water
1 strip kombu
2 shiitake mushrooms, soaked and ends of stems cut off
1 tablespoon tamari
2—4 tablespoons bonito fish flakes
fresh grated ginger
3 scallions, thinly sliced

Add the noodles, kombu, shiitake mushrooms, tamari, fish flakes, and grated ginger to boiling water and cook for 15–25 minutes or until soft. Do not cover.

Serves 4.

VEGETABLES

BAKED WINTER SQUASH

1 large acorn squash (or any winter variety)

Wash and cut the squash in half and take out the seeds. Place on a cookie sheet, cut side down. Bake in preheated oven at 350°–375° for about an hour. Test by pricking the center with a fork.

Serves 4.

BOILED VEGETABLE SALAD

Use any combination of three vegetables. Boil each vegetable separately, with a pinch of sea salt added to the water. The stronger-flavored ones (such as daikon, turnips, and watercress) should be added at the end, so that each vegetable maintains its distinct flavor. Boil for approximately 1 minute and remove. Leafy greens can be dropped into the boiling water and cooked for 30 seconds. All vegetables should retain their bright color with this method.

CABBAGE WITH CUMIN

> 2 tablespoons olive oil
> 1 head cabbage, chopped small
> 1 tablespoon sea salt
> 1 tablespoon cumin powder

Sauté all ingredients together for 5 minutes, then cover (add a little water, if necessary) and steam for an additional 5 minutes.

Serves 4.

CUCUMBER, WAKAME, AND WATERCRESS SALAD

> 1 4-inch piece of wakame, cooked for 15 minutes, and cut in small pieces
> 6 tablespoons brown rice vinegar
> 1 tablespoon toasted sesame oil
> 1½ tablespoons water
> 3 tablespoons tamari
> 3 cucumbers, julienned
> 3 bunches watercress, cut up

Mix oil, vinegar, tamari, and water. In a separate bowl combine the cucumer, wakame, and watercress. Add the sauce and toss.

Serves 3.

DAIKON RADISH WITH TAMARI

1 daikon radish, sliced
1 tablespoon tamari

Place daikon in a pot with water and tamari and cover. Boil until fork can be easily inserted into the daikon, about 15 minutes.

Serves 4.

LOVE THOSE LEEKS

5–6 leeks, washed and cut into 1-inch slices
1 carrot, diced
1 turnip, diced
1 tablespoon olive oil
1 teaspoon tamari
3 teaspoons prepared mustard
2 teaspoons brown rice syrup
1 teaspoon brown rice vinegar

Sauté leeks, carrot, and turnip on low flame, covered, for about 25 minutes. Remove cover and cook until there is no remaining liquid. Put rice syrup, mustard, and vinegar in a covered jar and shake. Stir into the vegetables.

Serves 3.

MARINATED VEGETABLES

Choose from some combination of the following vegetables: broccoli, cauliflower, brussels sprouts, zucchini, carrots, or green beans. Cut them small and marinate in a mixture of 1 cup lemon juice, ⅔ cup olive oil, and 2 teaspoons sea salt. Allow to sit in the refrigerator for 24 hours before serving.

RATATOUILLE

1 onion
3 large summer squashes (zucchini or yellow), sliced
2 tomatoes, diced
1 teaspoon sea salt

Place all ingredients in a pot with a little bit of water and steam a few minutes until vegetables are soft.

Serves 3.

ROASTED ROUND POTATOES

1 bag small yellow or red potatoes

Coat potatoes generously with olive oil. Add salt and pepper and bake at 350° for 1½ hours or until potatoes are soft.

Serves 6.

ROOT STEW

2 strips kombu seaweed
1 winter squash, cut in chunks
2 carrots, cut in chunks
1 onion, cut in chunks
1 burdock stalk, sliced

In an oven dish, layer kombu, burdock, onion, carrots, and squash. Add ½ inch water and sprinkle with salt. Cover. Allow to bake at 350° for an hour or until vegetables are soft.

Serves 4.

STEAMED CHINESE-STYLE VEGETABLES

1 large onion
4 cups cabbage
1 large carrot
1 cup snow peas
2 scallions
1 clove garlic, grated
1 cup cashews or almonds, roasted
1½ tablespoons umeboshi vinegar
1 teaspoon juice from grated ginger
1 tablespoon kuzu (diluted in one cup water)
1 tablespoon tamari

Thinly slice onion, carrot, and cabbage and place at the bottom of a skillet. Add grated garlic and 2 cups of water and simmer, covered, for 3–5 minutes. Add snow peas and scallions and simmer 2 minutes longer. Add umeboshi vinegar, tamari, ginger juice, and kuzu and stir until thick. To roast nuts, place on baking sheet and bake at 350° for 5–10 minutes. Sprinkle roasted nuts over vegetables.

Serves 4.

STEAMED LEAFY GREENS

1 bunch leafy greens
1 pinch salt
a few drops of toasted sesame oil, tamari, and/or umeboshi vinegar

Wash and cut greens. Place them in a pot with 1 inch of water and bring to a boil. Cover and cook for 2 minutes. Flavor with toasted sesame oil, tamari, and/or umeboshi vinegar. If you wish to include another vegetable in this dish, add the vegetable that needs longer cooking time first.

Serves 4.

SAUTÉED LEAFY GREENS

1 bunch leafy greens
2–3 tablespoons olive oil
a few drops of tamari

Wash the greens and cut them in half lengthwise along the side stem, stack them on top of each other, and cut again lengthwise. Turn them sideways and cut into ½-inch pieces. Heat oil and add greens, stirring gently until they begin to change color. Cover, add tamari, and simmer for 2 minutes.

Serves 4.

SALADS AND PICKLES

DAIKON RADISH SALAD

1 cup daikon radish, grated
1 cup carrot, grated
½ teaspoon sea salt
juice from one lemon
½ cup scallions, sliced thin

Mix together and serve.

Serves 3.

MACARONI AND BEAN SALAD

3 cups whole wheat macaroni, cooked
1½ cups kidney beans, cooked
4 scallions
2 celery stalks
handful of parsley

In a large salad bowl, combine the macaroni and beans. Chop the scallions, celery, and parsley finely and add to the macaroni and bean mixture. Toss with mustard dressing and allow to sit for at least 15 minutes before serving.

PRESSED CUCUMBER SALAD

4 cucumbers, peeled and sliced
1 teaspoon sea salt
1 teaspoon tamari
1 teaspoon toasted sesame oil
1 teaspoon brown rice vinegar
3 tablespoons toasted sesame seeds

Place sliced cucumber and sea salt in a pickle press or in a bowl with a weight on top. Press for an hour or more and drain the liquid. Rinse off the salt. Add mixture of tamari, sesame oil, and brown rice vinegar to the cucumbers and garnish with toasted sesame seeds.

Serves 6.

RUTABAGA PICKLES

2 cups rutabaga, cut small
2 cups tamari
2 cups water

Place sliced rutabaga in pickle press, small ceramic crock, or bowl. Prepare a mixture of half water and half tamari to cover the rutabaga. Put top on pickle press or some kind of weight on crock or bowl. Press rutabaga for 4 hours or overnight.

Serves 4.

BEANS AND BEAN PRODUCTS

ADUKI BEANS WITH SQUASH AND KOMBU

½ cup adzuki beans
2 stalks kombu
1 hard winter squash (acorn, butternut, buttercup, or Hokkaido pumpkin)
tamari

Wash and soak beans with kombu overnight. Place kombu, squash, and aduki beans in a pot. Add enough water to cover the squash. Bring to a boil and cook for 20 minutes. Cover and continue to cook until the beans are 80 percent soft. This usually takes about 1½ hours. When the beans are 80 percent soft, add a few drops of tamari. Cover and continue to cook for another 15 minutes.

Serves 4.

BLACK BEANS WITH ONION, CARROT, AND PEPPER

2 cups black beans
1 stick kombu
1 large onion, cubed
1 large carrot, cubed
1 green bell pepper, cubed
miso to taste

Pick over the beans, wash them several times, and drain. Soak overnight, if possible, or boil for 5 minutes and soak for 2 hours. Place beans in a pot and bring to boil with a stick of kombu seaweed. Turn flame down, cover, and simmer for 2 hours, or until beans are soft. Once soft, add the vegetables, and simmer another 20 minutes. Add miso during last few minutes of cooking.

Serves 4.

LENTILS WITH ONIONS, WINTER SQUASH, AND KOMBU

8 cups water
1 cup lentils
1 strip kombu
1 onion, diced
1 cup winter squash, cubed
tamari to taste

Bring lentils and kombu to boil. Reduce flame and cook on medium heat for 1 hour. Add onion, squash, and tamari and cook ½ hour more or until vegetables are soft.

Serves 3.

MARINATED CHICKPEA SALAD

3 cups chickpeas, cooked
2 tablespoons olive oil
3 tablespoons umeboshi vinegar
1 pinch of sea salt
6 red radishes, diced
1 small cucumber, peeled and diced
2 stalks celery, diced
½ cup watercress, sliced small
1 tablespoon fresh parsley
1 teaspoon fresh dill

Marinate the chickpeas in oil, vinegar, and sea salt. Combine with vegetables and add fresh parsley and dill.

Serves 4.

SCRAMBLED TOFU

1 onion, diced
1 carrot, diced
½ piece celery, diced
1 container of soft tofu
umeboshi vinegar to taste
1 teaspoon cumin
1 teaspoon turmeric
¼ teaspoon black pepper
½ teaspoon tamari

Steam onion, carrot, and celery in water for 3 minutes. Crumble up the tofu and add to the mixture. Add cumin, pepper, turmeric, and tamari. Cook covered for 10 minutes. Add umeboshi vinegar to taste.

Serves 3.

SWEET PINTO BEANS

2 cups pinto beans
1 strip kombu seaweed
½ cup brown rice miso (or another dark miso)
½ cup apple butter

Soak pinto beans overnight if possible, or boil for 5 minutes and soak for 2 hours. Bring beans and kombu to a boil, reduce flame, and cook for 2 hours. Mix miso and apple butter together. Put cooked beans with miso–apple butter mix into a glass dish and cook in the oven on 350° for at least ½ hour.

Serves 4.

TEMPEH WITH SAUERKRAUT

1 tablespoon olive oil
1 block of cubed tempeh

½ *medium cabbage, finely sliced*
½ *cup sauerkraut*
1 *cup water*
½ *teaspoon light miso, creamed in one tablespoon water*
¼ *cup finely sliced scallions*

Heat the oil in frying pan and brown the tempeh evenly on both sides. Add the cabbage and sauté with the tempeh for 5 minutes. Place the sauerkraut on top, add the water, cover, and steam for 20 minutes. Stir in the dissolved miso and simmer for 5 minutes. Mix in the scallions.

Serves 4.

TOFU WITH TAMARI AND GINGER

1 *package tofu*
a few drops of tamari
1 *teaspoon grated ginger*

Cut up tofu in chunks and add water to cover. Bring to boil, add tamari and grated ginger, and turn flame down to medium. Cook until water is almost gone. Garnish with sliced scallions.

FISH DISHES

BAKED SALMON

2 *pounds salmon fillet*
3 *tablespoons olive oil*
1 *teaspoon Worcestershire-style sauce*
1 *onion, minced*

Combine oil, Worcestershire-style sauce, and onion in a bowl. Place salmon in shallow baking dish, cover with sauce, and bake in preheated 350° oven for about ½ hour.

Serves 5.

BROILED WHITEFISH

2 pounds whitefish
2 tablespoons tamari
2 tablespoons sesame oil
juice from one lemon

Place fish on baking dish and add the other ingredients. Broil until fish flakes easily.

Serves 5.

FRIED RICE WITH SHRIMP AND VEGETABLES

1 tablespoon olive oil
1 clove garlic, minced
1 cup carrots, sliced thin
1 cup scallions, sliced thin
1 cup broccoli flowerettes
1 cup cooked rice
¼ pound shrimp, cooked
1 tablespoon tamari
¼ teaspoon umeboshi vinegar
1 teaspoon ginger, grated
1 sheet sushi nori, broken up in small pieces

Heat oil in a skillet and add garlic, broccoli, and carrots and stir for 10 seconds. Cover and cook a few minutes longer if broccoli is not yet tender. Add the cooked rice, scallions, shrimp, tamari, umeboshi vinegar, ginger, and sushi nori. Stir together until everything is well mixed and rice is coated with the sauce.

Serves 3.

WHITEFISH SALAD

> 1 pound white firm-fleshed fish
> 1 cup diced celery
> 1 cup sliced scallions
> 1 tablespoon Nayonnaise (tofu mayonnaise)

Steam fish, covered, in small amount of water until tender. Remove from heat and drain. Mix thoroughly with other ingredients. Serve on whole-grain roll with all the trimmings.

Serves 3.

SEA VEGETABLES

SEA VEGETABLE DELIGHT

> 1 package arame seaweed
> 1 tablespoon tamari
> 1 teaspoon grated lemon rind
> ½ cup ground roasted sesame seeds

Rinse the arame in a strainer under running water. Place the arame in a pot with enough water to cover and let sit for 3–5 minutes. Bring to a boil, cover, reduce the heat to medium-low, and simmer for 10 minutes. Remove the lid, add the tamari, and boil until all the liquid has evaporated. Add the lemon rind and sesame seeds and mix well. Serve with lemon wedges and garnish with fresh sliced scallions.

Serves 4.

SOUPS

FISH SOUP

½–¾ *pound firm-fleshed fish fillet*
2 *cups thin rounds leeks*
1 *cup bite-sized pieces Chinese cabbage*
1 *cup diced carrot*
6–8 *cups water*
1 *strip kombu, soaked and cut into thin strips*
1 *teaspoon salt*
1 *tablespoon tamari*
¼ *teaspoon freshly grated ginger*

Rinse the fish quickly under cold running water and cut into small pieces. Wash and cut the vegetables. Bring the water and kombu to a boil in a saucepan, add the fish and salt, cover, and simmer over low heat for 25 minutes. Add the vegetables, return to a boil, and simmer over low heat for 5 minutes. Season with tamari and grated ginger and simmer for 2 minutes. Stir with a wooden spoon to mix the vegetables and fish evenly. Garnish with chopped parsley.

Serves 6.

HEARTY GREEN LENTIL STEW

1 *cup green lentils*
1 *strip kombu*
1 *small onion*
2 *carrots*
2 *stalks celery*
6 *small potatoes*
1 *cup seitan (Optional. Can be purchased in a natural foods store.)*
1 *clove garlic*
1 *scallion*
tamari to taste

Boil 1 cup green lentils and kombu until soft. Cut vegetables up small and add to the lentils, along with seitan and grated garlic. Cook on medium flame, covered, for ½ hour. Add tamari and simmer for 10 minutes longer. Garnish with scallions.

Serves 4–6.

SIMPLE MISO SOUP

It is best to use barley miso for this soup. Experiment with various combinations of vegetables.

1 piece wakame, soaked for 5 minutes
4 tablespoons barley miso
1 onion, diced
1 carrot, diced
2 tablespoons scallions, sliced thin

Bring wakame and 6 cups of water to a boil. Add the vegetables and boil for about 5 minutes. Reduce flame to low. Add miso to soup and simmer for 5 minutes on a low flame. Do not boil miso. Garnish with scallions.

Serves 4.

MUSHROOM BARLEY SOUP

½ cup pearled barley
10 shiitake mushrooms
1 piece kombu seaweed
1 onion
2 carrots
7 leaves Chinese cabbage
½ cup barley miso
1 scallion
1 teaspoon grated ginger

Fill a pot with water. Add kombu, shiitake, and pearled barley. Bring to a boil. Turn down flame and after 20 minutes, take out shiitake with a spatula, dice, and return to broth. Add 1 onion, carrots, and Chinese cabbage to soup. Cover and simmer for at least an hour. Scoop out some broth and mix ½ cup miso into it. Return to pot and simmer on low for 20 minutes, but do not allow to boil. Garnish with scallions and grated ginger.

Serves 4.

RED LENTIL SOUP

> 1 cup red lentils
> 1 large onion
> 2 medium carrots
> 2 beets
> 1 bay leaf
> 6 cups water
> ¼ cup dark miso
> 2 tablespoons sesame oil

Wash and drain beans. Scrub veggies and slice in ½-inch pieces. Heat oil in soup pot and sauté onion 5 minutes, regularly stirring. Add lentils, water, bay leaf, and bring to a boil. Simmer for at least an hour. Take out bay leaf. Blend soup in a blender. Cream miso in small bowl with a little bit of the soup. Add to the rest of the soup. Garnish with croutons.

Serves 3–4.

SPLIT PEA SOUP

> 1 cup split peas
> 6 cups water
> 1 stick of wakame
> 1 onion, diced
> 1 carrot, diced

1 celery stalk, diced
tamari to taste

Wash the peas and bring to a boil, along with the wakame. Simmer for an hour or until the beans soften. Add the remaining vegetables and cook for 20 minutes. Add tamari and simmer for 5 more minutes.

Serves 3.

SQUASH SOUP

8 cups winter squash, cubed
1 large sweet potato, cubed
2 tablespoons barley miso

Cut the skin off the squash and remove the seeds. Place squash, sweet potato, and 1 cup water into pressure cooker. Bring to pressure and cook on low for 10 minutes. Allow pressure to come down. Remove the contents of the pressure cooker and blend in a blender. Transfer back to pot, add miso, and simmer on low for 5 minutes. If you would like a more liquid consistency, add more miso diluted in water and simmer a few minutes longer.

Serves 4–6.

VEGETABLE SOUP

1½ cups sliced thin rounds leeks
1½ cups cubed carrots
½ cup cubed daikon radish
1 strip kombu, soaked and cut into small strips
1 pinch salt
6 cups water
2 tablespoons tamari or miso

Wash and cut the vegetables. Place the kombu, carrots, and daikon in a saucepan. Add the salt and water and bring to a boil. Reduce the heat to medium-low and simmer for 15 minutes. Add the leeks, return to boil, and simmer for 8 minutes. Season with soy sauce or miso and simmer for another 5 minutes. (If you use miso, cream it with soup broth and add to the soup.) Garnish with parsley.

Serves 6.

SAUCES AND DRESSINGS

MISO DRESSING

> *3 tablespoons white miso*
> *1 tablespoon brown rice vinegar*
> *1 teaspoon toasted sesame oil*
> *1 clove garlic, grated*
> *1 teaspoon ginger, grated*

Blend or stir all ingredients together thoroughly.

Serves 2.

MUSTARD DRESSING

> *6 tablespoons lemon juice*
> *4 tablespoons tamari*
> *2 teaspoons mustard*
> *2 tablespoons tahini*
> *6 tablespoons water*

Place ingredients in a small jar and shake until blended.

Serves 2–4.

ORANGE MISO DRESSING

> ¼ cup freshly squeezed orange juice
> 1–1½ teaspoons white miso
> 1 tablespoon ground roasted sesame seeds (optional)

Cream the miso with the orange juice in a small bowl. Mix with the sesame seeds and pour over salad or leafy greens.

Serves 4.

PURE LEMON DRESSING

> 3 lemons, squeezed
> ½ cup tamari

Mix together and serve.

Serves 2.

SESAME-LEMON DRESSING

> 2 tablespoons sesame oil
> 2 tablespoons lemon juice
> 1 tablespoon brown rice vinegar
> 2 tablespoons tamari
> ½ cup water

Put all ingredients in a covered jar and shake until well mixed.

Serves 2.

SESAME SEED AND SCALLION CONDIMENT

> *1 cup sesame seeds*
> *1 cup onion, diced*
> *1 cup red pepper, diced*
> *1 cup scallion, sliced*
> *1 tablespoon olive oil*
> *1 tablespoon miso*

Sauté onion, red pepper, and scallion in olive oil until tender. Add miso and cook a few minutes longer. Toss with sesame seeds and use as a condiment on grain.

Serves 3.

TOFU DRESSING

> *½ teaspoon grated ginger*
> *1 cake soft tofu*
> *¼ cup water*
> *2 tablespoons white miso*
> *2 tablespoons umeboshi vinegar*

Puree together in a blender or mash in a suribachi.

Serves 3.

VINAIGRETTE

> *2 tablespoons onions, minced*
> *1 tablespoon mustard, prepared*
> *3 tablespoons brown rice vinegar*
> *½ tablespoon olive oil*
> *1 teaspoon tamari*

Put all ingredients in a covered jar and shake until well mixed.

Serves 2.

DESSERTS

APPLES WITH APRICOT SAUCE

8 apples, washed, cored, and cut in small pieces
½ pound dried apricots, soaked for an hour in a bowl with water
1 pinch of sea salt
handful of toasted walnuts

Place apricots in a saucepan with salt, cover with water, bring to a boil, and simmer for 15 minutes. Simmer the apples in another pot in ½ inch of water for about 10 minutes. Mash the apricots in a separate bowl and mix with the juice from the apples to make a sauce. If the sauce is too thick, you can add a little water. Dish out some of the apples, cover with the sauce, and garnish with walnuts.

Serves 5–6.

APPLE-LEMON KANTEN

10 cups apple juice
4 cups water
⅛ teaspoon salt
7 tablespoons agar flakes
6 medium apples, cored and sliced
1 tablespoon grated lemon rind
juice of 1 medium lemon

Place juice and water in a saucepan and heat. When the liquid comes to a boil, reduce heat and add salt and agar, stirring constantly. Stir in apples, lemon rind, and lemon juice. Simmer for 15 minutes, pour into a dish, and allow to chill until it sets.

Serves 5–6.

BLUEBERRY CRISP

> 4 cups blueberries
> 1 cup apple juice
> 2 tablespoons brown rice syrup
> 2 tablespoons kuzu, dissolved in 5 tablespoons water
> 3 cups rolled oats
> 1 pinch of sea salt
> 3 tablespoons maple syrup

Place blueberries, apple juice, and brown rice syrup in a pot and simmer. Add dissolved kuzu and stir until thickened. Place ingredients in a baking dish, adding mixture of oats, salt, and maple syrup. Bake at 350° for 30 minutes.

Serves 5–6.

COFFEE GELATIN

> 4 cups apple juice
> 2 ½ tablespoons grain coffee (such as Pero or some other grain coffee substitute)
> ⅓ cup agar flakes
> 2 tablespoons tahini
> ¼ teaspoon cinnamon
> ⅛ teaspoon salt

Whip all the ingredients in a blender. Bring to a boil in a saucepan, reduce the heat to medium-low, and simmer for 5 minutes. Rinse a bowl with cold water, add the hot apple juice mixture, and chill in the refrigerator until set—approximately 1 hour.

Serves 5–6.

KANTEN

1 quart apple or any other unsweetened fruit juice
1 pinch salt
½ teaspoon vanilla (optional)
⅛ cup agar flakes
1 tablespoon arrowroot or kuzu, dissolved in ¼ cup apple juice
1 pint strawberries, washed and quartered

Combine the apple juice, salt, vanilla, and agar flakes in a saucepan and bring to a boil, stirring constantly. Whisk in the arrowroot or kuzu mixture and continue stirring until the mixture returns to a boil. Reduce the heat to medium-low and simmer for 5 minutes. Rinse a square glass pan or bowl with cold water, place the strawberries in the pan, and pour the hot apple juice mixture over the fruit. Chill in the refrigerator until set—approximately 1 hour.

Serves 5–6.

STEWED PEACHES

4 pounds fresh peaches
water to cover
2 teaspoons vanilla
grated rind of lemon (organic)

Wash peaches and cut lengthwise, separating pulp from pit; cut each half into three slices. Place peaches in a saucepan, cover with water, and add vanilla and lemon rind. Bring to a boil, lower heat, and simmer, covered, for 5 minutes. Serve at room temperature or cool.

Serves 5–6.

Resource Guide to Healing Services and Natural and Organic Foods

Diet, Exercise, and Healing

For information about macrobiotics and residential programs and services, contact the following places:

The Kushi Institute
P.O. Box 7
Becket, MA 01223
800-975-8744
413-623-5742
www.kushiinstitute.org

The Vega Study Center
1511 Robinson Street
Oroville, CA 95965
800-818-8342
530-533-7092

www.vega.macrobiotic.net
e-mail: Vegastudy@cncnet.com

For information about the Pritikin Program and Residential Services:

The Pritikin Longevity Center
19735 Turnberry Way
Aventura, FL 33180
800-327-4194
305-935-7131
www.Pritikin.com

For information about the McDougall Clinic and Residential Programs:

The McDougall Health Center
P.O. Box 14039
Santa Rosa, CA 95402
800-570-1654
707-538-8509
www.drmcdougall.com

For Training in Natural Healing and Diet
Institute for Integrative Nutrition
120 West 41st Street
2nd floor
New York, NY 10036
212-730-5433
www.Integrativenutrition.com

Strengthening Health Institute
Philadelphia, PA
215-271-0158
www.strengthenhealth.org
info@strengthenhealth.org

Yoga, Personal Growth, and Healing

Kripalu Center for Yoga and Health
57 Interlaken Road
Stockbridge, MA
U.S. Mail:
Kripalu Center
P.O. Box 793
West Street, Route 183
Lenox, MA 01240
800-741-7353
413-448-3152
www.kripaiu.org
e-mail:reserve@kripalu.org

For People with Breast Cancer and Other Serious Illnesses Who Are Looking for Resources and Support with the Macrobiotic Diet

Meg Wolff, macrobiotic counselor and cooking teacher, is a wife and a mother of two children. She contracted bone and breast cancer and was given little chance of recovery. She used a macrobiotic diet and lifestyle to heal herself and now maintains a very active life attempting to help others with serious illnesses. In addition to her teaching, she maintains a Web site for people with breast cancer who are searching for resources to help them overcome the illness. Meg's Web site can be found at www.macrobreastcancersurvivors.com. Meg lives with her family in Portland, Maine.

Food: Whole, Organic, and Unprocessed

For people who are having trouble finding high-quality natural foods, the following suppliers provide organic, whole, natural foods and kitchen equipment by mail order.

Eden Foods
Full line of natural and organic foods
701 Tecumseh Road
Clinton, MI 49236
888-441-3336

888-424-3336
www.edenfoods.com

Diamond Organics
Organic produce, grains, fruits, and other foods
Shipped fresh overnight (guaranteed)
Kitchen equipment
888-674-2642 (toll free)
P.O. Box 2159
Freedom, CA 95019
www.diamondorganics.com

Jaffe Brothers
Organic Fruits and Nuts
28560 Lilac Road
Valley Center, CA 92032
760-749-1133 (tel.)
760-749-1282 (fax)
www.organicfruitsandnuts.com

Gold Mine Natural Food Co.
Full line of organic and natural foods
7805 Anjons Dr.
San Diego, CA 92126
800-475-3663
www.goldminenaturalfood.com

Natural Lifestyle
Full line of organic and natural foods
16 Lookout Drive
Asheville, NC 28804
800-752-2772
www.natural-lifestyle.com

Miracle Exclusives
Kitchen equipment
64 Seaview Blvd.

Port Washington, NY 11050
800-645-6360
www.miracleexclusives.com

Healing Touch
The issues are in the tissues, the mind is in the body. That, essentially, is
the axiom upon which therapeutic massage and other forms of bodywork
are based. The following is a guide to various types of healing touch and
massage techniques. Practitioners for most of these approaches can be
found in your local newspaper, telephone book, and locally published
guides to natural healing. Ask your doctor, local acupuncturists, local day
spas, and other health professionals for referrals.

ACUPRESSURE

Acupressure is based on the same principles as acupuncture, only the
massage technique uses fingers and hands to stimulate the flow of life energy along fourteen pathways, known in Chinese medicine as meridians.
The meridians flow along the body and provide life energy, or *Qi*, to specific organs. Along the meridian lines are many hundreds of acupuncture
points, which the Chinese say serve as generators of life energy when
stimulated. By increasing the life force to specific organs and tissues, the
acupressurist is able to strengthen organs and tissues, throw off waste
products and the underlying causes of illness, and restore health.

ALEXANDER TECHNIQUE

The Alexander technique focuses primarily on correcting posture and
the many disorders that can arise from distortions in posture. Practitioners maintain that poor posture is responsible for the creation of muscular
tension, pain, respiratory disorders, organ and hormonal imbalances,
and many forms of illness. Practitioners use hands, corrective exercises,
and teaching techniques to correct imbalances in posture and thus to restore harmony to the body and grace to movement.

CRANIOSACRAL RELEASE

Craniosacral release is fast becoming one of the most popular forms of
physical therapy and healing touch. The practice involves balancing the
craniosacral system, which includes the skull, spinal column, sacrum,

and all the nerves and tissues housed within these structures. Through very gentle manipulation of the body, the practitioner releases blocks within the craniosacral system to release trauma, old wounds, and sources of illness. Like other forms of healing touch, clients lie on the therapist's table while the practitioner holds the body in various positions. There are no extreme movements, and there is no stress placed on the body. Practitioners can be found in your local telephone book, newspapers, and health directories. They can also be found by calling the Craniosacral Institute (888-627-2642 or 650-369-3001) or on the Internet at www.cranial.org.

JIN SHIN JYUTSU

Brought to America by Japanese teacher and healer Mary Burmeister, Jin Shin Jyutsu is now taught and practiced throughout the world, having been spread primarily through the teachings of Mary Burmeister, her son David and his wife Alice, and the work of many teachers trained by Mary Burmeister. Jin Shin Jyutsu is based on the theory that pathways of life energy, known as flows, traverse the body and bring life force to organs, systems, and tissues. When the pathways become blocked, organs are deprived of adequate life force and illness arises. Along the pathways are specific energy-generating locations known as safety energy locks. These safety energy locks become closed, or blocked, when life force is diminished along the flow. A Jin Shin Jyutsu practitioner places his or her hands on the safety energy locks and channels life energy into the safety energy lock until it opens and generates additional life force to flow along the pathway or flow. When life force flows more abundantly along the pathways, organs, systems, and cells are restored to optimal function and health.

You can find out more about Jin Shin Jyutsu by turning to Jinshin jyutsu.com, or by contacting the primary offices of Jin Shin Jyutsu at 8719 E. San Alberto, Scottsdale, AZ 85258. You can telephone to find a practitioner near you at 480-998-9331, or fax a letter to 480-998-9335.

OHASHIATSU

Ohashiatsu, created by complementary healer Waturo Ohashi, is a form of shiatsu, the Japanese expression of acupressure. Ohashiatsu combines

shiatsu, exercise, meditation, and ancient diagnostic techniques to recognize imbalances, boost life energy along meridians, restore harmony
to organs and systems, and relieve tension. Practitioners use finger pressure to assess the hara, or vital center located below the navel, and to
stimulate acupressure points. Information about the Ohashi Institute can
be found at www.ohashi.com. The Ohashi Institute is located at 147
W. 25th Street, New York, NY 10001. Telephone: 800-810-4190 or
646-486-1187; fax: 646-486-1409.

PHYSICAL AND OCCUPATIONAL THERAPIES
Physical therapies combine stretching, massage, physical manipulation of
limbs and joints, and exercise to increase range of motion, release tension, relieve pain, and promote circulation and healing. Physical therapists are available through your doctor or local hospital.

REFLEXOLOGY
Reflexology is a form of acupressure that uses finger pressure to stimulate points on the feet. These points correspond to specific organs and
systems. By stimulating the points, life force is increased to various parts
of the body, thus relieving tension, restoring balance, and promoting
healing.

REIKI
Reiki is a Tibetan form of laying on of hands or palm healing. Practitioners, known as Reiki masters, channel life energy into the client's body by
placing their hands over specific parts of the body. As life energy is increased, organs are supported, mood is often elevated, and tension is re-
lived. Reiki practitioners, like many other types of bodyworkers,
maintain that by placing their hands on an injured part of the body, the
practitioner is reconnecting the client's consciousness with an injured
part of both the body and mind. Many Reiki practitioners encourage
people to speak from the injured part of the body, giving expression to
whatever feelings may be held there. Reiki practitioners are among the
most popular of alternative and complementary healers. They can be
found in your local telephone book, local newspapers, and natural-
healing directories.

SHIATSU
Shiatsu is the Japanese form of acupressure. Like acupressure, it has been practiced for thousands of years. Practitioners use finger pressure to stimulate acupuncture points and increase *Qi* along meridian lines, thereby promoting healing in organs and systems.

SWEDISH MASSAGE
Swedish massage is often referred to as deep tissue massage because practitioners often work the muscles extensively. They also use gentle rubbing and finger techniques to relieve tension and take muscles out of spasm. Swedish massage is among the oldest forms of massage practiced in the West. It has been used to relieve pain, increase range of motion, treat back problems, muscle injuries, and many other disorders.

YOGA, MOVEMENT, AND DANCE THERAPIES
Our physical movement is an expression of our state of mind and overall consciousness. Yoga, dance, and movement therapies are designed to help us experience, express, and release deep inner feelings and heal old wounds and traumas that may be held in the body and affecting our movement. Practitioners use movement exercises to gently and consciously place the body in direct contact with its tension and the feelings, emotions, and memories that may be held in its tissues. Dance and movement therapies also are designed to release that tension and the painful emotions or memories that may be held in the body. Among the most widely practiced dance and movement therapies are yoga, the Five Rhythms, and the Feldenkrais Method.

THERAPEUTIC TOUCH
Therapeutic touch is a form of laying on of hands. Practitioners either place their hands gently on the body, or just above the skin. They work on what they refer to as the energy body, or aura. Therapeutic touch has been subjected to extensive scientific studies, many of which have shown that the practice boosts immune function and promotes healing. Therapeutic touch has been shown to relieve pain and reduce stress, as well. Therapeutic touch is widely practiced in hospitals and other medical centers.

INTERCESSORY PRAYER

Most churches, synagogues, temples, and mosques offer prayer circles and intercessory prayers for people in their local communities. In addition, the following groups will pray for you and your loved ones. You can submit your requests to any of these groups by writing to them on the World Wide Web.

International Prayer Requests, at www.Prayer.LA. This site will connect you with people from all over the world who will pray for you or someone you love.

Beliefnet offers an array of groups that can be contacted on the World Wide Web for intercessory prayer. Beliefnet can be reached by logging in at www.beliefnet.com.

Almighty Power can be found at www.Almightypower.net. This is a Christian site that takes prayer requests.

International Directory of Spiritual and Healing, Meditation and Prayer groups. It can direct you to a wide array of prayer groups from all religions. This site can be reached at www.worldlightcenter.com.

Roman Catholic nuns and priests will take prayer requests from people of all faiths and will pray for you daily. The site can be reached at www.catholicprayerrequests.com.

The Carmelite Nuns are a Roman Catholic order of cloistered nuns with convents in cities and towns throughout the U.S. and all over the world. The singular purpose of the Carmelites is to pray for individuals and the world. You can find a directory of Carmelite nuns by logging on to www.ocd.pcn.net. You can also reach the Carmelites at www.e-prayer.org.

The Tehilim Hotline offers a twenty-four-hour hot line for Jewish people who seek to be helped through the power of prayer. You can reach the hot line by calling 1888-448-3445 or 718-851-2365 (in Brooklyn, New York). You can also log on to www.tehilimhotline.org.

Virtual Jerusalem is a Jewish magazine on the World Wide Web. It takes prayer requests and will place written requests in the Wailing Wall in Jerusalem. You can reach Virtual Jerusalem by logging on to www.virtual jerusalem.com.

The Healing Buddha Foundation is a Buddhist organization that accepts prayer requests from people of all faiths. Thousands of Buddhist monks will pray for any concern you have, including physical, emotional, and spiritual health. You can reach the Healing Buddha Foundation by logging on to www.healingbuddha.org.